Dear Bill –

This book is truly special.

How brilliant of you to go through the entire JFK Assassination in such poetic fashion!

– Dr. Cyril Wecht

THE QUATRAINS OF CAMELOT

by Bill Truels, M.D.

An Epic Narrative Poem Of The JFK Assassination

With additional poems on RFK, FDR, Huey Long, and Marilyn Monroe

The Quatrains of Camelot Copyright © 2023 by Bill Truels

All rights reserved under International and Pan-American Copyright Conventions.

Published in the United States of America.

No part of this book may be used or reproduced in any manner without written permission except in the case of brief quotations embodied in critical articles and reviews.

First published 2023

Graphics by Paul Hail

Email the author directly at btruelsauthor@gmail.com

Library of Congress Control Number: 2023905234

ISBN: 9798986956176

If you are ready for truth in a lyrical style,
Read Dr. Truels' book – it will bring you a smile!
But it also will bring you an assignation
To learn the facts of the assassination!

-- Jim Marrs
Author of "Crossfire: The Plot That Killed Kennedy"

*I wish to thank my wife, Maggie, and my three children,
Lisa, Tracy, and Michael,
for their unwavering support in writing this book.*

The Tale Of Camelot

Once upon a time, there was a place called Camelot, in the land of the West. It was a time of fantasy and imagination, for the leaders, King John and his wife, Jacqueline, were the heroes of the people.

Then, in the era of Sputnik, a great Red storm arose from the East, and the people did fear the Red tide, for Nikita the Red did threaten, "We will bury you!"

But King John knew the pain of War and sought to avoid it.

Thus, the Spymasters of Camelot did not trust King John to fight the Red Tide. Nor did the rulers of the Underworld trust King John nor Brother Robert, for he sought to contain them.

And so began the Great Conspiracy, which deceived the people, and replaced the Prince of Light with the Prince of Darkness.

This is the story of that Conspiracy — a tale of romance and love, but also of jealousy, rivalry, and greed —
      The Tale Of Camelot!

The logic of a trusted politician
Steeped in knowledge and erudition
Can easily refute a simple observation
If it can't provide the proper explanation!

We fill the empty spaces
That tragedy embraces –
Looking for a way
To keep the hurt at bay!

Those who live in the quiet suffering of a grievous loss
Carry a burden which can never be lost –
You toil in the present and smile at the last –
As flashes of memory break through from the past!

FOREWARD

The Quatrains of Camelot is an epic narrative poem which tells the story of the most famous assassination in American history, namely that of President John F. Kennedy. It is designed to be read by young and old alike, and has been popular both with researchers and students of all ages.

Dr. Bill Truels mixes his own knowledge and beliefs about the Kennedy assassination with what some have called "assassination philosophy" – the blending of a prominent historical event with musings about the role of God and man's role in the universe. He asks questions like, "When does God choose to intervene in man's affairs?"

I particularly like the Kennedy soliloquy in Chapter One, where JFK muses about his political opponents and society in general, before the Dallas parade begins. Lest the readings become too serious, Dr. Truels' sense of humor provides welcome relief:

> *If the government says a hole is small –*
> *Then it must be, after all!*
> *Who cares what the doctors say –*
> *The truth will wait another day!*

As a trauma surgeon, Dr. Truels adds his own insight into the controversial JFK shooting sequence. His explanation unifies the acoustics and the ballistic evidence for the first time.
From his many conversations with patients and other physicians, Dr. Truels presents a physician's verbal history surrounding the chronic illness and sudden death of FDR, which is unlike anything you will ever read.

Dr. Truels also presents his beliefs regarding the murder of Marilyn Monroe, and briefly discusses the assassinations of Senator Robert Kennedy, Dr. Martin Luther King, and Senator Huey Long.

Those who are hoping to find "absolute knowledge" will not find it here – Dr. Truels presents several scenarios in these poetic verses – it is up to the reader to choose which he believes to be the correct version.

There is even a chapter on UFO's, which is partly based upon an astronomy class that Dr. Truels attended in 1967 at Northwestern University by Dr. J. Allen Hynek, the civilian chairman for the Air Force's Project Bluebook.

Like the movie, *Casablanca*, history involves the interplay of multiple factions, and those hoping to pin the JFK assassination upon a single individual or group are ignoring the interplay of multiple forces which act upon our leaders. In many respects, the events leading to the death of JFK represent "the perfect storm."

For the first-time reader, *The Quatrains of Camelot* provides a well-detailed, descriptive introduction to the JFK assassination, and is a good starting point for those who wish to investigate further. Dr. Truels also pays tribute to many of the researchers who have dedicated their lives to unraveling the JFK assassination mystery.

Please note that, while the events depicted are based on historical information, John Kennedy's philosophical musings before the motorcade, Lee Oswald's words about being double-crossed, or David Ferrie's thoughts about the afterlife represent poetic license on the part of the author.

With the JFK assassination, we have one of the most important events in human history, which Dr. Truels uses as a starting point for thoughts about love, jealousy, rivalries, politics, religion, and even the nature of man and God. His insightful and compassionate poems provide therapy for anyone who has loved and lost!

I especially like the use of the narrative poem format with easy-to-read quatrains – it lends a certain nobility to President Kennedy and the entire Camelot experience!

John F. Kennedy, despite his flaws, is one of the great tragic heroes of our time, and an epic poem in his honor is only a fitting tribute!

– *The Editor*

TABLE OF CONTENTS

FORT WORTH 1
THE DALLAS PARADE 43
PARKLAND HOSPITAL 115
THE PLAYERS 147
THE MEETING AT MURCHISON'S 165
NEW ORLEANS, DALLAS, AND LAS VEGAS 173
THE SIMULATION 200
JIM GARRISON 223
THE RIFLE 246
CONTEMPLATIONS 256
THE QUATRAINS OF RFK 284
THE QUATRAINS OF MARILYN MONROE 290
THE QUATRAINS OF FDR 297
THE UFO QUATRAINS 304
THE KINGFISH QUATRAINS 311
THE "UNIFIED" SOLUTION 316
ANALYSIS OF THE JFK BACK WOUND 320
SUMMARY 335
COUNTER-ARGUMENTS 338
OUR HISTORY IN A NUTSHELL 340
DISCLOSURE TIMETABLE 346

ABOUT THE AUTHOR 350

Forbidden Knowledge

Thus, it came to pass that the Great Leader, the prince of Light, was killed by the Corruptors, while he did greet the People, and celebrate the Beauty of the Day.

Now, be it known that the dark forces of the Underworld did unite with the Spymasters to murder the King.

For each side did truly hate the King, and together they conspired to deceive the People.

The Tale Of Camelot

PRELUDE

Is truth some shining pillar in the night –
That shows itself with all its' might?
Or like nuggets of elemental gold –
Must truth be sifted from the fold?

Do we fool ourselves in the world –
With everything neatly furled?
With houses and cars and champagne –
Do we fool ourselves in the main?

Is there a world of great disorder
That lingers across the border?
With tears and anger and wars –
And people settling scores?

Is there a fine line or partition
That wavers on human volition?
Will there be a war to fight –
Or will the children sleep tonight?

All these philosophical musings
Are at times a bit confusing!
Better to face each day –
And accept what comes your way!

Close your eyes and clear your mind –
Let's travel back in space and time –
Let's view the Dealey Plaza station –
And watch a crime that shocked the nation!

WARREN COMMISSION MISTAKES

In pushing the Lone Gunman theory, which mandated no more than three shots, the Warren Commission made two mistakes. I call these the "Magic Bullet Theory" and the "Forgotten Bullet".

"MAGIC BULLET" THEORY

The Warren Commission knew there was a missed shot that nicked bystander James Tague's cheek at the triple underpass. They also knew there was a third and final head shot to JFK. That left only one bullet to explain the wounds to JFK's back and neck and to John Connally's chest and wrist. Yet, John Connally maintained that he was hit with a separate shot as he turned to look back and saw that JFK was already wounded before he, Connally was struck. Dr. Cyril Wecht was the lone dissenter on the Warren Commission and labeled this the Warren Commission's "Magic Bullet" because of its twisted path. Separate bullets to JFK and Connally required a total of four shots, which the Warren Commission would not accept!

THE "FORGOTTEN BULLET"

The second mistake by the Warren Commission was to ignore a frontal shot from the Grassy Knoll, which years later was further confirmed by the acoustic echo analysis. Railroad employee Sam Holland was standing on the Triple Underpass with an overhead view of the Grassy Knoll, when he heard a gunshot from the Grassy Knoll and saw gun smoke. He pinpointed the exact location of the shot as coming from behind the picket fence.

I personally talked to eyewitness William Newman, the closest eyewitness to JFK, who was standing at the Grassy Knoll with his family when a gunshot came from behind him. He and his family dropped to the ground, as seen on the Zapruder film. William Newman told me that JFK's right ear disappeared as a skin flap was created that flipped the ear back and blew out the back of his head.

Dr. Charles Crenshaw, a surgical resident at Parkland Hospital, told me that there was a small entry wound in front of JFK's right ear and a "baseball-sized" exit wound in the right rear. This Grassy Knoll shot became an inconvenient truth, and was dismissed by the Warren Commission as a loud echo – an auditory hallucination. Witnesses running toward the Grassy Knoll were ridiculed as "conspiracy theorists"!

I call this the "Forgotten Bullet" because the Warren Commission "forgot" to call Sam Holland, William Newman and many others to testify about this Grassy Knoll frontal shot. Of course, this would require two shooters in separate locations and prove a conspiracy to kill JFK!

FORT WORTH

*Though you may remember not
The day John Kennedy was shot –
The sound was heard above the fray
And echoes to this very day!*

*'Twas a sunny day in November –
A day I'll always remember!
The motorcade turned onto Elm
With the Secret Service at the helm!*

*Jackie joined John that fateful day –
Together they rode in the motorcade
Dressed in pink with a pill box hat
She was the favorite as people clapped!*

Red roses and asters were given as a treat –
Jackie placed them on the rear limousine seat!
The motorcade stopped to visit children and nuns
As the Kennedys basked in the warm Dallas sun!

They rode in a fancy Lincoln limousine
With an open top to enjoy the scene!
But Agent Rybka on the trunk was motioned away –
He was told he wouldn't be needed that day!

Henry Rybka then remounts the stoop –
And once again he gets the boot!
The man who could have blocked the shot
Is twice told he is needed not!

As the motorcade formed, LBJ declared
"I don't want Governor Connally sitting there!"
His rival, Senator Yarborough, was supposed to be
The one who sat in the right jump seat!

But Governor Connally resisted –
"I'll sit with the President!" he insisted –
So when the gunshots did resound
Governor Connally also went down!

The children greeted the motorcade cars –
Jackie and John were like movie stars!
The children asked for autographs –
And all around they cheered and clapped!

The Kennedys had in Fort Worth stayed
In preparation for the Dallas parade –
John looked out from the Texas Hotel
As the morning crowds began to swell!

John Kennedy opened the Dallas Morning News
And viewed an ad with malicious views!
He showed it to Jackie and explained –
"We're heading into nut country today!"

THE QUATRAINS OF CAMELOT

Bordered in black
The ad signaled that –
The men in the John Birch Society
Would soon achieve notoriety!

"How could they print this?" Kennedy queried –
"Such ads certainly aren't customary!"
"It's one thing to criticize my political views
But to implore my death, there's no excuse!"

The newspaper was owned by George Dealey
Whose right wing views were firm and steely!
The ad was placed by the John Birch elite
Before Kennedy rode down the Dealey streets!

Opinions at that particular time
Were really quite polarized –
And men like General Edwin Walker
Were more than just your casual talker!

Some people forget that in popular circles
Anti-Kennedy jokes would often swirl –
The divide between the East and South
Was more than casual word of mouth!

FORT WORTH

WANTED

FOR

TREASON

THIS MAN is wanted for treasonous activities against the United States:

1. Betraying the Constitution (which he swore to uphold):
He is turning the sovereignty of the U.S. over to the communist controlled United Nations.
He is betraying our friends (Cuba, Katanga, Portugal) and befriending our enemies (Russia, Yugoslavia, Poland).
2. He has been WRONG on innumerable issues affecting the security of the US (United Nations-Berlin wall-Missle removal-Cuba-Wheat deals-Test Ban Treaty, etc.)
3. He has been lax in enforcing Communist Registration laws.
4. He has given support and encouragement to the Communist inspired racial riots.
5. He has illegally invaded a sovereign State with federal troops.
6. He has consistantly appointed Anti-Christians to Federal office: Upholds the Supreme Court in its Anti-Christian rulings. Aliens and known Communists abound in Federal offices.
7. He has been caught in fantastic LIES to the American people (including personal ones like his previous marraige and divorce).

The ad in the Dallas Morning News
Reflected the radical views
Of Texas oilmen like H. L. Hunt
And their hatred of the Kennedy bunch!

Jackie was late in getting dressed –
"Let's get going!" John requests
"I'm getting organized!" Jackie declared –
Things must be right for the Dallas fare!

Jackie dreamed the other night
Of a vision that gave her fright –
"We're riding in an open top car –
The rain turned to blood from afar!"

"I dreamed we had to jump out –
For the blood was all about!"
Jack replied, "Don't you worry –
Dream meanings are often blurry!"

THE QUATRAINS OF CAMELOT

Jackie's pill box hat must be correct –
And her posture must be held erect –
Her pretty pink suit must fit just right –
In preparation for the Dallas rite!

We live our lives from day to day –
Not seeing what will come our way!
We plan each day all organized –
Never knowing when fate will us surprise!

Beauty is a relative thing
With large eyes and hips that swing –
Do we create artificial means
For judging our King and Queen!

Better that we should judge on action
And disregard the physical distractions
That make us judge on external whims –
And ignore the subtle beauty within!

What thoughts did John Kennedy entertain
As he looked out on the Fort Worth rain?
Do leaders ever think that they
Are looked upon as mortal prey?

"Sometimes I prefer to fantasize
And imagine a world that I surmise –
Than face the harsh reality
Of a world that might not come to be!"

"Will there be a war to end all wars?
And who will be left on distant shores?
Will the human race achieve world peace –
Or turn things back to the primitive beasts?"

"What heroes do we create –
That we also victims make?
Men march bravely off to war –
And are sometimes seen no more!"

"Perhaps I live in some confusion –
My life may be one great delusion!
The peace I see on yonder shore
May be the calm before the storm!"

"What machinations will fate impart?
Will I soon this world depart?
Will ill winds blow my way today
As we travel in the motorcade?"

"Blood pulsing through my veins
Warns me of a change –
Some people take delight
In causing others fright!"

"While others, out of an angry bent
Would rather see another spent –
Calling out the dogs of war
And causing sites that we abhor!"

"It's a race, you know –
To accomplish your task before you go!
Some are blessed with many years –
Others know not the end is near!"

"Will there be a laying on of hands
To protect my Presidential plans?
Will God soon intervene
To block the devil's schemes?"

"Perhaps I'm being a little mental
And maybe it's just coincidental –
But the man whose streets I've come to trace
Is the one, through ill, could me replace!"

"Sometimes, it's probably not worth
Meeting someone on his own turf –
You think that you can peacefully manage –
But you're always at a disadvantage!"

*"His views aren't the same as mine
A balanced ticket was our line!
There are rumblings, I must confess
Which are stirring up a hornet's nest!"*

*"And is a balanced ticket really balanced?
With opposing views that one can challenge?
Is this a formula for security –
Or a recipe for instability?"*

*"I've asked George Smathers to replace
Lyndon Johnson in the next Presidential race –
But if Lyndon's boys find out too soon
My chances for the Texas vote are doomed!"*

*"His ears are large – I know he hears
All the scuttlebutt that travels near!
He's only a heartbeat from the President –
He longs to be the White House resident!"*

*"One heart beating –
Time keeps fleeting!
Would that we
Could forever be!"*

*"What revenge does God bring
For foolishness in the spring?
We pay a lifelong lesson
For a moment's indiscretion!"*

*"I wish that I could choose
A profession with less to lose!
Doctors and lawyers at least
Have clients who keep the peace!"*

*"Lyndon visits me today
And says that everything's O.K.
There's no cause for my alarm –
No one here will do me harm!"*

*"But LBJ looks preoccupied
By plans that he would sooner hide –
At times I catch an icy stare
As if his temper soon will flare!"*

*"Do we use our reptilian brain
To mark and protect our terrain –
From the predators we eschew
With a different point of view?"*

*"Some rivalries are never seen –
Yet give rise to actions mean!
Buried deep within the heart –
They never do the surface part!"*

*"What primitive screams
Come from our Inner Being?
Is there some hidden turmoil
That would our ambition roil?"*

*"There's a wolf inside each man –
That tries to alter Nature's plan!
It lurks inside and plots and schemes
And takes away another's dream!"*

*"Will this continue to be my day?
Or will it turn into a Black Friday?
The future is a darkened room –
Is it full of joy or full of doom?"*

*"Is there a primordial anger
That could lead to my imminent danger –
A continual need for reliance
On quarreling and defiance?"*

*"Why not tax windfall profits –
Is that such a terrible process?
Do we want hundreds of oil millionaires –
Or hundreds of millions who toil to share!"*

*"The steel bosses would threaten
An inflationary recession –
Until I gave a frown
And forced them to back down!"*

*"Who will be the man on the white horse –
Able to change history's course?
Can he save our fragile democracy
From the military-industrial aristocracy?"*

*"National Security Memorandum #263
Is designed to get us out of the Vietnam spree!
While the Joint Chiefs still want to jibe –
My policy is 'All out by '65!'"*

*"I believe the Generals' prods
Are bigger than their proverbial nobs!
I just fervently hope and pray
That their views will not hold sway!"*

*"War just doesn't seem right –
Like fighting in the Dolomites!
Four thousand silent infantry graves –
Today they come to frolic and play!"*

*"And the Eastern bankers are upset
That I might dissolve the Fed!
But should the power to control interest rates
Be in the hands of magistrates?"*

*"As President, I issued silver notes –
Backed by the U.S. Treasury folks!
But John McCloy was quite perturbed –
He said I would ruin the Federal Reserve!"*

*"Now, the Federal Reserve is a money-making machine –
It can issue money – be it silver or green!
If you need greenbacks, for peace or war –
The Federal Reserve just prints up more!"*

"So the national debt continues to grow –
As the politicians lose control!
The Reserve can charge interest however it wishes –
While the bankers get to enjoy all the riches!"

"I'll continue to fight the Eastern lenders –
I personally think they're on a bender!
The people need to take control –
Or they'll forever be in the hole!"

"Sometimes the powered elite
Do not easily accept defeat!
They appear to easily cower –
But soon resent their loss of power!"

"I never cared for the Wall Street types –
Who trade paper stocks with lots of hype!
I'd rather rub shoulders with the blue collar crowd –
Productive citizens have a right to be proud!"

"Survival of the fittest
Means fighting to the finish!
You've got to stay the course –
And never show remorse!"

"Fame is such a fickle friend –
It leaves you when you don't know when!
Better to be lesser known –
With friends who never you disown!"

"A President with good rapport
Can often open many doors –
But if he tries to bull his way
Other countries will dismay!"

"Will Our Lady of Perpetual Help
Be able to call off the wolves that yelp?
Or will aggression have its way –
And keep the cooing doves at bay?"

THE QUATRAINS OF CAMELOT

"I will staunchly fight
For what I believe is right!
Though some might tricks avail –
My views will still prevail!"

"Things that go bump in the night
Never do give me fright –
But beware fellow politicians
With Presidential ambitions!"

"How do you put out the fire
When someone's full of ire?
It's tough to try and placate –
When they want you to vacate!"

"It's not a fair world –
Life can give you a whirl!
Just when you're about to settle –
You pack it up and hit the pedal!"

"What fate does man befall –
That one man's rise is another's fall!
Would that we could choose the path
And save us from our brother's wrath!"

"When you travel with the wolves –
Watch out for the gnarly hooves!
For if there is a weakness shown –
You'll find yourself out all alone!"

"Is there a hungry beast within –
That fights to keep us fit and trim?
That would have us grab for power
When the clock strikes ambition's hour?"

"What lies beneath
Can often defeat –
Thoughts of sedition
Can upset tradition!"

*"I don't like confrontations –
They create awkward situations!
For when the bulls do stare –
There's danger everywhere!"*

*"Is all this talk of conspiracy
Just a Bishop Berkeley fantasy?
Or do plans made by men
Herald inauspicious ends?"*

*"When I look into his eyes
Sometimes I do surmise
A look askance, as if to say
Don't look at me! I'm not to blame!"*

*"Is there a primordial anger
That forever keeps us strangers?
Actions in the past
That will always last!"*

*"Lyndon's voice bears a tone
Laden with testosterone!
Does his Southern drawl belie
A darker action he would hide?"*

*"Some say LBJ's ambition
Could one day lead him to sedition –
Does he harbor a maniacal urge
To plan a Presidential purge?"*

*"Is jealousy a reason
To plot with treason –
And achieve your dreams
With illegal schemes?"*

*"Am I right to be suspicious
During times so inauspicious?
It's always best to be on guard
When traveling in another's yard!"*

THE QUATRAINS OF CAMELOT

"Do we have a dark side
That we turn away and try to hide?
Are there rivalries and ambitions
That lead to murder and sedition?"

"Loyalty in politics is a lie –
A trait on which you can't rely!
Alliances constantly re-arrange
As each group tries the most to gain!"

"A dog remains loyal to his master –
To him alone will he answer!
But politicians are a fickle bunch –
They'll change their minds and head for lunch!"

"And the Wild West has a reputation
For resolving sticky situations
At the point of a loaded gun –
That's how New Frontiers are won!"

"Lions must be taught to kill –
Does murder go against man's will?
Is violence compatible with the soul?
Would that God could make us whole!"

"Is physical combat a language learned –
A way to deal with our concerns?
If we could find a better way
Maybe we could save the day!"

"Must we be pugilistic?
My views are realistic!
Surely we can hash things out –
Without the need for physical clout!"

"A leader with malicious intentions
Can steer a country in the wrong direction!
What can the world possibly do
To prevent a governmental coup?"

*"Who knows what motives lurk down deep?
At times they rouse me from my sleep!
Everyone's in a grab for power –
Is there a target on my collar?"*

*"Will a country's domination
Eventually be its ruination?
As lesser countries strive to grow –
Will each one fight to take control?"*

*"It's a universe of numbers –
Random chance makes thunder!
For if the dice don't land just right –
You'll soon feel the snake eyes bite!"*

*"What does it all mean
When we lose our dream?
Does it all end –
Or can you start again?"*

*"Are death and rebirth
The story of the earth?
Or do the gods of our creation
Spring from our imagination?"*

*"Can you blame God
For numbers others trod?
Each one is a small Creator –
Part of God's denominator!"*

*"It's better to suffer wrong than to do wrong –
That was Plato's philosophic song!
I choose to do no harm –
That was Hippocrates charm!"*

*"But if I die a martyr –
Will society be any smarter?
Marching off to war –
To settle all their scores!"*

THE QUATRAINS OF CAMELOT 15

President Kennedy in Fort Worth with John Connally, LBJ

"Who will be the King of the Hill –
As leaders vie for the people's will!
Each one promises more to give
To help the common man to live!"

"Some will ride on religious swells –
Others will on politics dwell –
But each generation trains a leader
Who promises to make life sweeter!"

"Will people ever be content
With what God has surely lent?
Will the loss of material possessions
Be our final teaching lesson?

"Is patriotism the real motivation
For my precarious situation?
Or does money have a voice
In the Presidential choice?"

*"The military-industrial complex
Doesn't seem to have a conscience!
Patriots march bravely off to war –
While profits rise behind closed doors!"*

*"My work is too valuable here –
I aim to give the people cheer!
I've asked them for 1,000 days
To get my policies under way!"*

*"Ask what you can do for your country –
That was my Inaugural plea –
Instead of resorting to the armory
Let's try once more for peace and harmony!"*

*"My decisions affect each and every one –
Can they afford to lose their Chosen One?"
Am I too important to be killed?
Why, the fate of man rests upon my skill!"*

*"The people in high-rise concrete caves
Gaze out hopefully for One who saves –
'Can you deliver us from our plight –
And help us make it through the night?'"*

*"Life can be a tragedy –
Judging from the people I see!
Dreams can often go awry –
But that's no reason not to try!"*

*"We're like clocks running out –
Of that there's not doubt!
Best to run and play
Before they take you away!"*

*"Life can be a comedy –
We laugh at what we cannot be!
Your life may be in tatters –
But your point of view still matters!"*

THE QUATRAINS OF CAMELOT

*"I choose not to be a doubter –
Nor a skeptic or a pouter!
Better things will come your way –
If you from your goals don't stray!"*

*"But he who thinks he's irreplaceable
Should know that politicians are irascible –
If anyone should cross their path
It's easy to incur their wrath!"*

*"Will God my general safety heed
In my hour of greatest need?
God watches every blade of grass –
But can he save me from man's wrath?"*

*"Lord, if this is your will, take me through it!
I've always been one to stick to it!
I don't mean to be a bother –
I won't go against my Father!"*

*"I'm not running the ship, Dear Lord –
If it's time for my ox to be gored –
I'll take my lumps and leave the stage
And let the others take the reins!"*

*"One day you're here and one day you're gone –
Not that you've done anything wrong!
But when the final bell has rung –
Your time on earth is quickly done!"*

*"Joe Jr. was the Chosen One –
To make the Presidential run!
But his plane exploded in a ball of fire –
Trying to vanquish Hitler's ire!"*

*"Is there a Kennedy curse –
That binds us chapter and verse?
Or is there a fatal attraction
That punishes men who take action?"*

"What is my place in the Universe?
Does my role as President make me averse
To the ravages of time and place
That would other mortals soon erase?"

"Some Egyptian Pharaohs claimed God's role –
People worshipped their heavenly souls!
But are claims of celestial ancestry
Nothing more than pompous sophistry?"

"Are we that different from times of old –
When royal families fought for gold?
A few people at the top
Make decisions for the lot!"

"Before he leaves office, a President is required
To help plan his funeral, for when he expires –
But if you die in office, before your term ends –
Who will plan your funeral and who will make amends?"

"Radio shows after dark
Are enough to give a start!
Is there a monster Loch Ness?
Or simply a Great Nothingness?"

"When we die, will our spirits
Be judged on our earthly merits?
Is there a Land Camelot –
Or a place where we'd rather not!"

"Is there a Great Destruction
That would create a giant eruption –
In the plans that we hold dear
And the people we keep near?"

"Will I return to the Ganges River
Where they say all life does linger?
Or will I cross the River Styx
And make my way to a heavenly tryst?"

*"Have a beautiful day!
That's what they always say –
But though we have the best intentions
We never know life's true direction!"*

*"And does God really care?
What happens on our earthly fare?
Are we alone or does he watch
As mortals knock each other off?"*

*"But should we blame God
For problems where man does trod?
In matters of our personal creation –
We must learn our limitations!"*

*"Praise the Lord, who gives and takes away –
Lead us down the path and not astray!
Help us put our trust in thee –
Ruler for eternity!"*

*"As the aging process unwinds
The body ever slowly declines –
The back pain that has plagued me for years
Already brings me to crutches and tears!"*

*"There's a natural sense of progression
That leads in the downward direction!
Would that I could reverse the flow
And make my body once again whole!"*

*"We are all in the process of dying –
It happens without even trying!
The process of natural erosion
Drives us to potions and lotions!"*

*"Some will die from malicious intents –
Others will die from pure accidents –
Some will die from foreign wars –
While others are killed on domestic shores!"*

"Death from a natural cause
Sometimes gives me reason to pause –
Wouldn't it be better to die while young
With all your faculties still undone?"

"Doctors and hospitals give me fright –
Twice they've given me the Last Rites!
It's not that I lack the constitution –
But who wants to linger in institutions?"

"Would that I could take a break
From this maddening cycle of fear and hate!
Is there a refuge to be found
Until men's passions cool down?"

"What will it be like
When all the noise and strife
Finally go away –
And children get to play!"

"The winds of change do blow –
Will they good or ill bestow?
Will my New Frontier prevail –
Or will all my plans derail?"

"Sometimes I hear a voice
That warns me of a fatal choice –
I must rely on all my friends
But can I trust them in the end?"

"There's a madness in human beings
That runs counter to all our dreams!
Would that our spirits could unite
And cease the endless wars we fight!"

"Sometimes I feel paralyzed
By all the jabs and all the lies –
All the negative publicity
Can affect one's sensibility!"

THE QUATRAINS OF CAMELOT

"Our task is to be strong at the broken places –
Those are words Ernest Hemingway graces!
Face up to the task at hand –
Everyone must make their stand!"

"We live our lives in quiet desperation –
Hoping for some major revelation
That will transform our tawdry lives
And let kings and queens arise!"

"I carry the world upon my shoulders
And my enemies grow ever bolder –
I take a measured, slow, deep breath
And wonder how many I have left!"

"Is this the Day of the Dead
That each person privately dreads?
Is this a dark situation
That will be my ruination?"

"Do I circle the Goddess of Death –
Will I soon take my final breath?
Will the conflicts that tear us apart
Soon take dead aim at my heart?"

"We are all like robot Beings –
With hearts that pump and lungs that breathe –
Would that these mechanical parts
Could withstand an assassin's darts!"

"Some people like to dream
That we're perpetual motion machines –
Doing our daily perfunctory chores
Until tragedy comes knocking at our door!"

"I wish that we were Supermen –
Bullet wounds would quickly mend!
And all the weapons man would make
Could never make our bodies break!"

Enter the Abyss!

*"Is there a dark Abyss
That all souls hope to miss?
Do we pass through some dark morass
On the way to our final path?"*

*"What if we could live forever?
We would leave this world never!
Our place on earth would be secure –
Would world peace then be assured?"*

*"Evil dictators would never die –
They might even multiply!
It seems that man is forever cursed
To battle in the universe!"*

*"Evil is a funny trait –
One man's devil is another's plate!
Good and evil will forever fight –
As long as each side thinks they're right!"*

*"It seems that every twenty years time –
Good and evil re-align –
Russia vows to cause our end –
But soon we'll be the best of friends!"*

THE QUATRAINS OF CAMELOT

*"If alien Beings came down to visit –
What kind of world would they elicit?
A universe that's full of strife –
With humans battling for their life!"*

*"In my dreams I'm swimming –
Trying to keep on winning –
Looking for that golden shore
Where I will have to swim no more!"*

*"We live our lives half asleep –
Not knowing what to throw or keep!
Overlooking what we have –
And on the hunt for more to grab!"*

*"Everyone's in a hurry, you know –
With no particular place to go!
Would that we could slow it down –
And take some time to look around!"*

*"I've been to Harvard and Princeton and London
But I'm still in quite a conundrum!
No matter the education –
It's still hard to run a nation!"*

*"You're the President, but you don't control
All the forces that swirl to and fro –
If people would simply together unite
We could solve our problems without a fight!"*

*"It's often nice to believe
That a change in policy is all we need –
That often just a tincture of time
Helps disparate forces re-align!"*

*"But just how much does man behold
The external forces that us mold?
The rise and fall of world nations
May be a property of civilizations!"*

*"There are certain rhythms in the earth
That have existed since mankind's birth –
Feast and famine, war and pestilence
Have bedeviled man since his existence!"*

*"There's a fundamental vibration
That permeates all creation –
A certain tranquility
Present in everything I see!"*

*"If man could tune his inner Being
To listen to the world unseen –
All souls might together soar
And put away the tools of war!"*

*"But Nature has an inner turmoil
That often makes spring water boil –
Perhaps the outer shell we see
Is the pause between catastrophes!"*

*"Was random chance extremely lucky
To fashion us so firm and plucky?
A mere speck among billions of stars –
Left to wonder who we are!"*

*"Divine action or random chance?
Are we victims of circumstance?
Is the genetic code God's instruction book –
Or did we arise from materialistic gook?"*

*"Is there a retreat from Copernicus
That should really concern us?
Can carboniferous creatures
Explain all our human features?"*

*"Is there a God delusion
That adds to my confusion?
Does one Prime Mover cover all –
Or does random chance make all the calls?"*

THE QUATRAINS OF CAMELOT

"Are periodic catastrophes
The way life was meant to be?
Like forest fires and tidal waves
Is mankind destined for the caves?"

"Do the gods drink merlot?
Sometimes I think it's so!
Disasters of giant dimensions
Could use Divine Intervention!"

"Will man's ability to reason
Overcome his destructive demons?
Will sanity rule the day –
Or will civilization just go away?"

"Will we live in a world of fire or ice –
A nuclear winter or everything nice?
In order to obtain peace and tranquility –
People must behave with a certain civility!"

"But enough of idle contemplation –
I must work to shape the nation!
Idle thoughts that through me pass
Must give way to cold, hard facts!"

"I've a parade today in Dallas
And though some would do me malice –
Thousands of citizens will me greet
As I travel through the Dallas streets!"

"Sometimes I wonder right out loud
As I wave to the frenzied crowd –
I'm just an ordinary soul
Trying to make the world whole!"

"Conspiracy theorists are quite active –
They're even trying to be proactive
In trying to prevent a fatal strike
That would take a President's life!"

*"Adlai Stevenson gave me a warning
That storm clouds were in Dallas forming –
He was hit by a lady with a picket sign
At a United Nations talk to express his mind!"*

*"A President lives in the fast lane –
Which brings additional toil and pain!
But if you've vowed to make a difference –
Be prepared for interference!"*

*"It's hard to believe conspiracy theorists
Are more suspicious than my Secret Service!
But then it's not truly paranoia
If someone's really out to destroy ya!"*

*"Certainly this is not
Part of a conspiracy plot!
I suspect I ponder needlessly
Over things that surely cannot be!"*

*"The Copperheads during the Civil War
Planned an insurrection at Lincoln's door!
They opposed slavery's abolition –
But were tried for murder and sedition!"*

*"Would that I could muster the force
To intercede and change history's course!
But my enemies grow ever stronger –
Can I hold out any longer?"*

*"When it's your time, there's no obfuscation –
Not that I believe in predestination!
But when the Lord your number calls
Start hoping for those hallowed halls!"*

*"There's a fickle finger of fate
That jabs me when I awake –
And reminds me of my impermanence
In this hallowed firmament!"*

*"I'm caught in a trap –
Like some hungry rat!
Trying to get away –
And live another day!"*

*"The greatness of a President
Is not always evident!
If I truly rate –
It may be seen too late!"*

*"Is there a manifest destiny
Of what I'm supposed to be?
Are things written in stone –
Or must I walk alone?"*

*"When is the end near?
It's often never clear –
We live until we die
And often wonder why!*

*"Does everything happen for a reason –
No matter the time or season?
Am I a part of God's Divine Plan
That makes me who and what I am?"*

*"How do we order our world –
With accoutrements and pearl?
Or with actions that relate
To every person's plate?"*

*"The missiles of October
Left everybody sober!
To raise your guns in anger –
Might trigger nuclear danger!"*

*The world faced annihilation
Over the Cuban nation!
Will the Lord rescue us
Before we turn to dust?*

FORT WORTH

*"Saving society from calamity
By resolving mutual enmity
Should always be our goal
To keep the country whole!"*

*"The bulls will fight
And split the night –
As battles rage
On the world stage!"*

*"Are we catchers in the rye –
Sparing nations before they die?
Catching children before they fall
Into a nuclear fireball!"*

*"Everyone's in a hurry to go nowhere!
Somehow, it doesn't seem quite fair –
We spend our lives making plans –
While the present slips from our hands!"*

*"If we're caught in the hubbub
Of the daily rub –
Will we miss the signs
Of an approaching demise?"*

*"Are we mere mechanical Beings –
Moving like some electrical machine?
Can we dream of worlds that lie beyond –
Or are we limited to our own pond!"*

*"Will Saint Christopher protect my travel –
Or will my Texas trip unravel?
I feel an undercurrent of dissent
As the American President!"*

*"Can I find security
From the forces of obscurity –
And save a nation
From utter devastation?"*

THE QUATRAINS OF CAMELOT

"You have to be suspicious
For signs so inauspicious!
Protests in the park
May lead to actions dark!"

"There's a battle within my chest
That warns me of great unrest!
Is there time to peace implore –
Or must we call the dogs of war?"

"People just don't get along –
That's the most unfortunate song!
They fight over politics and religion –
That's the human condition!"

"I'm a child of the Light
Trying to do what's right –
Hoping that one day
All can come to play!"

JFK points his finger at the hotel wall
And says, "Bang! Bang! Bang! – that's the end of it all!"
Did JFK have precognition –
Or was this merely a suspicion?

"We are embers in the night –
Glowing with delight!
Not knowing whence we came –
Or where we'll go again!"

"The pendulum of time
Isn't very kind –
It ticks away the days
That we have left to play!"

"But enough of death and dying –
I've got to keep on trying!
Create a world where people share –
With children playing everywhere!"

*"Sister Rosie was our special child –
She taught us how to laugh and smile!
Sister Eunice founded Special Olympics –
So handicapped kids could exceed their limits!"*

*"Sister Rosemary was an inspiration –
We all renewed our dedication –
To help kids strengthen their agility –
And make them believe in their ability!"*

*Arnold Schwarzenegger
Special Olympics Chairman*

MY SPECIAL CHILD

*Do you like my little boy?
He's cute enough for me!
I know he's not the perfect thing
That others want to be!*

*His eyes, you see, are turning in –
He may not ever walk –
His brain can't keep the signals straight –
He may not even talk!*

*He'll never be a doctor
Or a lawyer or a king –
He'll never rule the world –
Or fight for anything!*

*No, he's just my precious boy –
He loves me every day!
And each night when the sun goes down –
We fold our hands and pray!*

*The gift of life is very dear –
A treasure from above –
Thank you for my special child –
God shower him with love!*

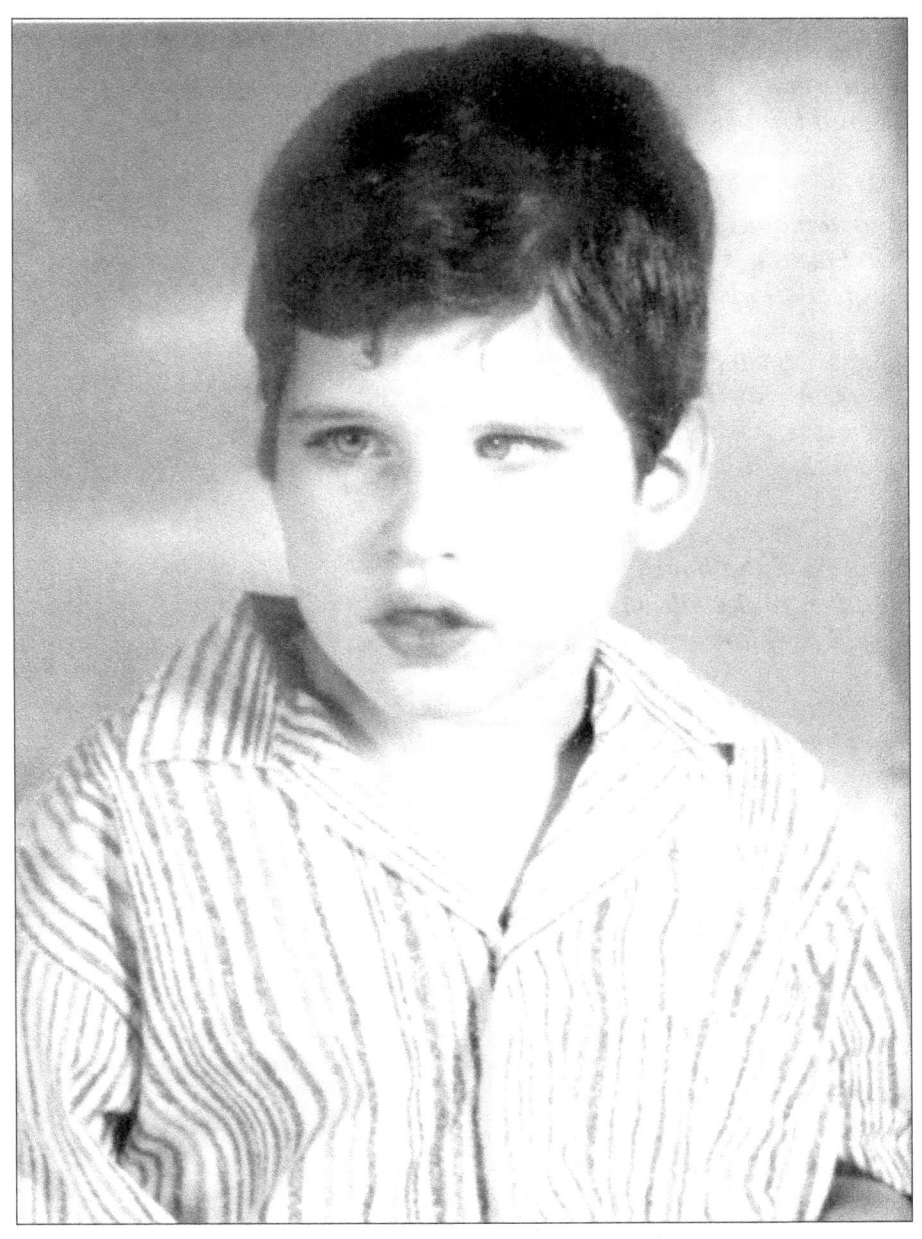

Isaiah Daniel Spencer, age 9, suffered from cerebral palsy. Danny was cared for by his mother, Paula, and loving brother.

"I started the Colonia Kennedy
In Tegucigalpa, Honduras I believed!
A little money goes a long way
To build houses made of clay!"

"'Man is clay and straw' –
Amenomope cared for all –
'God is man's builder' –
Respect all his children!"

"Are we born pure and become sinners –
Or are we born bad to become winners?
Are those Puritan beacons on the hill –
Or do they light the way for man's free will?"

"The Wall Street Boards
Steal from the hoards!
Bonuses in the billions
Could feed hungry millions!"

"Making lots of hay –   "Are my dreams slipping away?
That's the American way!   Will I have the time of day
But let's provide for the needy – To follow my ambitions
No need to be greedy!"   And carry out my missions?"

"How much time have I got left?
Will my campaign promises be met?
Will our reforms be carried out –
Or will the Old Guard have more clout?"

"Someday I'll leave the present scene –
Turn it over to someone green!
Let someone else have the satisfaction
Of trying to please the disparate factions!"

"How fragile are these bodies
That nature has endowed –
This fleshy skin and muscle
That does our souls enshroud!"

THE QUATRAINS OF CAMELOT

"If only we were made of steel
Protected from the night –
Bullets and knives and arrows
Never would take flight!"

"We are all like shooting stars
That streak a path from here to Mars –
Never noticing the embers of time
As they presage our fiery decline!"

"Life is such a transient phase –
A pause upon the cosmic stage!
Cherish each moment as you live –
And question not the One who gives!"

"And when death does come, we're surprised –
Like nobody ever really dies!
There's the miracle of our birth –
And the tragedy when we leave the earth!"

"But could it be that our birth is a tragedy?
We were after all created on God's parity –
But with a tragic flaw we could not quell
Are we destined for a living hell?"

"What bipedal animal would God create
To roam the earth and devastate!
To till the fields and plant the wheat –
Then burn the crops as he retreats!"

"In Nature there are no guarantees –
You live your life as God decrees!
But survival is not assured –
There's danger at every turn!"

"Nuclear weapons are everywhere
But no one really seems to care!
The eternal fires of damnation
Might be a nuclear conflagration!"

School Book Depository building with Howard Brennan seated on the wall, taken March 20, 1964 for the Warren Commission. Arrows indicate when Brennan thought each shot was fired. On a three-dimensional reconstruction, the first and second shots are blocked by the oak tree.

"What will my last day be like –
Will it be filled with heartache and strife?
Or will I peacefully pass away –
Content to my final day?"

"The highs and lows of Fortuna's wheel
Are enough to make a grown man squeal!
She showers her dice on the world below –
You never know what numbers roll!"

"Why do we relive the past?
Sailors swimming from a raft –
My patrol boat getting split in two –
Will this be my final crew?"

JFK in the Navy

"It's hard to tell a friend from foe –
The way all these alliances go!
Beware – the closest friend of all
Might be a traitor in the fall!"

THE QUATRAINS OF CAMELOT

"Did we outsmart ourselves –
With too many gadgets and smells?
And become so clever
That we will live never?"

"Are we headed for catastrophe
In this battle for nuclear strategy?
Is it safe to rattle our sabers
With so many nuclear neighbors?"

"Too 'oft I get perturbed –
Those Generals have a lot of nerve!
Urging for another war
On a far off distant shore!"

"Is this the true Dark Age –
With nuclear fallout and particulate haze?
Are we truly enlightened
When more and more people are frightened?

"Is it all about egg and sperm –
That makes us act like we're unlearned?
Is there not a higher purpose
For our existence in this circus?"

"Do we want a wolf on board
To lead our country into war?
Or can I find some other way
To keep the hungry wolves at bay?

"Have we created an efficient killing machine
That will wipe the slate totally clean?
Is win or lose the only game –
And will the nuclear genie tame?"

"Do we threaten mass genocide
When we nuclear weapons hide?
Exploding them on distant shores –
And hope our enemies will be no more!"

"The only real modern peace
Must through negotiation reach!
Talk of total domination
Does not fit the nuclear equation!"

"But how long do you negotiate
If someone's out to dominate?
Does conversation become a tool
When your enemy is out to fool?"

"And if both sides would rather die
With nuclear fireballs in the sky –
Then all the world that would remain
The cave man would again reclaim!"

"At times I sense a deep, dark cloud
That would envelope me and enshroud –
Is this a warning from some inner source
That would have me change my present course?"

"Are you blind? Are you deaf?
Are you of your senses bereft?
This is the kind of surly town
Where unseen dangers do abound!"

"I regret each passing hour –
My time on earth is still in flower!
Soon will come the chilly fall
And I must say goodbye to all!"

"Don't fear the Reaper! –
Life foils the meeker!
Live life with audacity –
And don't doubt your veracity!"

"Today is Friday – the goddess of Norse –
Would that she could change history's course!
She knows of the future and spins the thread of fate –
But will never reveal it, until it's too late!"

*"She lives in Asgard in the hall Fensalir –
Would that she could give us cheer!
The goddess asked nature for an oath not to harm –
But her son met his death at the mistletoe's arm!"*

*"November 22nd – is this a Catch-22?
You attempt to escape but never really do!
Sane or insane – the danger is clear –
There's no easy way to get out of here!"*

*"In Finland, November's the month of the Dead –
The sun passes through Scorpio, which all people dread!
Is there a scorpion hiding out there –
That would strike with a sting from some hunter's lair!"*

*"But all such late hour ruminations
Are probably needless speculation –
Sometimes we deal with too much fright
Over unfound worries in the night!"*

*"I can't afford to stew –
I've got too much work to do!
The people do me need –
I haven't got time to bleed!"*

*"I know there must be a God –
Yet I see a storm from the Southern quad!
If God has a place for me –
I'm ready to take my leave!"*

*"What's it like when it's your time to die –
Do you hang your head and silently cry?
Do you think of all that's gone before –
And wish that you could ask for more?"*

*"I don't want to be a tragic figure –
I hope my fate is something bigger!
I want to be thought a success –
Someone who tried his level best!"*

Jacqueline Kennedy

"Jacqueline has been a force
To help me stabilize my course!
Sometimes I watch with some hilarity –
As she steals my popularity!"

THE QUATRAINS OF CAMELOT

"Does her subtle smile
Belay a romantic guile –
Actions that would rather be
Held in tight security!"

"Where did you come from?
Were you sent from the stars above?
How could someone so pretty
Fill me with so much love?"

"How did Nature create you?
From water and sand and light?
How did God put you together –
Like a star that shines in the night!"

"I look into your eyes
And centuries of time transpire –
I view the wonder of ages –
That fills my heart with desire!"

"My hands caress your silken hair
Your skin so soft and warm
Your lips are like the honeydew
That wets the early morn!

"And as we close our hearts unite
You sweep me off my feet!
I thank my lucky stars today –
Our union is complete!"

"Did God create male and female
To help us with our human travail?
Or was this separate carnal creation
To divide hunting from procreation?"

"Is there a yin and a yang
That the universe does entertain?
A balance in the natural forces
Between creative and destructive courses!"

"You have to take what life dishes out –
There's no need to fuss or pout!
While others live a life complete –
Some will soon their Maker meet!"

"But enough of idle musing –
We are creatures of our own choosing!
I strove to become the President
And deal with human discontent!"

Kennedy left his medals on the shower that morn –
St. Christopher and St. Jude were quite forlorn!
The Saint who could guard against traveler's losses
Was left with the Saint of impossible causes!

We deal with tragedy as it arises –
And pray that God will not surprise us!
The enemies of death are luck and hope –
The best that we can do is cope!

Serious surprises may be expected –
That's what the horoscope directed!
November the twenty-second –
Kennedy's fate did beckon!

The Kennedys arrive at Love Field

Murder In Dealey Plaza

The King fell quickly, for the Trap was clever, and did not show its true source. With his Queen at his side, King John was struck down by the Lightning of the Corruptors.

And the King's Chariot did fill with blood.

> For thus spoke the Jester, "If you strike the King, you must kill him!'

And the People grieved mightily, for great was the Tragedy thereof.

The Tale Of Camelot

Breach Of Faith

And the Dark Prince took the Holy Oath that Somber day, and did become the Ruler of the Land.

For so it was written, that if the Prince of Light should fall, that the Prince of Darkness would follow.

Thus began the Dark Reign, sanctified by the blood of the Light Prince, who did become a sacrifice to his people.

The Tale Of Camelot

THE DALLAS PARADE

*Air Force One arrives in Dallas
But there's no real sign of malice!
The maddening throngs are cheering loud
As Kennedy waves back to the crowd!*

*The Lincoln limousine had a bubbletop
But they decided it was needed not –
The day was clear, although it might
Have helped to save the President's life!*

*What if the rain had persisted?
The bubbletop would be insisted!
And so the fact the day was bright
May have cost the President's life!*

*Would the Sun God looking down
Stop the bullets fired 'round?
Or will he merely turn away
While disparate forces have their day?*

*How many acts of sedition
Are influenced by Nature's volition?
Would that the gods had smiled that day
And spared John Kennedy from the fray!*

*George Bannerman Dealey must think it strange
To have such a famous plaza in his name –
What mischief did George's statue see
As it watched the murder of the century?"*

*Fifteen minutes before the motorcade
Jerry Belknap reported feeling faint –
He fell right down on Houston Street
With an epileptic seizure that was complete!*

*Was this some sort of premonition
Before this greatest act of sedition?
Or just a chance emergency
That created a diversion for all to see?*

*George Bannerman
Dealey Statue*

*Were the spirits feeling faint
As the President entered the plaza quaint?
I sometimes think the spirits cry
When great leaders are about to die!*

*Is Dealey Plaza Holy Ground –
With political forces swirling 'round!
Where spirits leave this hallowed earth –
A wormhole in the universe!*

*The motorcade entered Dealey Plaza
Past a reflecting pool made of terrazzo –
What murky shadows did the people see
Hunkering in the waters deep?*

*"The reflecting pool shines clear
Surely there's no need to fear!
I hope the gods of the sea
Will preserve my destiny!"*

Reflecting Pool

THE QUATRAINS OF CAMELOT

Dealey Plaza Computer Simulation

Is this the Día De Los Muertos?
When long-lost souls leave los cuerpos?
Do they dance along the Dealey Streets
Trying to warn the souls they meet?

With the Trinity River near its' berm
Dealey Plaza was at times submerged –
Would Neptune with his triad strike
In the Killing of the King rite?

The Depository looked solemnly down
With open windows all around!
Made of steel and ancient red bricks –
Was it man's repository for dirty tricks!

Now when the School Book Depository was constructed
Who could have predicted the furor that erupted?
When a hidden sniper from his lofty perch
Would fire a shot that echoed 'round the earth?

The people are not alarmed –
They sense no danger or harm –
Clandestine operations
Are oft' cloaked in celebration!

THE DALLAS PARADE

The Texas School Book Depository

If people were only aware
That trouble was in the air –
They might better fight
To make security tight!

The moment of action
Is oft' filled with distraction!
Was this a planned event –
Or just coincidence?

Were we lulled into complacency
That Dallas was a safe place to be?
That a popular President might
Make everything turn out right?

Popularity with the masses –
Like honey and molasses
Might to the taste be best –
But leave a sticky mess!

What fantasized smiles
Greet the Chosen Child!
People clap and cheer –
Others look and leer!

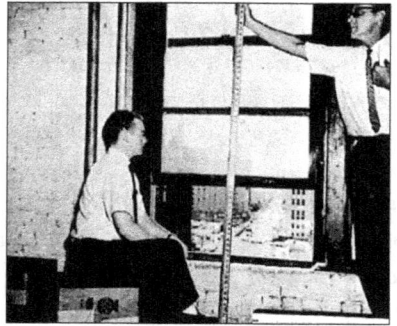

Sixth floor window
Not the best rifle perch!

A country unprepared
For wolves within their lair –
Might sit and contemplate
With barbarians at the gate

THE QUATRAINS OF CAMELOT

The King rides in his chariot
Amid joy and merriment –
But conspirators abound
Who seek to take him down!

Now the best opportunity for a shootin'
Was while the President was still on Houston –
From the sixth floor of the Depository –
Unless more shooters were in the territory!

Why didn't Oswald take the shot?
This would have been the perfect spot!
But was Oswald even on the sixth floor?
Or sipping a Coke by the snack shop door?

The motorcade turned from Houston to Elm –
A hairpin turn forced the cars to slow down!
The air was fresh and the sky was blue –
Nellie Connally said to Jackie, "Dallas loves you!"

As John Kennedy rode in the Dealey air
Would he think no more of Harvard Square?
Of dating co-eds and boats a-rowing
And wild times with parties throwing!

Children along the Motorcade Route

*While at Harvard, Kennedy charted his own course –
The Boston Brahmins thought him coarse!
But there he learned to think for himself –
And not be swayed by those with wealth!*

*"I'm not button down wealthy-
All trim and fit and healthy!
I challenged the Brahmins
To help all the Commons!"*

*The Establishment has its' own intentions
And believes it knows the best directions –
But a President following his own instincts
Can save a nation from the brink!*

*Kennedy waves and smiles at the crowd
As they continue clapping loud –
"It's nice to be the President
When everyone seems so content!"*

THE QUATRAINS OF CAMELOT

*"We wear fancy clothes and colored hats
With dapper coats and fancy spats –
Then we march in long parades
And cheer ourselves upon the stage!"*

*"I sometimes think that we
Create our own royalty –
Endowing them with the power
That helps our lives to flower!"*

*"I view the Dealey Plaza scene –
A pretty park that still is green!
I see the children run and play
Will they lose their innocence today?"*

*"People waving as you greet –
Knowing you will never meet!
A common bond enjoyed by all –
As we celebrate the coming fall!"*

*"Life forms perpetuate –
As I look across the 'scape!
Young people in the emplacements –
Soon will be our replacements!"*

*"There's a transience to this scene
That permeates my Being
We flicker in the light
Like fireflies in the night!"*

*"Do we have premonitions
That raise our suspicions?
Why do our thoughts range –
Over matters we cannot change?" "*

*"I hear church bells ringing in the distance –
Do they warn of the devil's persistence?
Does the Lord try to warn
Ahead of a violent storm?"*

*"Is there a parabellum
Headed for my cerebellum?
Must we always prepare for war
To keep the savages from our shore?"*

*"Do I suffer absinthian dreams
Of twisted worlds and political schemes?
Specters hiding in the shadows
With fire sticks and hidden gallows?"*

*"I was foolish in my younger days –
I cheated death in many ways!
But through the years I've come to know –
The fragile nature of life's road!"*

*"Gone are the times when you always win –
Those days are gone, gone with the wind!
We are entering tumultuous times –
With misdemeanors and high crimes!*

*"Do you remember
When life was simple –
Coke was a dime
And gum was a nickel!"*

*"Old time cars
Were once brand new –
With rear jump seats
And whitewalls, too!"*

*"Saddle shoes
And bobby socks –
Rock and roll
And record hops!"*

*"The Fourth of July
Was a day to play –
With baseball games
That went all day!"*

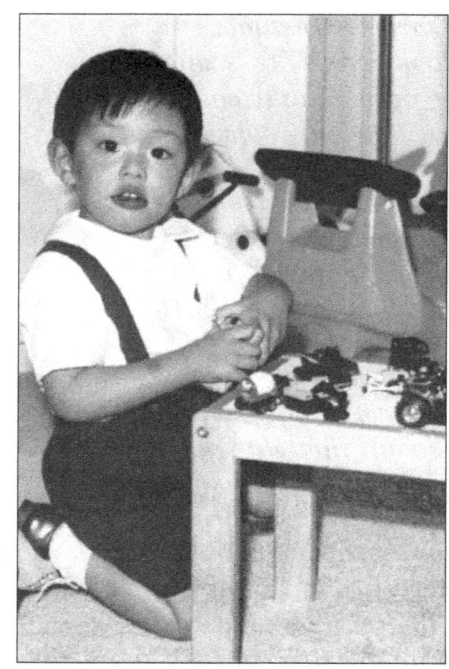

THE QUATRAINS OF CAMELOT

"For twenty five cents
You could buy hot dogs –
Or ride the subway
All day long!"

"We never spent
More than we earned –
A balanced budget
Was our concern!"

"We had our problems –
That was true –
But way back then
We could solve them, too!"

"Is there a Legion of Decency
That determines how we should be?
Distinguishing right from wrong –
And how we should get along!"

"I view the storm clouds that passed today –
They linger in the northern way –
Might they yet reverse their course
And trigger yet a devilish force?"

"Harsh winds blow today
Will evil have its' way?
Will the winds of change –
My life rearrange?"

"Where did Elijah go?
Into the whirlwind he stole!
He ascended into the clouds –
Where mystery still enshrouds!"

"What happened to the Immortals?
Did they pass through some Ancient Portal –
Never to be seen again
And curse us with a finite end?"

*"Do we worship heavenly orbs
And pray that Nature stays the course?
Do we create celestial gods
Where the imagination trods?"*

*"Was Jesus mortal –
Passing through some earthly portal?
Or was He divine –
Lasting until the end of time!"*

*"Is there a dark omen in the sky –
Was the morning storm a warning cry?
Or do I dwell on faulty premonitions
Born of unreasonable suspicions?"*

*"Is yonder rainbow God's proclamation
To protect us from devastation?
Or will there be another Flood
Of bullets and brain and blood?"*

*"Are catastrophes a necessary force
That alter a political course –
Is sudden change a way of life
In a world of fear and strife?"*

*"Death – I put you on pause –
Don't show me your angry claws!
I've got too much work to do –
I don't have the time to stew!"*

*"The mind goes to ugly places
When ghoulish nightmares it traces!
Better to think in the light
Than chase thoughts that linger at night!"*

*"I hear voices that sometimes shout –
What wild thoughts do run about!
Do they speak of premonition –
Or is it merely my condition?"*

THE QUATRAINS OF CAMELOT

"How much time have I got left –
Before my senses are bereft?
Will I make it to the end –
Or will fate my life upend?"

"Blood pulsing through my veins
Warns me of a coming change!
Are the Generals pushing hard
For a changing of the guard?"

"We spend our lives repairing wounds
Suffered since we left the womb –
Hoping for some saving Grace
That would make our pain erase!"

"Do I suffer from the silence of God –
Bearing thoughts where others won't trod?
Do I live in some grand illusion –
Riddled by own confusion?"

"What a chore to be human –
With religion and politics dueling!
Do we kill for the gods above –
Or do we act with brotherly love?"

"Does Nephthys come to protect the Pharaoh –
And spare him from the fatal arrow?
Or spread her wings in preparation
For yet another funeral oration?"

"Is there a logic or reason
In a political season?
Or does blind ambition
Lead to sedition?"

White Stone Cenotaph

"I see people waving as I pass –
Hoping to be led out of their morass!
We make copies of ourselves in spasms of delight –
Then walk a weary path before the endless night!"

THE DALLAS PARADE

*"Does the beauty of the day
Belie a deep dismay
By the generals and the spies
Who would seek my quick demise!"*

*"Is our fate ruled by a black swan theory
That unexpected events quite dreary
Are the ones that shape our lives
And often catch us by surprise?"*

*"I keep hearing interference –
Is it some kind of deterrence –
Warning me not to proceed –
Dare I stop and take heed?"*

*"Do the spirits that surround me –
Constantly trying to hound me
Speak of unknown danger
From some hidden stranger?"*

*"Will the CIA take schadenfreude
If the motorcade should loiter –
Allowing the shooters time to aim
And end my Presidential claim?"*

*"Does God play dice with the universe
Or are we born with a fatal curse –
That the One who guides us on our path
May not spare us from His wrath?"*

*"The leaves turn from green to red
Do they bring changes that I dread?
With the fall comes winter's snow –
And the Grim Reaper takes his toll!"*

*"Must we be without knowing –
And keep the Gnostic fires glowing?
Or will there be one sunny day
When all our doubts are washed away?"*

THE QUATRAINS OF CAMELOT

*"What do you do when your world falls apart –
It's not that easy to make a new start
When every day you reminisce
About the loved ones that you miss!"*

*"What message do the gods portray
With people dying every day?
Is there some rationalization
For our gradual annihilation?"*

*"Time goes by so fast –
The future becomes the past!
Would that I could stop this motorcade
And revel in some quiet shade!"*

*"There lies a hidden pain
Within each one's domain
A quiet, inner yearning
To keep the juices burning!"*

*"To realize that it's the end –
To bid farewell to friends –
To see your loved ones cry –
It's tough to say good-by!"*

*"Of course, nothing goes on forever
But with each and every endeavor
You wish that it would last
Until your time has passed!"*

*"When my sun goes out
Will you be about?
As I near the end
Will you be my friend?"*

*"I know not where we go
Will it be hot or cold?
Will it fulfill my dreams
Or will I just hear screams?"*

THE DALLAS PARADE

The pistons reciprocate
While the wheels gyrate –
The Lincoln machine
Knows not where it leans!

Will our mechanical devices
Spare us from our sins and vices
Or be the parting knell
On our road to hell?

"Living the dream
Is not what it seems –
You've got to adjust
To life's little ruts!"

"To die in your prime
Is not very kind –
But who can ignore
What fate has in store?"

"Is the end of the world really near –
Is that something we should fear?
Will an apocalyptic insistence
Shorten my existence?"

"Is this the Hopi doomsday –
When catastrophic forces play?
Or do I needlessly wonder
Over conspiratorial thunder?"

"There's something about the fall –
A quiet peace before winter's maw--
A time to reflect upon things done
And future goals that are yet unsung!"

"I feel my heart beating
And the moments fleeting –
Do I sense an urgency –
Some dire emergency?"

*"Or am I fooled
By thoughts unschooled –
An ancient warning
From prehensile formings?"*

*"When we close our eyes and sleep
In a slumber calm and deep
Are there hints of something more
From long lost friends on distant shores?"*

*"There's always competition
For that coveted first position –
But keep a wary eye
On those who you rely!"*

*"There are millions of damaged souls
Trying to make things whole –
Working with all their might
To make the world seem right!"*

*"Will we ever know the truth –
Will the curtain fall and show the booth
Where manipulators behind the scenes
Crush our hopes and steal our dreams!"*

*"Can the rites of ablution
Achieve restitution
For the misdeeds of man
In a prodigal land!"*

*"Will Hermes escort me on high
With Gabriel at his trusty side –
Or will Ash-bedi and his anger
Put my soul in real danger?"*

*"I think about the loved ones gone
And whisper them a little song –
I'll be crossing there one day
And all my cares will wash away!"*

THE DALLAS PARADE

*"You roll with the punches
Of life's daily crunches –
Hoping to find
Your own peace of mind!"*

*"Life is a series of misses
Trying to avoid the abysses –
Until tragedy strikes
And takes your life!"*

*"Marty, ignore those rumors--
Dallas is a city of bloomers!
Don't listen to those warnings
Of storm clouds that are forming!"*

*"In order to obtain their fill
Animals must learn to kill –
Is the key to our survival
The murder of our rival?"*

*"Each person is a heart beating
Counting the time fleeting –
You've got to keep on going
Until the blood stops flowing!"*

*"Value the air you breathe
Each day is a reprieve –
Another chance to shine
Before the end of time!"*

*"Dancing with the devil
Can leave you quite disheveled –
Best to play it straight
So angels congregate!"*

*"Will Rama with his bow and arrow
Make me walk the straight and narrow –
Dare I wander from the path
And inculcate his holy wrath?"*

THE QUATRAINS OF CAMELOT

"Even Ra, with all his glory
Descends down into purgatory –
Then rises each and every day
To face whatever comes his way!"

"Does Lyndon have a giant ego
That might consider acts illegal?
If cajoling and arm twisting won't work –
Then dirty tricks might not be shirked!"

"Did he make a deal with Faust
To the President oust?
And grab the reins of power
In history's darkest hour!"

"There are always forces that disunite –
That's part of a President's fight!
But those within our coast
Are the ones I fear the most!"

"Is there a code of action that applies
To all our actions as a guide –
Or must we constantly seek shelter
From a world of helter-skelter?"

"Is God in control
Or do the dice roll?
Do we live in a world of chance –
Ruled by happenstance?"

"I live in a world of generals and spies –
Constantly checking the look in their eyes!
Do they support or do they portend –
And are they plotting my early end?"

"Is there a dark force
That wound change history's course –
And take control
Of the mind and soul!"

THE DALLAS PARADE

"Will Surya protect me
From man's adversity?
Will the light of day
Keep conspirators away?"

"I saw Diogenes in the night
Wandering with his light –
Traveling through the land
Seeking an honest man!"

"Does Queen Nefertiti bring the North wind
To herald her next of kin?
Do regal figures from ages past
Try to warn of tragic paths?"

"Is envy the silent sin
We harbor deep within –
That would dare to kill a man
For possession of his land?"

"The Depository time is twelve twenty nine –
Do tragic forces seek to malign?
Will my enemies strike with impunity –
Trying to create a world of disunity?"

"Water – the symbol of life
The Trinity River flows through the night –
Would that the waves that roll
Could warn of their human toll!"

Who did this to us –
And created all this fuss?
Was it one man's alienation –
Or conspirators against the nation?

A simple twist of fate –
Or a conspiracy debate?
Which one shall it be
In American History?

THE QUATRAINS OF CAMELOT

Do we live in a quantum foam
Trying to protect our home –
In a world where creation and destruction
Are part of a universal function!

Could we travel in a time machine
And re-create the Camelot dream?
Stop the bullets before they strike –
And act to save a President's life!

Do we pay for sins of the past –
Constantly looking back
Haunted by dreams at night –
Trying to make things right!

Do we pay for yesterday's sin
With a future dark and dim?
Do yesterday's manipulations
Cause today's tribulations?

We live in a world of misgiving –
Hammering out a living –
Trying to live a life
In a world of heartache and strife!

Do we live by rules and taboos –
Constantly hiding the truth?
Working to make ends meet
Even if we have to cheat?

Is it mere chance –
Or just happenstance –
That the motorcade rides down Elm
With Lucifer at the helm!

There will always be parts of history
That remain shrouded in mystery –
Secrets so dark and deep
That the proletariat must not keep!

THE DALLAS PARADE

Did JFK time it right?
With war and racial tensions at their height –
He became a martyr for idealistic hopes –
While society still tries to cope!

The motorcade rides down Houston street –
Past the Old Red Courthouse where people greet –
A white stone cenotaph would nearby be placed
As an open tomb tribute to Kennedy's final race!

The Depository shooter aims his gun
As the motorcade makes its' Elm Street run –
What thoughts must rumble through his head
That would make him shoot a President dead?

Was he a Lone Nutter out for glory?
Or could there be a different story?
Was he mad about the Bay of Pigs –
When Kennedy refused to send the brigs!

Or was he taking orders from a Mafia chief
Who would Kennedy's War on Crime defeat?
Or was the shooter really a covert spy –
Acting with the knowledge of the FBI?

Perhaps it was just fortuitous
That security that day was ludicrous –
Or were key figures at the top
Part of a conspiracy plot?

THE QUATRAINS OF CAMELOT

Who does God choose to save?
Does Divine Intervention rule the day?
Does the Lord ever choose to intervene –
Or must He leave us to our means?

The Hertz sign on the roof of the Depository
Recorded the Dallas time at 12:30 –
We never know when our time is done
And when the Lord will end our run!

We are all like clocks running out –
Our sojourn is limited, there's no doubt!
We do the best, and in due time –
We hand the baton to the next in line!

A Presidential assassination
Is really an attack upon the nation –
Though one man takes the fall
The pain is surely felt by all!

The day was clear, the north wind was stout
And little children ran about!
Would that Nature could give a warning
Of the storm that was now forming!

What might otherwise be
In this day in history?
Life is full of what-ifs –
We have to take what Nature gifts!

We are transient creatures
With ever-changing features –
Trying to have fun
Before our day is done!

Is there a script in the genetic code
With actions that might forebode
The beginning of a new Dark Age
With humans knocked off center stage?

The Oklahoman

"Do I see a face among the trees
That puts my senses ill at ease?
Or is it just my imagination
That plays with darker situations?"

"Does something not smell right?
Are there actions out of sight?
Did I hear the click of a gun –
Or is my imagination overrun?"

"Open windows in the square
Could hide a lone gunman there!
The sorcerer has warned me twice
Of those who seek to take my life!"

"Flowers, flowers everywhere –
One way to express your care!
Everywhere you take a breath –
Flowers for life and flowers for death!"

"Does the pretty fall
Conceal a maw –
That might devour
A life in flower?"

THE QUATRAINS OF CAMELOT

"Does a tiger lurk at will
Anxious for a hungry kill?
Does he spot a prey
That will make his day?"

"The world's coming to an end –
Won't you be my friend?
Let's make music in the park
Until our world turns all dark!"

"Does the food chain of life
Explain our world of strife –
With each destructive deal
Just another person's meal?"

"Is there a shark
Within the park –
That might attack
And strike in back?"

"Do voices in my head
Warn of danger just ahead?
Or are these mere delusions
That add to my confusion?"

"Does the appetite of man
Create the tragic plans
That ruin nations
And bring utter devastation?"

"Do things happen for a reason –
Or is this just hunting season?
Is there a purpose to our life –
Or do we suffer needless strife?"

"Friday – the day of Venus' love –
Beauty and peace from God up above!
But actions by people with devilish schemes –
May soon give rise to freshly quashed dreams!"

"I see the rising quarter-moon in the East –
Does it herald war or hopes for peace?
The moon shows half its' brighter side –
But darker actions it would hide!"

"The moon tells a tale
Of brutality regaled!
Craters on the moon –
Do they portend our doom?"

Rising Quarter Moon

THE DALLAS PARADE

*Will God intervene in history
And spare us from this misery?
Do we live in Messianic times –
Foretold by Ancient Mariner rhymes?*

*The forces of darkness were gathering strong
As John Kennedy waved to the eager throng!
Was Dealey Plaza a repository for evil
That led to the New Frontier's upheaval?*

*"Is there a Brutus in the crowd?
Someone who claps and cheers out loud –
But deep within his heart
He carries poison darts!"*

*"The winter sun hangs low at solar noon –
The days grow shorter as the night does loom!
The shadows lean toward winter's North –
Will darker actions soon spring forth?"*

*"Are the gods displeased?
Will they hear my pleas?
Will the stars align –
Or is this just my time?"*

*"Is there a comet in the sky
That would portend an evil ply?
Some celestial warning
Of a political storming?"*

Dallas Motorcade

*"Feast day – the 22nd of November –
St. Cecilia we do remember!
The Patron Saint of musical traits –
Was martyred for her religious faith!"*

*"Will another martyr die
On the day Cecelia cried?
Does history repeat in kind
When the stars and moon align?"*

THE QUATRAINS OF CAMELOT

"With the sun entering Sagittarius –
Is my situation precarious?
Do the solar signs
Foretell evil times?"

"Is our universe based
On a destructive face?
Or is it rife –
With rekindled life?"

"Will the rain bring good or evil –
Does it signal an upheaval?
Or with each new drop of rain
Will a new seed grow again?"

View down Houston Street
(Greg Jaynes)

"Was the morning storm
Intended to warn
Of actions dark
Within the park?"

"Do we live from day to day
In a normal sort of way –
Denying with great insistence
Our very mortal existence!"

"Do we sometimes have premonitions
That warn us of evil volitions?
Do we have a sixth sense
That hints of coming events?"

"People die at the wrong time –
There is no reason or rhyme!
One day you're doing your lifelong work –
The next they're putting you in the dirt!"

"When you're in your final days
Can you see right through the haze?
Travel to the other side –
And see the folks who long ago died?"

THE DALLAS PARADE

"Do I see 'Kick' and brother Joe
Standing by the Grassy Knoll?
My eyes it seems are playing tricks
As visions from the past do fix!"

"Kick would always say to me –
Become the man who you can be!
Come out from Joe Jr.'s shadow –
Soon you'll be revered and hallowed!"

"I see little Patrick in his bed –
Will he rise up from the dead?
Would that he could come to life –
And help resolve our family strife!"

"The fabric of society   *Will there be a Black Swan event*
Is filled with impropriety –   *Involving our President?*
Primitive sounds   *Some unexpected occurrence*
Oft' abound!"   *Arising from disparate currents?*

"The moment of creation
Is filled with exclamation!
As the new soul
Does enter whole!"

"But the moment of our demise
Is filled with sobs and cries!
As the weary soul
Does exit whole!"

"There's a lot more intrigue
Than people believe –
When it comes to politicians
With Presidential ambitions!"

"Should I be the President –
The White House resident –
When the Illinois tally
Was a contrived reality?"

THE QUATRAINS OF CAMELOT

*"The heart of darkness is near –
Where all hope disappears!
The forces are gathering strong –
Will my life be short or long?"*

*"I dallied with Cord Meyers ex –
Surely that does him vex!
Will he seek retribution
Through his spooky institution?"*

*"Do heroic people have tragic flaws
That give the imagination pause?
When you strive to be the best
Will your character meet the test?"*

*"There's a violent difference of opinion
Between myself and Landslide Lyndon!
I picked LBJ to balance the ticket –
But it's really left me in quite a thicket!"*

*"Is there a continuity to consciousness –
Or a dark and empty Nothingness?
When we cross the great Unknown –
Do we reap the seeds we've sown?"*

*"The wealthy merchants march to the grave
At the same rate as the lowly knave!
So gather your acorns as you will –
But be prepared for the final chill!"*

*"It's a race, you know –
To see who gets the dough!
So jump on the treadmill
Until you've had your fill!"*

*"I see the monarch butterflies
Heading for the Southern skies!
What danger does entail
When a northeaster does prevail?"*

THE DALLAS PARADE

*"Will my soul travel ahead
As they celebrate the Day of the Dead?
Las mariposas carry the souls
Of our ancestors long ago!"*

*"What will my final days be like –
Will there be heartache and strife?
Will I suffer in the end –
And will I ever see you again?"*

*"What would God say
If this were my final day?
Does mankind ignore obvious warnings
Of storm clouds that are forming?"*

Day of the Dead Mask

*"Should notice be served to God
That we're not happy with the path He trods?
Can a summary judgment rule
Against a world that's cold and cruel?"*

*"But when God closes one door, he opens another –
Will I get to heaven with my older brother?
Joe died a hero and went down in flames –
Will I die a martyr, so peace finally reigns?"*

*"Are human beings predatory –
Like lions and tigers, all bloody and gory?
Can we assuage our primitive past –
And dream of civilizations that will last?"*

*"We are all casualties –
Living in a false reality!
Dark memories of war-torn days
Keep filtering back through the haze!"*

*"Are we just dust in the wind –
Born to rise, then fall again!
Like flowers planted, we celebrate our birth –
Before winter comes, and we return to earth!"*

THE QUATRAINS OF CAMELOT

"These are the good old days
Looking for fun in the haze!
Not knowing what lies in the distance –
Or who will be the resistance!"

"There's a peace in the morning
That belies a warning
Of trouble ahead
And actions I dread!"

"When I contemplate my end
Is this the final bend?
Or will there be new roads
Lined with silver and gold?"

"Don't try to understand
Deal with life as you can!
No matter what you dread
Don't fear the road ahead!"

"I feel a pounding in my chest –
Does it warn of some unrest?
Or just a minor palpitation
From some passing situation?"

"I fight battles in my dreams
With heavy breathing and screams –
I hear warnings and admonitions--
Could they be premonitions?"

"Is there a primal fear
That senses trouble near –
A warning from our genes
Of danger that's not seen?"

"Sins of the past
Threaten my path –
Though I offer restitution
They threaten retribution!"

THE DALLAS PARADE

*"Perhaps it's in the air –
The smell from someone's lair –
A sense that all's not right
From trouble out of sight!"*

*"This will be the day that I die –
When women scream and children cry!
The end of the prophecy
For one thousand days of democracy!"*

*"When I fancy my demise
Will it come as a surprise?
Or will it be a gradual progression
To yet another world dimension?"*

*"Man is aware of his mortality
And must face the reality
Of a life that ends
And say good-by to friends!"*

*"Is there a reason for death –
Does it keep life fresh?
With each generation
A new iteration!"*

*"Is all hope lost
And at what cost –
Can we make amends
Before the world ends?"*

*"Am I a wayfaring stranger
Not aware of the danger
That lurks in the air
From some tiger's lair?"*

*A deception within a deception –
It's all about perception!
But what the eye does see
Is all just make-believe!*

THE QUATRAINS OF CAMELOT

The Depository was a misdirection
With bullets from a different section –
The rear shots from the Dal-Tex
Would the President hex!

Oswald would get the blame
For an act he never claimed!
The magic trick from the CIA
Would never know the light of day!

Did the Illuminati make the kill –
Did Kennedy act against their will?
Do they claim a divine right
To fully exercise their might?

Our life's a tragic act
With images of the past
That float upon our mind
And haunt as they rewind!

"Life is a kaleidoscope of scenes
Passing within my dreams –
Trying to make things right
In a world of fear and fright!"

"Is there an animal creature in my past
That warns of danger in my path –
Dare I take the turn down Elm
And enter yet another realm?"

"Is there a parallel universe
Where lies the Kennedy curse –
Did Kick and Joe and Patrick find the way
To yet another world at play?"

"Is there a death Star
That circles from afar –
And crushes all our dreams
With tragedy and screams?"

*"Talk of a traitor
By Kennedy haters
To the best I can tell
Just poisons the well!"*

*"I see the umbrella going up and down
My father knew well the sounds
Of people clamoring for war
In order to settle the score!"*

*"My Father had the best intentions
To settle political dissension
By coming to mutual agreements –
Which were later called appeasement!"*

*"We follow in each other's path
Trying to avoid God's wrath-
But could there be another way
To keep the howling wolves at bay?"*

*"One car follows another
Is there safety in numbers?
But if we travel the wrong road –
Then all will pay the toll!"*

*"Is there a bullet with my name
Headed for my brain –
Or will it miss the mark
And spare me from the dark!"*

*"I survived the vicissitudes of World War II.
And saved some members of my crew –
But still I sense a danger
From some dark and hidden stranger!"*

*"Do we head down the yellow brick road
Where ends the colored rainbow?
Or is this the parting knell
Where we enter the gates of hell!"*

THE QUATRAINS OF CAMELOT

"We can never know about the days ahead –
Will there be sunshine or storms we dread?
Will there be trouble on the road we take
That would sabotage the plans we make?"

"Am I ill at ease
As the wind blows through the trees –
Did I catch a passing glance
Of a gunman in his stance?"

"As I enter Dealey Square
Do I cross the Rubicon there –
The point of no return
With all your bridges burned!"

"Do I, like Icarus with waxed wings
Soar to heights where angels sing –
Only to fall to the seas
Over deadly rivalries!"

"The morning rain leaves freshened air –
No sign of trouble anywhere!
The Dealey Park is quite serene –
Will Venus or Mars portend the scene?"

"Is it accident or fate that my stars don't align –
Do they seek to warn me of dangerous times?
Dare I be strong and enter the fray
Or should I stay home for the rest of the day?"

"If tomorrow never comes –
We frolicked in the sun
W had a love affair
The two of us could share!"

"Will Jesus return
Before the world burns?
And spare our lives
From compromise?"

THE DALLAS PARADE

*"Am I a catcher in the rye
Saving countries before they die –
Wandering too close to the abyss
In a world of hit or miss!"*

*Official history is a joke!
The establishment could never cope
With a true accounting of the facts –
They'd be labeled unnatural acts!*

*"Is the Abyssal plain
Where souls remain –
The lowest ebb
Of Nature's web?"*

*"When we grow old
We think of life's toll –
And try to fill the spaces
Of life's empty places!"*

*"We live a life of transience
With parades and pageants
To mark the time of year
And treasures we hold dear!"*

*"Do we live in Paradise Lost
With suffering and death the cost?
A struggle for persistence
In a Darwinian existence!"*

*Would Dulles and McCloy and the Bilderberger crew
Seek to consider what no one else would do –
A Presidential assassination
For financial considerations!*

*Printing dollars by the Treasury
Without the Federal Reserves usury
Might be considered a risk
By those who hold the chips!*

THE QUATRAINS OF CAMELOT

*"Some people don't make it –
They say they just can't take it –
Perhaps they know more
What fate has in store!"*

*"We fill in the spaces
Of life's empty places –
Trying to make sense
Of lost innocence!"*

*"We're players on a stage
Taking turns expressing rage –
Shuffling in and shuffling out –
Wondering what it's all about!"*

*"There will always be Kennedy haters
Like swamps have alligators!
But the best you can do
Is to your ideals be true!"*

*"Balance the ticket!" is what they say –
"Pick someone of a different sway –
But if you fall into disgrace
He'll step right up and take your place!"*

*"When I leave this planet
Will I be remembered like granite?
Or will my memory be washed away
Like sandstone into clay?"*

*Run, Clint Hill, run –
Save our President from the gun!
Run with all your might
In dreams that haunt the night!*

*"The falling leaves
Put me ill at ease –
Will winter's eyes
Be my demise?"*

"Some people are damaged and never recover –
Like losing your one true lover –
Others are able to heal their wounds
And give rise to the flowers that bloom!"

"I keep getting older
My enemies are bolder!
Like circling hawks –
They stare and gawk!"

"We are all born with a death sentence
No matter your sins or penance –
So enjoy the world while you can
Before life's race is ran!"

"The disappointment of unfulfilled dreams
Leaves me with failed schemes –
How can you make things right
When you can't sleep at night?"

"They stone the devil
To keep him disheveled--
But will he rise again
In another ken?"

"We live a life of near misses –
Trying to avoid the abysses!
Hoping to live out our days
And die in natural ways!"

"Are we tortured by the past
With thoughts that ever last –
Awful situations
That trigger ruminations!"

"You know that life isn't fair –
You must have the strength to bear –
Life is a series of traumatic events
Caused by Nature or ill intents!"

THE QUATRAINS OF CAMELOT

"Do craters on the moon
Portray eventual doom –
Or do violent acts give way
To yet a brighter day?"

"Is God everywhere –
In the ground and in the air--
Or do we imagine protection
From a heavenly direction?"

"I see Helios travels today
And looks down upon the fray –
What tales will he bear
That give the gods a scare?"

"The days are shorter
In the fourth quarter –
When nights are longer
You must be stronger!"

LBJ bends over before the shooting starts –
And Rufus Johnson jumps upon his parts –
Did LBJ have precognition –
Or was he part of the coalition?

Will chaos reign supreme
Before the Mahdi makes the scene?
And can they hasten his arrival
By killing all their rivals?

Did evolution shape us to be good –
Must we always do what we should?
Or must we sometimes slip away
And let the devil have his way?

"People say good-by
And ask you not to cry –
Soon there'll come a time
When you can come and rhyme!"

*"Each one has their fun
To frolic in the sun –
And after every fray
There comes a brighter day!"*

*"In the epic of Gilgamesh
The king mourns Enkido's death
Is immortality
A false reality?"*

*"We live our daily life
Never knowing when our time is ripe –
Living each passing day
Hoping to keep the gods at bay!"*

*"Your life is in transition
Hoping for a new position –
Getting more education
To start a new vocation!"*

*"Eggs and sperm
Our bodies constantly churn –
Making future replacements
For our embattled emplacements!"*

*"Birth, death, and renewal –
Am I some kind of fool?
Trying to play the game
In a world I cannot tame!"*

*"Life is over so quick –
Careers, children – it's a trip!
But in the blink of an eye
You have to say good-by!"*

*"Will Leon Trotsky be remembered
For the revolution he engendered –
Or must idealism pass
Under the dictator's ax?"*

THE QUATRAINS OF CAMELOT

Would the CIA toast with champagne
The end of the Kennedy domain
And the rise of the military-industrial complex
That would the nation vex!

"My heart is pounding in my chest –
Do I sense a deep unrest?
Do I see an icy stare
From a shooter in his lair?"

"I wish that we
Could always be
And never know
The final blow!"

"Why the big rush
To be doctors and lawyers and such
When the real world situation
Is a global disintegration?"

"Don't' try to understand –
Live life the best you can!
No matter what you dread
Don't fear the road ahead"!

"I feel the pain
Of the human strain
To live a life
That's full of strife!"

The earth does shake
And reverberate
From the shock and chill
Of a kingly kill!

Are the pleasures we share and take
Merely tricks of nature to procreate?
Are we victims as a nation
Of our cerebral stimulations?

THE DALLAS PARADE

*"It's twelve thirty and all seems well
As our Lincoln makes the turn down Elm –
Will another President meet his fate –
Or will the gods commiserate?"*

*"Is life just a confabulation
Of impossible situations –
With quirks and turns ahead
That sometimes we must dread!"*

*"There's a transience
To our existence
That belies the slowing tide
As we pursue our daily grind!"*

*"Do we fight battles today
Left over from yesterday--
Perceiving in today's disgraces
The memories of yesterday's faces!"*

*"Will Athena spare me
From the fate of royalty –
And spare the nation
From assassination!"*

*"Can't people co-exist
Without raising clenched fists?
Why, in every civilization
Is there a threat of annihilation?"*

*"My Father rang the bell
That war cries we could quell--
If only other nations
Would accept the invitation!"*

*"Now they blame me
For a lack of rivalry
When I try to make things right
And resolve without a fight!"*

THE QUATRAINS OF CAMELOT

"This isn't some schoolyard altercation
We're talking nation against nation!
The stakes are much higher
When you play with nuclear fire!"

"I see open windows in the Depository
Could it be a repository
For shooters who could strike
Or a decoy on the right?"

"Perhaps I'm being paranoid
From watching too much celluloid –
But the advance surveillance team
Should have checked the scene!"

"If my safety is compromised
It could lead to my demise –
Was this just an oversight –
Somehow things just don't seem right!"

"Are my senses dulled with age?
I see a vision in the haze!
The angel sends a warning
Of storm clouds that are forming!"

"Somehow it seems a little queer
To see Ed Lansdale walking here!
What mischief might the CIA
Be planning on this sunny day?"

"We all circle the sun
Until our day is done –
Like moths circling the flame
We worship what we cannot tame!"

"With the Mafia and the CIA
We tried to quell the Cuban fray –
But after the Bahia de los Cerdos
We had angry spies and guerreros!"

*"Showing self-respect
Is what everyone expects –
The loss of self-esteem
Can leave you tough and mean!"*

*"Is it accident or fate
That my stars don't' relate?
Do they herald dangerous times
When malicious forces align?"*

*"When you've been given the last rites
And survived twice –
You want to have some fun
Before your time is done!"*

*"Is there a line between right and wrong
Or does each person sing his own song?
Those who live a life of adversity
Are more aware of life's diversity!"*

*"Each day is a gift
So please don't be miffed
If all isn't right
By the end of the night!"*

*"Do we live our lives shackled in chains
Re-living yesterday's pains--
Looking in each new path
For a solution to yesterday's wrath!"*

*Do you believe in divine intervention –
That God would enter our dimension
And protect our nation
From assassination?*

*Or must man rely on his own instincts
To keep from becoming extinct?
For the laws of the universe won't alter
If yet another species should falter!*

THE QUATRAINS OF CAMELOT

"Is there a cancer in my house –
Someone who has sold me out –
Or do I needless reason
Over non-existent treason?"

"Everybody reaches for the limelight
No matter who they have to fight –
Like trees reaching for the sun
They care not who they overrun!"

"Is there a sentient evil force
That would alter nature's course –
That plots and undermines
The plans of noble minds?"

"Can you see through the looking glass
And view our ancient past –
From whence came our aggression
And our territorial protection?"

"Is there a planet X
That would our people vex –
Every 26 million years
That would bring us to tears?"

"Why do we suffer
Without a buffer
To shield the pain
From the devil's domain?"

"Are there secrets so deep
That they must always keep –
And conspiracies so rare
That we need not beware?"

"Like salmon swimming upstream
We try to fulfill all our dreams--
Planting the seed for the new generation
Before giving way to the next iteration!"

"Do we live in a world of deception
Blinded in either direction
By a parliamentary elite
That keeps things nice and neat?"

"What in the world is God doing
With people cheering and others booing –
Why the great dichotomy
Over a difference in philosophy?"

"Did Ananias and Saphira deserve to die
For telling Peter a little lie?
Don't we all want recognition
Despite our imperfect condition?"

"I am tormented by enemies that I cannot see –
With visions of angels coming after me!
What mischief does the mind constantly play –
That seeks to warn me of my final day?"

"Has the resurrection defeated death –
When I take my final breath
Will there be a world free of strife
That promises eternal life?"

"Will God intervene
And alter the scene –
Or will God demure
And let havoc occur?"

"The wind has changed from south to north –
What mischief might be coming forth?
Does nature warn of changing times
When blustery gales blow winter chimes?"

"What trick of the gods would promise me
One thousand days of destiny –
Then leave me to be suddenly killed
With all my promises unfulfilled?"

THE QUATRAINS OF CAMELOT

"How quickly we enter the afterlife!
Is it free of pain and free of strife?
Do we enter a world that's calm and serene –
Or do we enter another battle scene?"

"Life is a silly carnival game
That you hope your luck will entertain –
But if you're in the wrong place at the wrong time
The rings will never fall in line!"

Did Lyndon have ESP?
He ducked before the shooting spree!
He claims he bent over to listen to the radio –
At least, that's how the official story goes!

Some say Lyndon was paranoid that day –
That perhaps the bullets might go astray!
Lyndon, too, had enemies in Texas –
Was he part of a fatal nexus?

LBJ later joked that Divine Intervention
Was how he achieved Presidential dimensions!
But is it really a divine attraction
When human beings take all the action!

The Depository oak tree
Looks down upon the scene!
Looking somber, with boughs that bend –
It holds the secret of a President's end!

Did bullets whistle through its' leaves
From a crazed lone gunman in the eaves?
Did the oak tree stand and cry –
As it helplessly watched a President die!

And what did the Triple Underpass see –
As the royalty approached with glee?
Was there a gunman in the drain –
Waiting to cause the President pain?

And did the Grassy Knoll just stare –
With gunmen hiding in its' hair?
Would the ground could stomp and quake
And help to change a President's fate!

But Nature chose to hold its' peace
And let the killers do their deed!
Divine Intervention was not at hand –
Man's free will would rule the land!

People waving – that's the norm
But is this the calm before the storm?
Scenes of peace and tranquility
May harbor hidden hostility!

We're in a giant wave machine
With ups and downs and in-betweens!
We ride the highs and then the lows
And what will happen no one knows!

The people along Elm Street were cheering loud –
As Jackie and John waved to the crowd
Rosemary Willis ran with her Pops –
When she suddenly heard several loud shots!

Little Rosemary runs back and forth
Does she know history's course?
"I want to run fast
And make circles in the grass!"

"Let my heart run free
And circle every tree!"
When the gunshots do resound –
Rosemary stops and looks around!

Rosemary Willis suddenly stops

What does Rosemary Willis see –
As she looks at history?
A President will be replaced –
A lone gunman will be disgraced!

THE QUATRAINS OF CAMELOT

Innocence was lost that day
As little Rosemary ran and played!
Would that we could live our lives
Minus all the screams and cries!

Will anyone remember
This day in late November
When people cried
And a President died?

Into the Valley of Death
Rode Royalty's final breath!
Unaware of the present danger –
And the plans of perfect strangers!

As the car turns from Houston to Elm –
Is God or fate at the helm?
Is the road we travel predestined
Or filled with shooters clandestine?

"When will unresting death
Come to take my final breath?
Elm Street looks quiet and peaceful –
But will it lead to an upheaval?"

"How do we face the ugly realities –
Do we live in a world of dualities?
When things get bad, we turn away
And think about those happy days!"

"Is our life a deception –
Headed in the wrong direction?
Just when things seem right –
Reality takes a bite!"

"Why does God let people die?
Can't He hear the people cry?
I've been praying hard at night –
But the answers don't seem right!"

90   THE DALLAS PARADE

"Is there a principle of uncertainty
That covers all humanity?
Are actions planned by mice and men
Doomed to fail in the end?"

Do we live in a steady state
With a universe sedate?
Or do we face sudden destruction
From another Big Bang eruption?

Can we shape the world with platitudes
And encourage positive attitudes?
Or is our future destined to falter
By actions we simply cannot alter?

Is reality just an illusion
Arising from some quantum confusion?
Are the particles of creation
Just mathematical equations?

THE QUATRAINS OF CAMELOT

When the bullets resounded in Dealey Square
A flock of pigeons took to the air!
As they suddenly left the Depository roof
Did they wonder what mischief was aloof!

The dictabelt preserved the sounds
Complete with echoes from the rounds!
Five shots rang out in Dealey Square
As shooters fired from their lair!

Hugh Betzner snapped a picture (Z-186) before the first sound
Phil Willis took his photo (Z-202) after the first round!
Kennedy looks to his right as he waves –
When the first shot is fired from the conspirator's cave!

But a shot around Zapruder 190
Is blocked by the Depository tree!
So the Dal-Tex becomes the spot
Where gunmen fired that early shot!

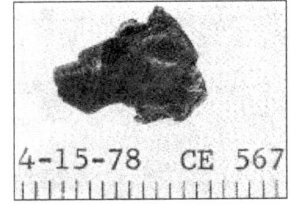

The first shot was fired too low
And almost was a fatal blow –
It skipped upon the limo's rear
And sent sparks flying everywhere!

The people who were standing 'round
Thought they heard a firecracker sound –
With sparks and a metallic clank
They thought that it was just a prank!

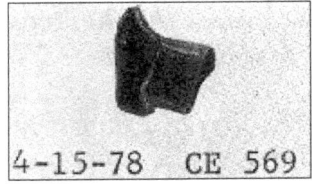

The bullet then entered Kennedy's back –
And traveled upward out his neck!
He clasped is throat in agony –
And wondered, "Who did this to me?"

The Dal-Tex building was the spot
Where gunmen fired that early shot!
It struck John Kennedy from behind –
And echoes 'til the end of time!

THE DALLAS PARADE

Altgen's Photo (AP)

*Sheriff Decker turned around
When he heard the first rifle sound –
He saw the second shot hit Elm Street
And spread a cloud of fine concrete!*

*The second shot was a near miss
And scared the limousine occupants!
It headed toward the Main Street way –
And hit the curb in front of Tague!*

*James Tague stopped his car to get a glance
And stood beneath the Triple Underpass –
But when the shooting was complete –
He was told of blood on his right cheek!*

*The first two shots were way too close
For a single shooter to fire both!
1.6 seconds was not enough time
For a shooter to reload and fire on line!*

*The shot to Tague created a conundrum –
It meant the shooting wasn't humdrum!
You must have more shooters than Lee –
Unless one bullet does the work of three!*

THE QUATRAINS OF CAMELOT

"Why did God do this to me?
Haven't I had enough adversity?
These people who want me dead
Should think about what lies ahead!"

Kennedy leaned forward and grabbed his neck –
Then he turned to Jackie and said, "I've been hit!"
John Connally then turned around
To see whence came that dreadful sound!

Connally saw Kennedy grab his throat
And cough as if his neck was choked –
Perhaps he does remember not
But Connally claimed he'd not been shot!

"The bullet that hit John Kennedy
Was not the one that went through me!"
Then, as Connally turned, his face was racked –
As the third shot fired went through his back!

The bullet then shattered Connally's right wrist –
At least that's the official media blitz!
It fractured his wrist, and that was that –
But he still held on to his Stetson hat!

Then there was a fatal pause
That gave the Secret Service cause –
Driver Greer did all astound
And slowed the car as he turned 'round!

Jackie said later, "Get a good driver
If you're going to be a survivor!"
Agent Clint Hill jumped off the trailing car
With bullets he would try to spar!

Archduke Ferdinand with his wife beside
Was on a Presidential ride –
The driver went straight instead of turning
And World War I. would soon be burning!

THE DALLAS PARADE

Seconds count when shots are fired –
Did the Secret Service conspire?
Open windows everywhere –
But no one really seemed to care!

The Secret Service that previous night
Had gone out drinking to near daylight!
The only hotel guards, to everyone's ire
Were two firemen, in case of fire!

Vince Palamara studied the Secret Service
And saw some things that made him nervous –
An open car was an invitation
To a Presidential assassination!

Doesn't it seem a little strange
That the Secret Service was never made
To account for it's ineptitude
For mistakes of such great magnitude?

Vince Palamara

Abraham Lincoln suffered the same lot
When his security guard left his spot –
Was this a planned situation
Or just an unlucky deviation?

"Et tu, Lyndon?" did Kennedy say
As shots were fired that fateful day?
Sometimes your greatest enemies
Are in the closest proximity!

Colonel Reich of the 112th Military Intelligence Group
Was told to stand down on the day of the coup!
From Fort Sam Houston they would have assured
That the motorcade route was better secured!

The Black Umbrella went up and down
As the Umbrella Man twirled it round and round –
"Kennedy does the communists please
Which puts us Texans ill at ease!"

THE QUATRAINS OF CAMELOT

Joe Kennedy had supported Neville Chamberlain
Who tried to please Hitler before World War II. began!
Neville Chamberlain had tried to appease –
Such diplomacy could never succeed!

But what's wrong with negotiation
To avoid a nuclear confrontation?
Mutual talks should be the potion
To help prevent a nuclear explosion!

Did the umbrella fire poison darts –
A product of the department of black arts?
If you aimed the umbrella just right
A poison flechette would take to flight!

Years later, the Umbrella Man came forth
The man, Louis Witt, brought his umbrella to court!
But the umbrella ribs didn't match the Zapruder film –
So the truth behind the umbrella may never be known!

Others claimed there was a manhole cover
Where a silent shooter could patiently hover –
He could fire his gun from a spot discreet
And disappear beneath the street!

Some placed a shooter near the triple underpass
Who shot from the front before Kennedy passed!
Others placed a shooter near the pergola wall –
The "Black Dog Man" was the strangest of all!

Then there's the story of Agent George Hickey
Who rode in the follow-up car with an AR-15 –
Did Hickey accidentally fire a shot
When he really intended not?

But the most amazing feat of all
Is that after three shots, the President didn't fall!
Now the back-up man would play his role
And fire his gun from the Grassy Knoll!

*Kennedy wore a rigid back brace –
It was made of canvas with metal stays
After the neck shot, he was still upright –
'Cause he couldn't duck out of the rifle sights!*

Vigil at St. Eduards

*Can you interfere with God's plans –
And stop a bullet before it lands?
Clint Hill sought to block the force –
And interfere with history's course!*

*Agent Hill jumped from the motorcade
And tried to give the President aid –
But the fourth shot from the Knoll ahead
Would shortly leave the President dead!*

What Abraham Zapruder saw.
Courtesy of Josiah Thompson

Sketch of Zapruder frame 237

> *"I've got orders to kill the Ruler –*
> *Can anything we do be crueler?*
> *Yet another coup d'état –*
> *Framed as a lone gunman plot!"*

THE DALLAS PARADE

The hunter hid silently beside the tree
And viewed his quarry behind the leaves –
Would he hesitate and let him go?
And spare the President from his fatal blow?

What thoughts must a gunman think
As his quarry descends into the rink?
"Is this ambush really justified?
And why do I feel mortified?"

"Will God look kindly upon this attack –
Or will He punish us with His wrath?
Have we a right to usurp the King
And invoke the policies that we bring?"

"Or will this attack upon the nation
Merely result in destabilization?
Will the policies we put in force
Put us on a dangerous course?"

"The Navy ships were set to land
At the Bahía de Cochinos was the plan –
That's when Kennedy lacked the will –
I saw my comrades all get killed!"

"With the communists you cannot reason –
That's why they're in hunting season!
It's not enough to talk the talk –
You've also got to walk the walk!"

"These are thoughts I must not harbor
If I'm to do my job with ardor!
A soldier's performance will surely lessen
If he takes the time to thoroughly question!"

His finger trembles on the trigger
As through his sites he sees a figure –
The President descends the Elm Street Lane
As the young assassin takes dead aim!

THE QUATRAINS OF CAMELOT

Sometimes I wonder late at night
As God looks down upon our plight –
Couldn't God perform a little magic
And make the world a little less tragic?

Do we have destructive desires
That would fill our lives with fire –
And early end our fruitful days
Born of guilt from early ways?

How many times do tragic scenes
Play over and over in our dreams!
Would that we could have some respite
And make our lives a little less desperate!

But if God were to intercede
To prevent the occurrence of evil deeds
Would mankind ever learn a thing –
And would we be puppets on a string?

Over and over and over again
The list of tragedies never ends –
I construct a world of great illusion
In order to lessen my confusion!

God decides who lives and dies –
It's not for us to reason why!
We play our role and cast our net –
We never know who might be next!

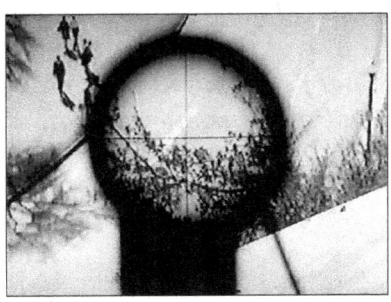

Shots are blocked by tree
from Z-166 to Z-210

We do our best from day to day
And help each other along the way –
We never know when our time has come
And when our work on earth is done!

Somehow it doesn't seem right
That an entire country's plight –
That the people's dreams of peace should linger –
Around one man's quivering trigger finger!

THE DALLAS PARADE

Or was the man so resolute –
So steeped in what he thought was truth –
That never would he doubt his deed –
So determined was he to succeed!

And what did John Kennedy say that day
Before he died in the Dallas parade?
Was there time for a last goodbye
With words to Jackie at his side?

Six seconds isn't much time
To say what's really on your mind!
So often we wait too late –
To say good-bye to our lifelong mate!

Too oft' we never get the time
To utter final words and lines –
To bid farewell to our loved one
Before the final bell has rung!

"Shall I make a supplication –
A prayer for our sacred nation –
That peace might soon prevail
And spare us more travail!"'

Jack with Jacqueline

"Take my hand
We're going down
Our ship of life
Has gone aground"

"All our hopes
And all our schemes
Are but the stuff
Of what we dream"

"We'll make our peace
With hands that bind
Our luck, our fate
Has not been kind"

THE QUATRAINS OF CAMELOT

"We'll never part   "So take my hand
I promise you   And don't be sad
And when I go   Let's thank the Lord
I'll think of you!"   For what we had!"

I wish I had another minute
Of our love that had no limit!
I'd say, "I love you – please don't cry!"
We never said our last good-bye!

Boom! *The shot was heard so loud*
That people jumped down to the ground!
Witnesses to the ground were flattened
And people all around were saddened!

And the splattered remnants of the dream
Go flying about as people scream –
"Bring our leader back –
And leave our world intact!"

The shot was heard around the world
As flags at half-mast were unfurled –
Someone's killed our President!
And people all around just wept!

William Newman with his family
Was the closest to the shooting spree –
"I saw his right ear disappear
As blood and brains went to the rear!"

*"We all fell flat upon the ground –
I know when I hear a rifle round!
I was in the military and I know
The fatal shot came from the Grassy Knoll!"*

William Newman lies down with Family after Grassy Knoll Shot

*William Newman was only fifteen feet
Where the President met his final defeat –
But the Warren Commission didn't want to hear –
William Newman was never asked to appear!*

*"I thought the shot came from the garden behind me –
I do not recall looking toward the Depository!"* –
*Those were the words William Newman would say –
But the Warren Commission never gave him his day!*

*Lee Bowers was watching from the railroad tower
And observed commotion at the Grassy Knoll bower –
He heard shots and saw smoke behind the fence
But the police said it was no consequence!*

*Gordon Arnold was at the Grassy Knoll
And fell down when the shots took their toll –
"They came from behind me," he later declared
"And I must admit that I was scared!"*

*Was Jesus just a little late?
These are words I contemplate –
Do the gods supervise
Every moment of our lives?*

THE QUATRAINS OF CAMELOT

*Are there times that we perceive
When our gods have taken leave?
Or do we fail to understand
The inner workings of God's plan?*

*From a distance, Marie Muchmore and Orville Nix
Photographed the motorcade with action pics –
But some of the motion seems a little too fast –
Could some of the frames have been dispatched?*

*Beverly Oliver was only 50 feet removed
When the Grassy Knoll gunman made his fatal move –
When the shot was fired, the Babushka Lady cried –
Then her movie camera was confiscated by the FBI!*

*The people have a right to know
What happened on the Grassy Knoll!
What right has the FBI
To confiscate evidence and let it die?*

Beverly Oliver

*Motorcyclist Hargis thought he'd been shot in the chest
As blood and bones embedded in his patrolman's vest!
Riding left and rear he felt the might
Of a bullet fired from the front and right!*

THE DALLAS PARADE

Kenny O'Donnell and Dave Powers
Were two of Kennedy's closest followers –
They both said shots from the front were taken
But the FBI told them they were both mistaken!

Now when you conduct an investigation
Into a Presidential assassination –
Should the FBI be influencing a witness statement
By telling him that he's mistaken?

A fifth shot was heard right after that
And Connally dropped his Stetson hat!
"They're trying to kill us all!" he declared
As bullets echoed in Dealey Square!

What's it like, to watch your loved one die?
To cradle him, then watch the pieces fly!
Jackie climbed the trunk to retrieve a bone –
Would that she could make him whole!

"May you all burn in hell!"
That was Jackie's parting knell –
The words still echo in the shooter's ears
As he contemplates his final years!

A white stuffed dog was in the seat –
Between Jackie and John it did retreat!
A gift from a little girl that day –
It was washed in the blood of JFK!

"Would it be so unfair
If we could our love repair –
Put the pieces back in place
And let you feel my sweet embrace?"

When a sudden catastrophe
Ruins your view of reality –
What do you think and say
As you face each daunting day?

THE QUATRAINS OF CAMELOT

Frame From Muchmore Film – Clint Hill dashes toward the limo, as JFK slouches and Jackie climbs on the trunk

What forces of chance
Are looked at askance –
With body parts
And broken hearts!

"Something has happened on the motorcade route!"
Those are the first words that came from the South –
"John Kennedy has been shot on the motorcade path!"
And all the world just stopped in their tracks!

"Hold everything secure!"
Sheriff Bill Decker demurred –
"Until the homicide and other investigators get there!"
Those were the orders in Dealey Square!

Then police Chief Jesse Curry offered –
"We're going to the hospital, officers!
We're on our way to Parkland Hospital!"
Those were words almost inaudible!

THE DALLAS PARADE

Aerial View of Dealey Plaza

*One minute you're waving to the crowd –
The next you're covered with a shroud!
Sometimes I ponder in the night
When sudden tragedy takes a life!*

*To die in such a violent way –
It wasn't meant to be that day!
But vendettas have a way of striking
When men of power engage in fighting!*

*The official view would be promulgated
That a lone gunman had assassinated –
Firing from the Depository window
At a moving target the size of a pinhole!*

*The heads of the Secret Service men
Were present in the shooter's ken –
Standing on the running boards of the trailing car
Their bobbing heads would a clear shot mar!*

THE QUATRAINS OF CAMELOT

Seven witnesses saw smoke from the Knoll –
They smelled it and saw it, but what did they know?
The Warren Commission gave them no heed –
They said they saw smoke, but it must have been steam!

Now there was a steam pipe farther away
But Stewart Galanor gave it no sway!
Nor did the Warren Commission convince –
It's never leaked before, nor has it ever leaked since!

Missed shot from Dal-Tex hits pavement, then nicks James Tague

(Re-creations from JFK Reloaded)

Z-190
JFK hit

THE DALLAS PARADE

Z-238 Connally Hit – Trajectory 27 degrees downward

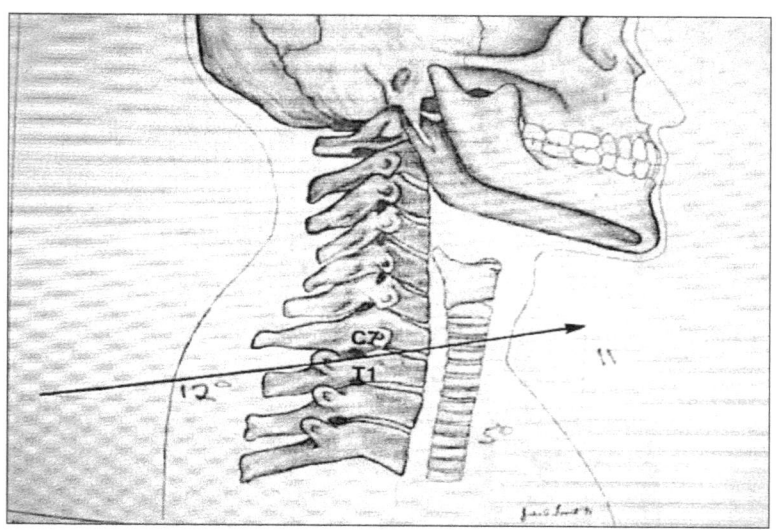

Z-190 JFK Neck Shot   Illustration by Julie Foont

*Did we inherit a lizard legacy –
Or is this just an evolution heresy?
Will ambition kill to get ahead
And commit the acts that we all dread?*

THE QUATRAINS OF CAMELOT   109

Grassy Knoll and Picket Fence Prior to Headshot
(At this point, Jackie has turned and is almost directly in front of JFK)

Sixth Floor East Depository View
*(Note that the heads of the Secret Service men
in the trailing car come into the shooter's view.)*

THE DALLAS PARADE

*One man was stopped who only spoke Spanish
But the Dallas police only spoke English!
"What should we do?" they thought and they thought
As they watched the suspect slowly walk off!*

*Is there justice in the universe –
Or is this just a thought perverse?
Are the scales of justice truly blind
And will the criminals do their time?*

*Twelve persons were arrested in Dealey Plaza that day –
But any official records soon faded away!
Police were required to file reports without fail –
But on November 22nd there was no paper trail!*

*Now there was a man named General Charles Cabell
Who led the Bay of Pigs and efforts to kill Fidel –
His brother, Earle Cabell, was the Dallas Mayor
In charge of the motorcade and police behavior!*

*The FBI conducted interviews
Of what the witnesses heard and viewed –
But when the final reports came back
The witnesses revealed, "I never said that!"*

*Witnesses can't be trusted
Or the government will be busted!
So you're forced to accept alterations
To avoid a government provocation!*

*Keep in mind it only takes
A small number of people to a conspiracy make –
A few people at the top
Can many a reputation blot!*

*Life magazine printed a lead story –
Stating Kennedy looked back toward the Depository!
But with the Zapruder film in their possession
They knew that this was a blatant deception!*

THE QUATRAINS OF CAMELOT

Josiah "Tink" Thompson

*Josiah Thompson spoke of Six Seconds In Dallas –
The Warren Commission he did challenge!
Two shots fired 1.6 seconds apart
Meant two shooters in the Dealey park!*

*Josiah Thompson did study and suggest –
That the Connally shot came from the Dal-Tex!
As Connally looked back and turned to his right –
A Dal-Tex shot matched the trajectory flight!*

*Because this is the Presidency
You cannot say conspiracy!
A lone gunman must assume the blame
In this most dangerous political game!*

*Right after the Kennedy assassination
There was all sorts of speculation –
That Kennedy had been very sick
And wouldn't have much longer to live!*

*But the reports were exaggerated –
Kennedy's illnesses were overrated –
The only thing that threatened his life
Was the fatal bullet from the front and right!*

THE DALLAS PARADE

Now Kennedy did have Addison's disease
Which put some people ill at ease –
But with modern steroids to replace cortisone
Kennedy could maintain his own!

Some days Kennedy walked with a crutch –
The back pain was, at times, too much!
But never did his symptoms give
A reason for him not to live!

Standing at the corner of Houston and Elm
Phil Willis viewed the assassination realm –
He said the limousine came to a temporary stop –
Before fatal gunfire from the Grassy Knoll plot!

William Newman, as he to the ground vaulted –
Said the limousine temporarily halted!
But the Zapruder film shows the limo never stops –
Are there frames missing from the Zapruder shots?

Even J. Edgar Hoover was surprised –
"A splicing error" he did surmise!
That caused the Zapruder frames to be reversed
And give the false impression of a rear shot burst!

A previous splice did also vex –
Where JFK was shot in the neck!
During the two times when John Kennedy is shot –
The film happens to break at just the wrong spot!

Three giant steps did Clint Hill take –
That only a kangaroo could make!
Missing frames in the Zapruder shots
Belie a limousine that stopped!

Disinformation is supreme
In the Spymaster's scheme!
Trust no one –
Or you'll be undone!

THE QUATRAINS OF CAMELOT

*Will our world mend
After seeing John Kennedy's end?
And can any real thesis
Put back the broken pieces?*

*Does God transcend time?
Will he spare mankind
From a nuclear Armageddon
And let us into heaven?*

*Or will the Illuminati lead the way
And spare us from the fray?
Acting just in time
To keep our world sublime?*

Abraham Zapruder

**Computer Simulation of Grassy Knoll View
Bony fragments embedded in Officer Hargis' vest to the left and rear of JFK
*(Computer Simulation from JFK Reloaded)***

THE DALLAS PARADE

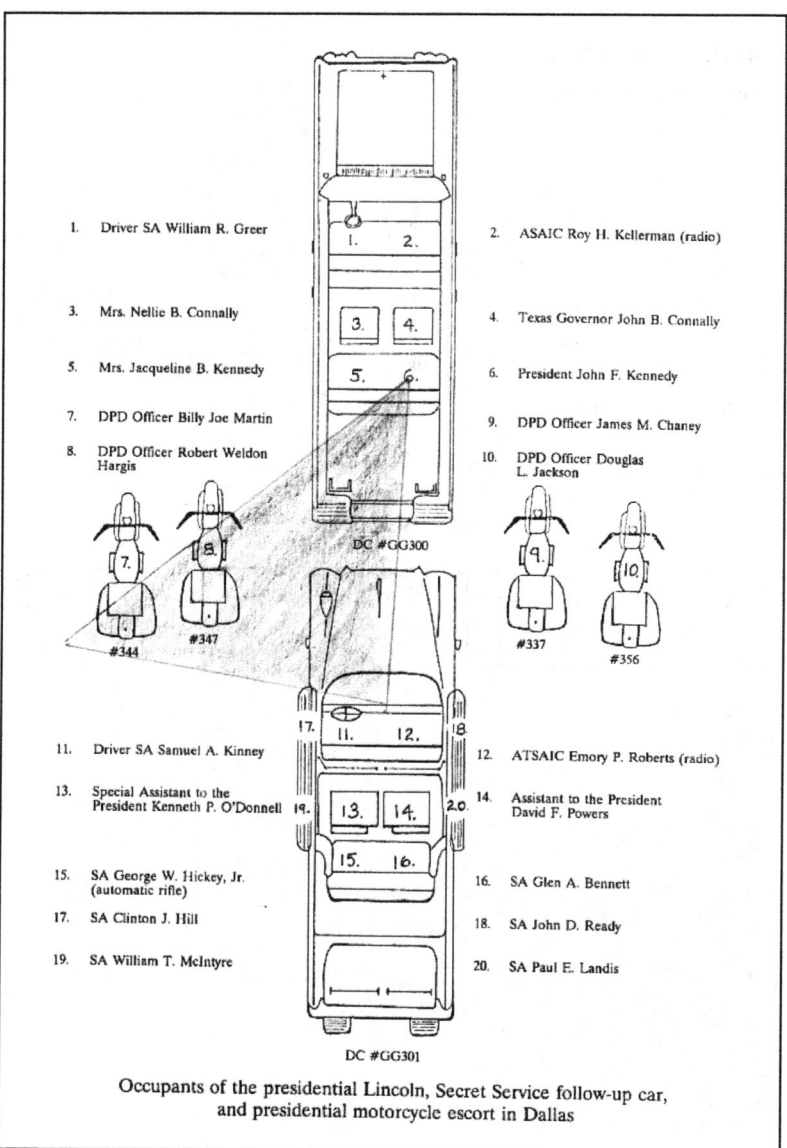

Occupants of the presidential Lincoln, Secret Service follow-up car, and presidential motorcycle escort in Dallas

Splatter pattern from Grassy Knoll shot.

Shooter was ahead and to the right of JFK.
Multiple bone fragments were embedded in Office Hargis' vest, riding behind and to the left of President Kennedy.

PARKLAND HOSPITAL

The Motorcade Arrives At Parkland

*Sirens blasting everywhere –
It's enough to give a scare!
What tragedy has befallen
With ambulances calling!*

PARKLAND HOSPITAL

The motorcade sped toward the underpass –
Would that God could make this moment pass!
Traveling down the Interstate, they arrived at Parkland –
"The President's been shot within the Texas heartland!"

"Oh no, no!" Jackie cried –
As the limousine down the Interstate flied –
"They've killed my husband!" she decreed –
John Kennedy – may you Godspeed!

"My hands touch your hair
As it blows in the wind –
Your skin touches mine
As we embrace once again!"

"Sometimes I think
When I look in your eyes –
Was it good that we met –
Does God really cry?"

"For though our paths cross
As we sail in the sea –
Now I suffer the loss
Of what cannot be!"

Everyone was quite forsaken
As Kennedy to the hospital was taken –
Jacqueline held onto a rose
With blood all over her hands and clothes!

"Please don't fall asleep –
I've got enough reason to weep!
If you should finally die –
I know I'll cry and cry!"

A mixture of blood and roses
In the limousine reposes –
As all our idealistic views
Take on realistic hues!

THE QUATRAINS OF CAMELOT

Jackie sat down and took a rest –
"Can I please have a cigarette?"
Sometimes it's good to take a pause
In the middle of a tragic cause!

"I never got to say good-by!
Jack just broke apart and died!
One minute you're alive and talking –
The next you're in a nightmare walking!"

"I never thought you'd leave so soon –
It seemed like yesterday we swooned!
At least I held you in my arms –
The days we shared were surely charmed!"

"Jack fought to the very end –
Mortal wounds he would transcend!
But we are made of mortal stuff –
That's the curse of flesh and blood!"

"All the landmarks changed
As my life was re-arranged!
Signposts I have known for years
Change their name as people cheer!"

"Out with the old, in with the new –
I'm not ready for a different view!
I like things the way they've been –
Don't throw them into history's bin!"

Senator Ralph Yarborough was dismayed –
"Excalibur has sunk beneath the waves!"
Jackie Kennedy sat in Trauma Room One –
And would not leave 'til the doctors were done!

The Parkland doctors did their best to revive
But Kennedy was no longer alive!
Dr. Kemp Clark looked at the back of the head
And saw cerebellum hanging on by a thread!

A large wound in the back of the head he did see –
He was a specialist in neurosurgery!
But the Bethesda pathologist then history re-wrote –
Dr. Humes said a small hole, then burned his first notes!

Rev. Oscar Huber

Reverend Oscar Huber gave the Last Rites
To send Kennedy's soul on its upward flight!
No longer was he shackled to the earth –
It was at once an end, but at once a rebirth!

What does John Kennedy's spirit see
As it rises above the Dallas scene?
His days on earth have suddenly ended –
Does he enter a world where wrongs are mended?

"I made it to a world
That no one else has seen –
It's just the kind of place
You'd find in someone's dreams!"

"The world is at peace –
There is no need for war –
There is no use of weapons
To settle any score!"

"There are no starving children –
There's food for everyone!
The children run and laugh and sing
And frolic in the sun!"

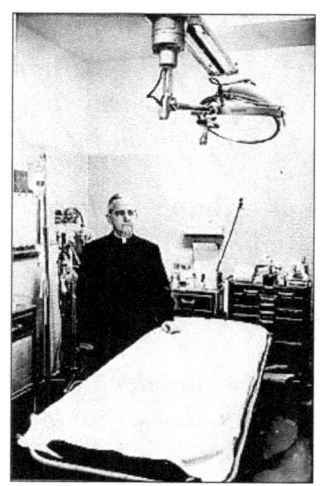

Trauma Room One (AP)

THE QUATRAINS OF CAMELOT

"The air is clean and fresh and pure –
It smells of flowers in spring!
It really does my heart some good
To hear the robin sing!"

"The water flowing in the brook
Plays against the stones –
The fish are jumping at my hook –
It's nice to be back home!"

Nurse Diana Bowron of Derbyshire washed the wounds
And the President's body was to a bronze casket removed –
She noticed the back wound two inches below the neck –
But the location was moved – the Magic Bullet to protect!

"The projectile couldn't have exited his throat
If the bullet entered so low on his coat –
It doesn't make sense!" Gerald Ford hollered –
"So let's move the entrance up to his collar!"

Now, does a politician have the right
To alter the truth just a mite?
"If things don't quite make sense –
Let's just alter the measurements!"

Kennedy's casket was wheeled down Parkland's hall
With doctors and Secret Service Agents both in haul –
But there soon arose an argument
Over where the casket should be sent!

Then the Parkland doctors engaged in a tussle
With Secret Service Agents flexing their muscle –
"A homicide needs an autopsy!" Dr. Earle Rose glared –
"You'll not take the casket anywhere!"

The cross on the casket began to wobble
As the doctors and Agents furiously squabbled!
"Release the President!" Roy Kellerman squared –
"We'll lose the chain of evidence!" Dr. Rose declared

PARKLAND HOSPITAL

The casket wavered back and forth –
A battle of wills was in full force!
"Texas law says you must stop!"
But the federal agents would listen not!

"Release the President!" *This most sacrilegious event*
"There is no precedent – *Was no way to handle a President!*
Texas state law decrees *But nobody could agree*
There must be an autopsy!" *What the proper procedure should be!*

For fifteen minutes that cross did shake
As doctors and Federal Agents debate!
Kennedy proved more controversial in death than life –
As the various groups continued to fight!

Then the Agents bared pistols on their hips
And the doctors were forced to release their grip!
Bullets, you see, will always rule
No matter how long you went to school!

Kellerman's submachine gun threatened a burst
As Agents loaded the casket into the hearse!
"'Tis a tragedy," Dr. Rose then cried
"To see the President's body so maligned!"

The casket was taken to a Love Field ramp
Where Air Force One was patiently camped –
They loaded the President for his final ride
With Jacqueline Kennedy standing by his side!

Departing
Love Field

THE QUATRAINS OF CAMELOT

Windshield with Crack at Parkland

*The Secret Service took the limousine
And decided they would wipe it clean!
The windshield with a hole was then replaced
And clues to the murder were soon erased!*

*Lyndon asked for Judge Sarah Hughes
Who, as a Federal Judge, was imbued
To swear in Lyndon Johnson as President
And the White House had a brand new resident!*

*The military went to DEFCON FOUR –
The nuclear codes unlocked the doors!
The officers were ready to flush the birds –
But no one ever gave the word!*

*Judge Sarah Hughes swears in LBJ
aboard Air Force One*

PARKLAND HOSPITAL

Jacqueline insisted on wearing her blood-stained dress –
They suggested she change – it was such a mess!
She wore her blood-stained suit with her pill box hat –
"I want them to see what they've done to Jack!"

"Forgive and forget – that's what they say
But some things just won't go away!
You plan your life around one man –
And then they take him from your hand!"

"The perpetrators get off free –
That's just not right to me!
Where's the justice in this nation
When they hide a Presidential assassination!"

"Feelings of loss
Oft' make me cross!
At times I will cry
Without knowing why!"

"Each person goes through life
Hoping things will turn out right –
Knowing that one final day
Each life must surely pass away!"

"Life is a series of adjustments
We make for each abutment –
We must learn to adapt
As we travel life's slippery path!"

Something is special about that blood-stained dress –
It bears the blood of a martyred President!
It's stored in the Archives for all to see –
A snapshot of this terrible moment in history!

"After you're gone
Will I see you again?
Will we dwell in a place
Where life never ends?"

THE QUATRAINS OF CAMELOT

"Will we go to a land
With streets lined with gold
Where we never get hungry
And we never grow old?"

"Will your soul and my soul
Come together as one?
Will we join hands again?
Will we play in the sun?"

"Will we go to a world
Where peace rules the state –
Where there's no room for war
And no room for hate?"

"As I think of our love –
How great it has been!
If I were with you
I'd be happy again!"

Jim Marrs provoked the media's ire
When he dared to use the word, "Crossfire"!
"It's clear that Oswald didn't act alone –
Yet this is what the media drones!"

Harold Weisberg of the Wilmington Morning News
Was one of the first to discuss conspiracy views –
He described the Warren Report as a Whitewash –
And feared that the truth would forever be lost!

Did LBJ deal with key members of Congress –
To hold the establishment completely harmless?
And did LBJ appoint the Warren Commission
Knowing that there would be sins of omission?

A conspiracy is kind of scary –
It implies that change is necessary!
With lone gunmen, there's no need to react –
After all, it's only a random act!

PARKLAND HOSPITAL

After the Kennedy assassination
There was a mad chase to find Oswald's location!
Officer Tippit was agitated and raced around a lot –
From the Gloco station to the Top Ten Record Shop!

Now, why they looked for Oswald is not clear –
Several Depository employees disappeared!
The witnesses all ran toward the Grassy Knoll –
So why did they check the Depository role?

Officer Tippit was nervous that morn
When his girlfriend served him his biscuits and corn!
He broke out in a sweat – that was plain to see –
Was he aware of conspiracy?

A police car stopped by Oswald's house –
J. D. Tippit's car was the only one about!
But Oswald refused to leave –
Was he suspicious of the scene?

J. D. Tippit visits the Top Ten Record Shop
The time was just after one o'clock –
He makes a phone call but doesn't talk
And quickly leaves with a rapid walk!

Roger Craig was a Sheriff's Deputy –
Who saw Oswald at the Dealey Plaza scene!
Deputy Craig saw Oswald get into a Nash station wagon –
But the Warren Commission said it never happened!

Roger incurred the wrath of his boss, Sheriff Decker –
Who said Craig was just a conspiracy heckler!
Roger assisted Jim Garrison in the trial of Clay Shaw –
And was a victim of suicide – or so they thought!

Some say Oswald took a cab to his house in Oak Cliff –
And shortly after was blamed for killing Officer Tippit!
He ran to the Texas Theater and saw "War Is Hell!"
And was arrested by the police after a little pell-mell!

THE QUATRAINS OF CAMELOT

Did Officer Tippit suffer an untimely fate
When he stopped Frank Schweis by mistake?
Knowing the police might shoot Oswald on sight –
Did Schweihs kill Tippit to save his own life?

Tippit had already stopped
At the Top Ten record shop –
Was Tippit searching frantically
For a man that he wound never see?

"Poor dumb cop!" the killer said –
As Officer Tippit lay dead!
Schweihs and Oswald were tall and lean entities –
Was it a case of mistaken identity?

Witnesses then said the killer "sort of ran"
As he left the scene in a jacket tan –
Frank Schweihs was known to run with a limp –
When he took a bullet from a Chicago hit!

Do our genes tell a tale
Of brutality regaled?
Or has the process of evolution
Refined our very constitution!

Are there black holes in the universe
Where death and dying are rehearsed?
Where people clap and cheer away –
While disruptive forces rule the day!

Oswald received payments from Hunter Leake –
Who was second in command to the station Chief!
But the day after Lee Oswald died –
Richard Helms told Leake to have the records fried!

Leake worked with Bannister at his CIA station
Where they helped train troops for a Cuban invasion!
When the order came through to shred the plans –
Langley had them hire a rental van!

Oswald Boarding House

Texas Theater

"I'm not resisting arrest!" Oswald declared
As pistols were brandished in the air!
He sustained several bruises to his face
Before the final arrest took place!

But Oswald never fired a shot
This you will remember not –
The news media with much pretense
Will rob you of your common sense!

Oswald was taken to the Dallas police station
Where he faced a lengthy interrogation –
His demeanor was calm and quite composed –
But nobody bothered to take any notes!

The police mentioned a trip to Mexico
That Oswald took several weeks ago –
Oswald became irate and mad –
"How did you ever learn about that?"

Oswald said, "You've blown my cover!"
But, after a while, he discovered –
"I'm just a patsy!" he declared –
He could have spilled the beans right there!

There was a news conference late that night
When the Dallas police announced with delight –
"We've got our man, it's plain to see!"
"He's the man who killed President Kennedy!"

Dallas District Attorney Henry Wade
Had made up his mind that very day!
"Oswald killed President Kennedy!
To further an international communist conspiracy!"

"I didn't kill anyone!" Oswald replied –
"And I'll prove I haven't lied!
Please call lawyer John Abt in New York –
"And I'll prove I'm innocent in a legal court!"

What's it like to be a patsy?
To face the glare of the paparazzi?
What did Oswald think as he sat in jail?
"I don't deserve all this travail!"

PARKLAND HOSPITAL

"We live in a world of deception
Where people disguise their true intentions!
I played the part of a communist Red –
Not knowing that I might end up dead!"

"You do whatever your country asks –
You play the role and do your task –
You lay false trails – it's a black art –
People never are who they say they are!"

"How did I get into this predicament?
On killing Kennedy I'm totally innocent!
But I know the men who pulled it off –
Should I show my cards and get them caught?"

"I was supposed to follow the group
And report their actions as an FBI snoop –
David Atlee Phillips was the CIA entity
Who told me never to reveal my identity!"

"Jack Ruby stands at the corridor's end
Is he a foe or still a friend?
Sometimes I get a little confused
Was my life just one big ruse?"

"I guess I was a little naïve
To be so easily deceived!
To think that all the friends I made
Would disappear into the haze!"

"I'm amazed they went to all this trouble –
They even created an Oswald double!
A phony rifle from a mail order store –
And Jack Ruby stalking the police corridor!"

"I'm a walking dead man, I must conclude –
My days on earth will be misconstrued!
I played the role my handler requested –
Little did I know I'd be arrested!"

THE QUATRAINS OF CAMELOT

Lee Harvey Oswald

*"It's not easy being a spy
When your government hangs you out to dry!
I did my work at the government's insistence –
Now they want to deny my very existence!"*

*"We live in a culture of cover-ups –
Designed to protect the upper crust!
The people must have faith in their nobility –
Or the government will lose its credibility!"*

*"Despite my vociferous insistence
The CIA will deny my existence!
I'm just a lone gunman, don't you see?
That's the official reality!"*

*"You perform your role like an artist
And play the game of a Marxist –
Then they pull the plug and let you die –
While the common folk your name decry!"*

*"We were trying to kill Castro
But that turned into a fiasco –
Now they want to blame me
For the murder of John Kennedy!"*

"People see what they want to see –
That's not the way it's supposed to be!
We live in a world of deceptions –
Created by our own imperfections!"

"Everybody wants their piece of the pie –
Weaving their circles in the sky –
Stopping for a moment to pray –
As each one drops by the way!"

"I guess I was too malleable –
Like working in a crucible!
I did the work that I was told –
And then they go and sell your soul!"

"Restore my name – that's all I ask –
Let the truth come out at last!
The people have a right to know
The real players in this show!"

"People now will spit on my grave
And never know the contribution I made –
I reported faithfully all the assassination plans –
Little did I know that I'd be canned!"

"We're like lemmings walking toward the cliff –
Following our leaders as we see fit –
Trusting our own predilections
To lead us in the right direction!"

"Governments create their own reality –
The truth you're not supposed to see!
Conspiracies are a myth, you know –
When framed lone gunmen steal the show!"

"Do I see the ghost of Mary Surratt?
Hanged for a crime that she did not!
Blamed in a conspiracy for Lincoln's death –
She swore she was innocent with her last breath!"

THE QUATRAINS OF CAMELOT

"Where do we go when we die?
Nobody really knows –
Is there a heaven above us
Or only a cold wind that blows?"

"If only I could remember
Long before I was born –
Where did my soul arise from
At the dawn of my morn?"

"I wish that I had a Father
Growing up as a toddler –
I've been roaming this eternal land –
Searching for a paternal hand!"

"I hope that I'll have the answer
To where I might journey some day –
For surely we go where we came from
If I could remember the way!"

"Too bad our life's not that simple
Like a tapestry long ago sewn –
We live in a world of mystery –
Surrounded by the unknown!"

Two days later, Jack Ruby feigned indignation
And shot Lee Oswald at the Dallas police station!
J. Edgar Hoover exclaimed, "There'll be no trial!"
So he told his Agents to burn their files!

Lee Oswald was rushed to Parkland emergency
Where Dr. Charles Crenshaw assisted with the surgery –
He received a phone call during the case
From President Lyndon Johnson, who was quite irate!

"I want a death bed confession!" Johnson declared
As he talked to the surgeons in Oswald's care –
Now, did Johnson really want a death bed confession?
Or rather Oswald's death in rapid succession?

PARKLAND HOSPITAL

Unfortunately, this type of injury
Was not amenable to successful surgery –
Lee Oswald shortly after died
And Marina and her daughters sat and cried!

The hurt doesn't go away –
No matter what people say!
Though less often when it strikes –
It still maintains its' painful bite!

Now the FBI took the opportunity
To remind Marina that she had no immunity!
If the right answers were not reported –
To Russia she could easily be deported!

The Men In Black arrived that day
And took the Dallas files away!
It's a federal matter, it does appear –
And the files were classified for 75 years!

A lone gunman must this surely be!
That's what they'll write in history!
A chance event, there is no doubt –
Has nothing to do with political clout!

Will reason predominate –
And save the present head of state?
Or must there be a grab for power –
As we near the final hour!

"Who's to gain?" some people say –
But let's not make political hay!
Murder's never on the plate
In a democratic state!

Decisions are made by popular selection
With properly run democratic elections!
Debates are held in a manner sedate
To elect the incoming Chief of State!

Governor John Connally Greets the Kennedys

*Croft photo of JFK Motorcade on Elm Street at Z160
Moments Before the First Shot*

*There's not much time
To fashion rhyme –
We make our mark
And then depart!*

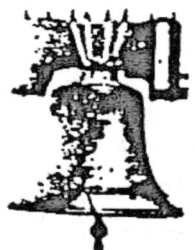

DISCUSSION UNLIMITED INC. presents

THE WARREN REPORT: THE WHOLE TRUTH?

MR. MARK LANE, Attorney and former New York State Assemblyman, does not accept the findings of the Warren Commission Report and will present a critical analysis of the Report.

A PANEL OF PROMINENT ATTORNEYS WILL CROSS-EXAMINE MR. LANE:

MR. JOSEPH A. BALL, attorney for Warren Commission during the investigation.

MR. HERMAN F. SELVIN, former president L.A. County Bar Association.

MR. A. L. WIRIN, noted civil liberties and constitutional attorney.

8:00 P.M., Friday, December 4, 1964 Beverly Hills High School Auditorium 241 So. Moreno Drive, Beverly Hills

Admission: $1.50   Students: $1.00
For ticket information call NO 3-0424

THE QUATRAINS OF CAMELOT

Dr. Cyril Wecht

*The Warren Commission conducted a test
And fired a bullet into a human wrist –
The bullet broke into several pieces
And shattered the Commission's original thesis!*

*"It's a Magic Bullet!" Dr. Wecht declared
"That sailed in the Texas air –
To hit both Connally and the President
And suffer only a minor dent!"*

CE399

*The Magic Bullet was nearly pristine
Yet it left fragments in Connally's chest, wrist and knee!
Seth Kantor talked with Ruby at the Parkland venture –
Did Jack place a bullet on the Parkland stretcher?*

*As a trauma surgeon, I'm a witness
That bullets don't fall out of victims!
The skin is elastic and recoils back
Which traps a shallow bullet within the fat!*

*Now Ruby had a dilemma at the Parkland scene –
No bullets showed up with the X-Ray beam!
Ruby was under a lot of pressure –
Until a bullet showed up on the Parkland stretcher!*

PARKLAND HOSPITAL

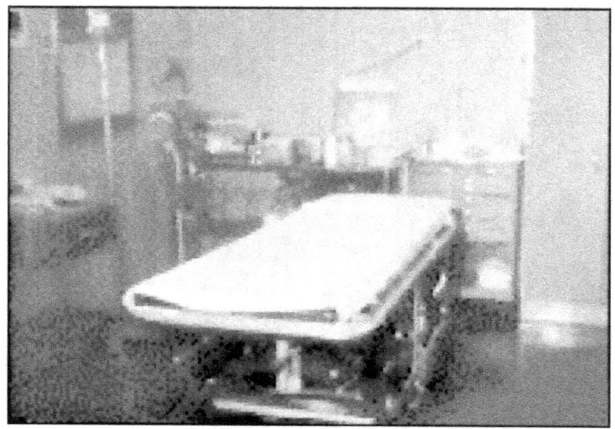

Parkland Stretcher – Trauma Room One

*The bullet was found on the stretcher of a little boy –
Which makes it sound like some sort of ploy!
Others say it was Connally's stretcher –
But, why was there no blood to measure?*

*With the Magic Bullet there's a funny lesson –
It seems it lacks a chain of possession!
Bardwell Odum – the FBI agent on record –
Said he never saw a bullet from a Parkland stretcher!*

*With the bullet, you could now prove
That it matched with Oswald's rifle grooves!
But was it fair with the evidence to trifle?
And was this really Oswald's rifle?*

*Was Jack Ruby worried
That no evidence could be curried?
Did he place that bullet on the Parkland gurney –
To plant false evidence for the District Attorney?*

*The Warren Commission did a trajectory exam
With Representative Gerald Ford as the lead man –
But in order the Magic Bullet to protect
He moved up the back wound two inches to the neck!*

THE QUATRAINS OF CAMELOT

Bullets don't go straight, you see
In this land of make-believe –
Some will call it Political Correctness
That made the Warren Commission so feckless!

Years later, the government had a fit
With Dr. Wecht, the forensic pathologist!
They confiscated his assassination files
And put them in their classified piles!

Wouldn't Albert Einstein think it crass –
The idea of a bullet that didn't lose mass –
Leaving fragments in Connally's wrist and knee
Conservation of Mass says that cannot be!

And what did God in truth intend
By sending Kennedy to his end?
Do we live in sin and temptation –
Or was this merely predestination?

Nostradamus, in one of his quatrains
Predicts lightning shall fall on a great man –
They will accuse an innocent man of the deed
With the guilty one hidden in the misty small trees!

Does some divine force control our fate?
Or are we doomed to contemplate
Whether tragic events are meant to be
In a world of uncertainty?

Did John Kennedy die for our transgressions?
A sacrifice to the gods in heaven?
Or was this just a random act
With the laws of nature still intact?

Cardinal Cushing celebrated the Requiem Mass –
He had married Jackie and John ten years past!
The horse-drawn caisson drove to Arlington Cemetery
Where an eternal flame was lit to Kennedy's memory!

THE QUATRAINS OF CAMELOT

John John, his son, then saluted his Dad
As the caisson slowly rumbled past –
How does a little boy deal with separation
With hardly any preparation?

"I miss you, Dad
I knew I would –
I'd bring you back
If I but could!"

"I think of days
When I would play –
And you would call me
From the fray!"

"It's time to eat!"
You'd yell to us
"So come inside
And quit the fuss!"

"We'd sit around
The glowing fire
And you'd remove
Our wet attire!"

"We had the time
To run and play –
Tomorrow seemed
A long, long way!"

"But now the days
Go by so fast –
My thoughts of you
Are in the past!"

"And when I look
At your rocking chair
Sometimes I think
I see you there!"

John John Salutes

Ten witnesses saw a mid-air explosion
Before John John's plane went into the ocean!
But the official government explanation –
Is that John John suffered from disorientation!

*"It seems a shame
That I can't play –
And hear your voice
Above the fray!"*

*"I wish that we
Would never cry –
I wish that we
Would never die!"*

*"The last days when
You felt the pain –
I wish that I
Could live again!"*

*"I'd talk about
A love so true –
I'd take the pain
Away from you!"*

*"But through it all
Our love will shine –
And carry us
Through tougher times!"*

*"I know not where
We come or go –
We play the game
And never know!"*

*"I miss you, Dad
I knew I would –
I'd bring you back
If I but could!"*

John F. Kennedy, Jr. (AP)

THE QUATRAINS OF CAMELOT

Jackie gave John one final kiss
And said that you I will always miss!
It's always tough to say goodbye
When all you want to do is cry!

"*I miss you every day –*
I miss you in many ways!
Would that I could turn back time –
For once again, I'd make you mine!"

JFK with Macaroni

"*If I should count the stars*
That shine in our heavenly sky –
They say I wound never finish
Though I count 'til the day I die!"

"*Like the stars, my love has no limit –*
It is timeless, endless and bright!
Like a rose that blooms in the sunshine –
Your beauty is my delight!"

"*Some things go on forever*
Though I will never know why –
Yet true lovers like you and me
Are the flowers that blossom and die!"

"*But why count the grains of sand*
Or even the stars above?
Though Nature may long outlast me –
It's you I always will love!"

"*Sometimes I ponder as I travel through life –*
Why is there so much heartache and strife?
Does God allow tragedies for some greater good –
Or is He basically misunderstood?"

"*Don't forget to remember me –*
I hear your voice but cannot see!
Will we meet once more in the afterlife –
And will I once again be your wife?"

PARKLAND HOSPITAL

*"There's a gaping hole where that memory has been –
I've been looking for a way to fill it back in!
If you don't rake it over and plant something new –
You'll spend all your life looking in the rear view!"*

*"It takes time for the pain to go away –
It doesn't happen in a day!
But, more than time, it takes the hope
That you will someday learn to cope!"*

*What's it like to lose everything –
To start over again with nothing?
To see your friends and hear them tell –
As you go back to the wishing well!*

THE QUATRAINS OF CAMELOT

Wishing Well at Indiana University

*Those who live in the quiet suffering of a grievous loss
Carry a burden which is never lost!
You toil in the present and smile at the last –
As flashes of memory break through from the past!*

*The schoolchildren come to Dealey Square
With box lunches they sit everywhere –
The teachers talk of a day in November
When a President died, and how we must remember!*

*And Robert Groden, like a watchful sentry
Hands out leaflets to the gentry –
Forty years he's been in Dealey Square
He tells the history to all who care!*

*"The world's not what it seems to be
Believe not all that you may read!
Oswald never fired a shot –
He's just a patsy in the plot!"*

PARKLAND HOSPITAL

"There is a weltschmerz –
It's like a world hurt!
A kind of universal pain
I feel again and again!"

"Is it the human condition
That creates such a sad rendition?
Do we go in the wrong direction
Because of our imperfection?"

"Are we a jackpot nation –
Betting on each coronation?
Who will be the next king –
And will somebody take a swing?"

Robert Groden

"I'm not a betting man –
I know God has a plan!
But can Divine Intervention
Supersede man's intentions?"

"The Magic Bullet doesn't go straight
It breaks into pieces, but doesn't lose weight!
It zigzags back and forth, don't you see?
That's how one bullet does the work of three!"

Under the Freedom of Information Act
The government should release the facts –
But with all the names so heavily redacted
You can never tell who really acted!

And so Robert Groden spends his time away
Hoping that one final day
The government will soon reveal
All the facts that it conceals!

Reveal the truth, the people cry!
Reveal the truth before I die!
But the years pass ever slowly on
And one by one, we all are gone!

THE QUATRAINS OF CAMELOT

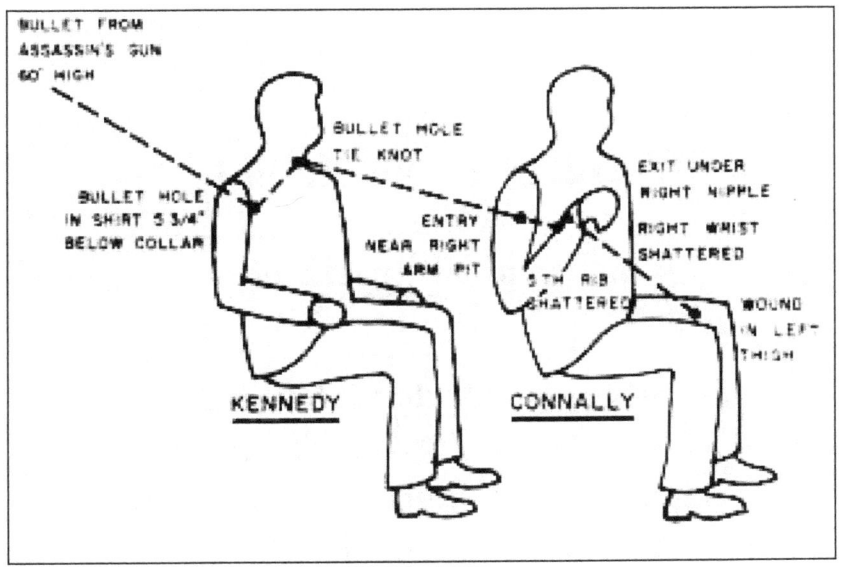

*My days are numbered
Before my final slumber!
Is it a large number or small –
Before my final fall?*

*When will I die
And make my final cry?
Will I be young or old –
Will I be timid or bold?*

Robert Groden in Dealey Plaza

*We are all like animals caged –
Fighting to quell the hidden rage!
Looking all about –
Trying to get out!*

*The truth, like cream, will rise to the top –
Though it reveals a conspiracy plot!
The people always yearn to know –
Who made those footsteps in the snow!*

Protecting The Myth

Thus did the people trust their Leaders.

But the Leaders stubbornly refused to tell the People, for fear that their office might be tarnished, or they might themselves perish in the Revelation.

For great was the Secret, and deep were its roots.

And the Mystery did remain.

The Tale Of Camelot

THE PLAYERS

The assassination is a puzzle
That's caused many a soul to guzzle –
But if you manage to solve the crime
You'll discover the true nature of mankind!

Bannister and Martin were at the Katz and Jammer Bar
When the two of them argued and began to spar!
Martin accused Bannister of JFK's downfall –
And was treated for trauma at the Charity Hospital!

Jack Martin talked of Bannister and Ferrie
And thought the New Orleans police should query!
But after the assassination, when he talked to the FBI –
He met with intimidation and the evil eye!

Bannister had contacts with Permindex –
Which funneled money to Algerian extremists!
They tried to assassinate Charles DeGaulle
Eighteen months before John Kennedy's fall!

The NATO military machine
Didn't like DeGaulle's political lean!
So Permindex said "La-di-dah –
Let's arrange a coup d'etat!"

Now here was a military-industrial complex
That was enough to make a President vex!
President Eisenhower warned of such an apparatus –
That was capable of actions quite erratic!

Ambition and jealousy must play a role
As each man vies for his control!
The Mafia, the Cubans, the CIA –
Each one had their role to play!

Bay of Pigs Cubans

The Cubans were an angry lot
When Kennedy put them on the spot!
They invaded at the Bay of Pigs
And then John Kennedy pulled the brigs!

The Mafia, as well, are suspects prime
With Robert Kennedy's war on crime!
He shipped Carlos Marcello across the border
Without his shoes or any water!

Keep in mind that Robert Kennedy
Could be vindictive as could be!
If you didn't sing his tune –
You might end up in Cameroon!

Robert asked Colonel Burl Boatman
To compromise a political opponent –
When the Colonel said that wasn't his position
Kennedy proceeded to take away his commission!

THE QUATRAINS OF CAMELOT

The Mafia and the Cubans, too
Were used by the CIA and their crews –
They conspired to put an end to Fidel
And spare Cuba from a communist hell!

Now Castro was a vicious man
Who sent his opponents to the firing stand!
"I'm a socialist, don't you see?
But with me you must never disagree!"

Castro would spend hours talking to his foes
Promising them he would relieve their woes –
But as he left, since he was paranoid still
He'd give the signal to have them killed!

The easiest way to avoid suspicion
Is to pretend to form a coalition!
When they later pass away
People will look the other way!

Did Fidel Castro decry
That he would need a JFK alibi?
Jean Daniel interviewed Fidel that day –
Who duly recorded his shock and dismay!

Dr. Rafael Silva knew Fidel as a child
And traveled with him in the mountains wild –
But when Fidel turned to communist ways
Rafael headed to the Florida bays!

The socialists all thought Fidel was great
Young minds he could ingratiate –
He says he hates the capitalist Yanks
While he keeps millions in offshore banks!

Fidel was on a Batista raid
When all his followers were betrayed –
Only Castro managed to swim to shore
But he would trust the CIA no more!

Did Castro a Castro kill –
While he was in law school still?
If he couldn't play it by the book
He'd still win – by hook or crook!

Did Fidel have an assassination squad
That on U.S. soil did trod?
Did they infiltrate the Cuban exiles –
And report back to the Cuban Isle?

Fidel talked to the Harvard elite –
At the Dillon Field House he did speak –
On the River Charles he spoke of Operation Truth
While his brother, Raul, was forming communist roots!

Fidel Castro was still irate
That he wasn't admitted to Harvard in '48!
What a different world this would be
If Fidel had received a Harvard degree!

The CIA was in a cold war –
With Russia they would settle the score!
But Kennedy just talked and talked
And never would he walk the walk!

"We must learn to negotiate
Or we will all incinerate!
We must learn to compromise
Or we will meet with our demise!"

Is there a tit for tat?
You bombed this, so I'll bomb that!
Call it even-steven –
And spare the nuclear demons!

But the CIA would not listen –
Kennedy couldn't beat the competition!
He let Krushchev build the Berlin Wall –
And the Bay of Pigs Cubans take the fall!

THE QUATRAINS OF CAMELOT

*Some accused Kennedy of limpdickedness
During the Bay of Pigs predicament!
But he inherited a poorly planned invasion
Which put him in an awkward situation!*

*In the fall of 1962
The Cuban Missile Crisis began to brew
RFK secretly met with Russia's Georgi Bolshakov
And got the Pentagon generals all hacked off!*

*"That's treason!" they yelled, "That's for sure!"
And wondered if there was a Kennedy cure –
His father, Joseph, was sure an appeaser
And JFK was proving even weaker!*

*The Pentagon Generals pushed for war –
They wanted to invade the Cuban shore –
But little did they know they'd meet
Nuclear weapons on Castro's beach!*

*During the Cuban Missile situation
John Kennedy was on multiple medications –
He was taking pain pills and flat on his back
So Robert Kennedy went to bat!*

Robert Kennedy

*Cooler heads finally did prevail –
Nikita Khrushchev agreed to curtail
Nuclear missiles on Cuban soil
And thus a nuclear war was foiled!*

*Some people of course will ask
If John Kennedy was up to the task –
But while his private life was subject to derision
He had the insight to make the right decisions!*

*Now, being Catholic did some provoke –
Would Kennedy take orders from the Pope?
But such fears proved totally unfounded –
The anti-Catholic sentiment was totally ungrounded!*

In ages past, the Ancients created booths
Where people prayed – their gods to soothe!
Now we go to our confession –
And hope that we can learn a lesson!

Does God cry
When man goes awry?
Does he commiserate
With Heads of State?

Does the Pope talk to God?
And then give us a nod--
A Papal dispensation
From the Maker of Creation!

Teddy Kennedy would take the reins
When John and Robert left our plane –
He was the real politician
'Cause he could get both sides to listen!

Senator Edward Kennedy

John, Bobby, and Teddy

THE QUATRAINS OF CAMELOT

In 1924 Irish mobster Dean O'Banion was mum
As he trimmed his flower shop chrysanthemums –
One Capone gunman shook his hand
While the other sent him to the Promised Land!

Beware the handshake of the Mafia clan –
They'll shoot you with the other hand!
Secret deals in secret rooms
Helped to seal the President's doom!

A funny thing happened that fateful day
The plans were cancelled by the CIA!
"It's a walk-off," Johnny Roselli declared,
"So pack your guns and clear the square!"

Now, why would the CIA call things off
When they would Kennedy's orders scoff?
It seems that Jackie was a late arrival
And the CIA was worried about her survival!

John Kennedy

Everything, you see, has to do with appearance
And nobody had been given clearance –
If our beloved First Lady was accidentally shot
The government might be forced to reveal the plot!

But higher elements within the CIA
Got wind of the assassination that day –
They sent Roselli to cancel the plan –
But Giancana just ignored the command!

For mobster deals should give you pause –
Their loyalty's for a different cause!
The War on Crime – it had to stop –
The President would still take a shot!

Sam Giancana

Now, if the CIA called it off
Was the assassination still their fault?
The short answer has to be 'Yes' –
They helped lay the groundwork for the rest!

THE PLAYERS

LBJ was a paranoid man –
He didn't trust the assassination plans!
He sent Mac Wallace to the sixth floor loft
To make sure no one tried to knock him off!

They found Mac Wallace's fingerprint lines
Next to the shooter's nest on Box 29 –
Was LBJ's right-hand man
Part of the assassination plan?

Walt Brown has researched the story
Of Mac Wallace in all his glory –
Over many years, fifteen people have died
Yet only once has Mac Wallace ever been tried!

Barr McClellan talked of Edward Clark –
LBJ's lawyer for duties dark!
Lyndon's foes would be investigated –
And, if necessary, eliminated!

Walt Brown

Barr McClellan

Judge Henry Marshall was investigating Billie Sol Estes
Who was LBJ's confidante in the state of Texas –
When Judge Marshall refused to lay off
Mac Wallace decided to finish him off!

THE QUATRAINS OF CAMELOT

The assassin waited at Judge Marshall's farm
Where he made his plans to do the judge harm –
Shot five times, with his bolt action rifle at his side
Sheriff Stegall declared, "It's obviously suicide!"

Oswald's rifle was in the sixth story
Of the Dallas Book Depository –
The rifle was a Mannlicher-Carcano
From Klein's Sporting Goods in Chicago!

Two shells were found on the window's run
A third, unfired, had jammed the gun!
Two shots were fired, the police decreed –
But the Warren Commission would make it three!

Craig Roberts tells the story how
The police report was altered now –
Instead of two shells on the ledge
A third appeared – a magic hedge!

Craig Roberts

Dr. Charles Crenshaw was in Trauma Room One
At the Parkland Hospital Emergency run –
He saw a small hole in front of the President's right ear
And a large hole to the right and rear!

Yet Dr. Crenshaw had to go to court
When an outside doctor tried to deny his report!
It seems the Journal of the American Medical Association
Was involved with political obfuscation!

Dr. George Lundberg, the editor, with much fanfare
Claimed Dr. Crenshaw really wasn't there!
"I was present!" Dr. Crenshaw did retort
Dr. Lundberg apologized and settled out of court!

"I was there in Trauma Room One
And participated in the work that was done!
I saw the large hole in the back of the head
And agreed that the resuscitation should end!"

THE PLAYERS

Dr. Charles Crenshaw

Dr. Charles Baxter, with the sternest of looks
Said, "You must not publish any books!
What you've seen in these Parkland Halls
Must remain behind these walls!"

There seemed to be a tendency
For anyone who had the audacity
To offer an alternate explanation
To meet with ridicule and denunciation!

The doctors at both Bethesda and Parkland
Observed one thing which left them disheartened –
There was a large hole in the back of the head
That left our beloved President dead!

Dr. Kemp Clark was a neurosurgeon
Of one thing he was very certain –
He noted a large hole in the right occipital –
An observation that proved quite pivotal!

THE QUATRAINS OF CAMELOT

But the Warren report that finally came out
Placed a small hole in back, and said there's no doubt –
A shot from the rear – it had to be –
From the Dallas Book Depository!

Thomas Evan Robinson was the embalmer that day
And noted a large hole in the back head of JFK –
A smaller wound was noted in front of the right ear –
With a three inch flap facing toward the rear!

Mr. Robinson described the back wound as well –
Two inches below the shoulder it did dwell!
"Sitting to the right of the backbone!" he hollered –
But the Warren Commission moved it up to the collar!

Two small shrapnel wounds in the face
The embalmer also did trace –
Did these dissect from the back –
Or was there a frontal attack?

David Lifton looked for the best evidence –
The autopsy photos didn't match the President's!
Either the body on its way to Bethesda was altered
Or two different sets of pictures were proffered!

Now, who was in charge of the autopsy?
A uniformed military man, that's plain to see!
Sitting in the gallery, he was making decisions –
He told Dr. Finck, "Don't make that incision!"

"You examined the neck wound?" Dr. Finck was asked –
"I did my best to complete the task –
But when I picked up the knife to make the cut –
A military man said I'd done enough!"

Floyd Riebe, an autopsy photographer
Said the photos had obviously been doctored!
There was a large hole in the back of the head –
That disappeared when the films were read!

THE PLAYERS

The autopsy photos were not the norm
For what you'd see at the Bethesda morgue –
There's a black phone on the background wall –
That never existed there at all!

Mark Lane wrote of a Rush to Judgment
But the Warren Commission wouldn't begrudge him!
He offered to defend Oswald before the Commission
But the Committee members refused to listen!

Connally's right wrist was left in tatters –
The radius bone was completely shattered!
Additional lead fragments remained near his hip
But the Magic Bullet had barely a nick!

Dr. Charles Gregory removed three lead wrist fragments
And testified that a fourth from his hip was splattered –
The Strange Commission ruled the Magic Bullet defunct
But Arlen Specter would them all debunk!

Now Albert Einstein would be amused
At the Warren Commission's ruse –
To defy the Law of Conservation of Mass
To a physicist is just plain crass!

But politicians don't give pause
To anyone who bends the laws –
Bullets can violate the laws of Nature
If they meet with approval from the Legislature!

Is there a fundamental equation
That would solve our present frustration –
That would separate wrong from right
So disparate forces could then unite!

Dr. Gary Aguilar was mortified
When the doctors' notes were classified –
Decades later they finally revealed
What the House Select Committee had concealed!

THE QUATRAINS OF CAMELOT

"It must be a small hole," Arlen Specter declared
"If it was fired by Oswald from the shooter's lair!"
An entry wound, it seems quite clear
Allows the government to cover its' rear!

But the doctors' notes would contradict
Arlen Specter's little trick –
The rear scalp wound was really huge –
An exit wound you must conclude!

One way to change history's course
Is to remove a leader with force!
But why won't the government go public –
Would we be labeled a Banana Republic?

George Orwell called it "protective stupidity"
That keeps your mind from thinking heresy –
Any new breakthrough revelation
Is treated like an aberration!

If the government declares a hole is small
Then it must be after all!
Who cares what the doctors say?
The truth must wait another day!

If you don't believe the gist of this
You must be a conspiracy theorist!
Great harm may come to those who doubt –
The government, you see, has much more clout!

If the government says something didn't occur
Then we mustn't be demure!
Why should we the government disgrace –
If they're only saving face!

Jack Valenti and the Ex-Presidents
Decided to hold a news conference
"You must never view this conspiracy tape –
It's full of lies and full of hate!"

But even if the tape is true
Certain things you must never view!
The government would be embarrassed –
Our democracy might even perish!

"Whatever you do, don't read this trash –
It's full of lies and tends to bash!
But even if the words are true –
They're still not very good for you!"

The truth, you see must be altered
Before it's to the public proffered!
Truth must be palatable for all to read
Before it becomes part of history!

How does the intellectual
Deal with the unmentionable?
That's very plain to see –
You just deny conspiracy!

And so the secret files grow –
Presidents don't even know
What really happened way back then –
Who knows what and who knows when?

"We must not exhume the bodies of Ex-Presidents –
That's just gruesome and doesn't make sense!"
For if they died from a sinister group
We must keep the public out of the loop!"

Thomas Jefferson traveled with Miss Sally
No one thought he ever dallied!
"It's against all his principles!" the historians said
"He would never take Miss Sally to bed!"

"The red-haired offspring are of no consequence –
We think that's just plain coincidence!"
But centuries later, when the DNA came in –
The Presidential historians had to change their spin!

THE QUATRAINS OF CAMELOT

*Jean Hill was closest to the crime
"How many shots?" Arlen Specter opined
"Four to six shots I did hear –
Both from the front and from the rear!"*

*"Surely this can't really be –
I think that there were only three!
Three shots is all that I'll explore
'Cause Oswald couldn't have fired more!"*

*To tell the truth can hurt your credibility
In a world of false sensibilities!
Listen to the pundits roar –
As they do the truth deplore!*

*A crooked path is straight you see
It's called the Single Bullet Theory –
Arlen Specter explains it all
And so Lee Oswald takes the fall!*

*Now was Arlen Specter just a bad sleuth
Or was he intending to hide the truth –
To save the world from utter destruction
If there should prove a Russian deduction?*

THE PLAYERS

Mixing politics with science
Places an undue reliance
On government trust and stability
At the cost of truth and civility!

Eyewitness reports
The government retorts
Are not reliable –
And are easily deniable!

The logic of a trusted politician
Steeped in knowledge and erudition
Can easily refute a simple observation
If it can't provide the proper explanation!

They checked Lee for powder burns on his face
But needless to say, they found not a trace!
Now how can you fire a Mannlicher-Carcano
Without facial nitrates from an old Italian rifle?

Robert Morrow modified four Mannlicher rifles
By altering the forepiece of each just a trifle –
The guns could now be quickly disassembled
So the murderers would ordinary people resemble!

Ed Hoffman observed two men from the railroad overpass
After shooting, one rifle to a rail worker was passed –
The man bent down, took the rifle apart
And the two men from the Grassy Knoll did depart!

Now Ed Hoffman was a deaf and dumb mute
Who tried to talk to one of the Secret Service brutes!
He flashed a submachine gun and told Ed to scram –
And turned a deaf ear to this handicapped man!

The CIA's Robert Morrow modified four walkie-talkies
That could fit in your pocket while you're walking –
They were ordered by Del Valle, the Cuban mercenary
And picked up in a private plane by David Ferrie!

THE QUATRAINS OF CAMELOT 163

Robert Groden shows the picture of a Dealey Plaza lad –
With a bulge in his back pocket, he's the radio man!
Was there radio communication among the team?
Or were they just listening to their favorite audio stream?

Billie Sol Estes tells the tale of a body in store
They kept all preserved in a refrigerated morgue!
Placed in a shipping casket with shots in the head
It was flown to Bethesda in a small private jet!

Two bodies arrived at Bethesda that night
Paul O'Connor viewed them with absolute fright!
"And two different coffins," O'Connor did say –
"One was of bronze, the other military gray!"

One of the bodies arrived in advance
With shots from the rear – the government's stance –
Then came Jackie and Bobbie with the coffin in hand
To give JFK his final exam!

The government itself would later agree
It dropped JFK's bronze coffin down into the sea!
They said it was of no consequence –
So there went another piece of evidence!

Dr. David Mantik examined X-rays of the head
And said, "They're the strangest I've ever read!
When I look at the films with a stereoscopic fix
There're two different people in the mix!"

"The optical density in the back of the head
Is much higher than it should be read –
There's really a large hole, I do believe –
Covered up by someone trying to deceive!"

The skull X-ray shows a 6.5 mm shadow
In the back of the head, but the object is shallow!
Was this a sheared-off fragment from the skull impact?
Or was it added to the X-ray after the fact?

*The proof would lie in the films by Pitzer
Who took hundreds of autopsy pictures!
But the key photos were all suppressed –
And William Bruce Pitzer met an untimely death!*

*Dr. James Fetzer talked of assassination science
And how there was entirely too much reliance
On faulty reasoning over the events in Dallas –
With a lack of true scientific analysis!*

*The Warren Commission did not employ logic
And treat this as a scientific project –
The politicians did not use reason or deduction
So the Warren Report became a political production!*

*Sir Isaac Newton believed that religion and science
Were part of the same one-world alliance!
He believed in a certain unproven duality –
That God and Nature both formed reality!*

*Do the laws of the universe
Follow chapter and verse?
And does every action
Meet with God's reaction?*

*Is democracy a multi-headed Chimera
That will lead us to a dry Sahara?
With factions pulling different directions –
Can we ever hope to find perfection?*

*Two days after the assassination
Nicholas Katzenbach made a proclamation –
"The public must be satisfied, in some fashion
That Oswald was a lone assassin!"*

THE MEETING AT MURCHISON'S

With a meeting at Murchison's the night before –
The final plans they would explore!
Oilmen, spies, and the Mafia too –
With Hoover and Johnson at the head of the crew!

The oilmen were so worried, they almost cried!
What if the oil depletion allowance died?
If LBJ is President, then
Who'll break the tie as the Senate Pro Tem?

Now Richard Nixon deserves a mention –
He was at the Pepsi bottlers convention –
Nixon left Dallas early that morn –
But he can't quite remember anything more!

Richard Nixon was the Bay of Pigs Action Officer
As Vice President under Dwight Eisenhower
He helped to train the Cuban swifties –
Until he lost the election in 1960!

George Bush moved from Connecticut to Texas
And got involved with the big oil nexus!
If you're friendly with the CIA –
An oil well might come your way!

George Bush owned an oil company named Zapata –
Which bore no relation to Operation Zapata!
A CIA plan to help the Cuban martyrs –
With transport ships named Houston and Barbara!

Now, when Lyndon Johnson had his heart attack
It was a most unusual circumstance!
He was spirited out of his secretary's house
Before the news media came about!

THE MEETING AT MURCHISON'S

Dr. Bill Truels with Madeleine Brown

There was a room near the post office tunnel
Where politicians liked to rumble!
It was built for Lyndon to recover
And play with his significant other!

Lyndon cavorted with Madeleine Brown for a while
She raised her son, Steven, with his LBJ smile –
Another Valentine raised a child unhindered –
As long as wily Lyndon would never by fingered!

Madeleine Brown tells the story of LBJ's peeve –
How Robert and John would pay him no heed!
He was, after all, the Vice President –
You'd think they'd show him a little respect!

"Instead, they're trying to put me in prison
Like some old worn out politician!
With Billie Sol Estes, Mac Wallace, and Cliff Carter
You'd think I'm a crook by the way they dishonor!"

THE QUATRAINS OF CAMELOT

Bobby never liked LBJ –
The two of them would never play!
So even though Lyndon was the Vice President –
He was "Colonel Cornpone" to the Eastern establishment!

Now what were Bobby's credentials
To be the U.S. Attorney General?
Lyndon had won political campaigns –
While Bobby on his brother's coattails did reign!

Robert Kennedy had a strong compunction
To meticulously weed out greed and corruption!
He was opposed to political favors –
Unless, of course, they were Kennedy players!

Bobby had a vision of racial equality
That transcended the contemporary political reality!
But when the Kennedy civil rights bill failed –
With Lyndon Johnson's help it finally prevailed!

When LBJ was Senate Pro Tem
He would appoint all the committee chairmen –
But because of the East-South rivalry
Few assignments were given to John Kennedy!

But Senator John Kennedy didn't help –
He rarely answered the voting bell!
When a vote was about to be cast –
He'd usually end up taking a pass!

Kennedy and his friends were really cool –
They'd frolic naked in the White House pool!
But when Jacqueline was back in town
Never would they come around!

"My husband has a wandering prod –
Sometimes I think he needs a bob!
Would that he could settle down –
And spend some time with kids around!"

THE MEETING AT MURCHISON'S

"When people are in their bloom
They never seem to have the room –
For quiet thoughts and gentle ways –
Instead they act like people crazed!"

Alfred Kinsey conducted investigations
Into human sexual procreation –
Did he open Pandora's box –
And set the stage for Camelot?

Or was it simply the birth control pill
That gave people the will
To give up customs of the past –
And pursue a hedonistic path!

Now, Johnson had a scandal called Box 13
Where his victory margin was mighty lean!
They "found" 200 votes for Lyndon in '48 –
And he became Senator of the Texas state!

And did you hear about Lyndon's Silver Star?
In New Guinea, he didn't have to travel far!
Lyndon told the tale of a daring, heroic mission –
But his plane returned due to a mechanical condition!

President Johnson would say, "I beg your pardon" –
And relieve himself in the Rose Garden!
With the White House parties going strong –
The bathroom lines were way too long!

Now, should a revered Presidential figure
Pull out the Royal Phallic Finger –
To moisten the hallowed White House grounds –
Where gents and ladies do abound?

Kennedy met with irritation
From the Southern delegation –
To them, he acted debonair –
A rich man's son who didn't care!

THE QUATRAINS OF CAMELOT

But to the people of Massachusetts
The Kennedys were like Confucius!
They could never fail or wrongly act –
You'd think they wrote the Mayflower Compact!

To the Eastern establishment
Lyndon was subject to banishment!
His western ways and southern beam
Left him out of the Kennedy team!

So why did Kennedy pick LBJ?
The two never got along anyway!
It was at father Joseph's insistence –
'Cause LBJ would balance the ticket!

So the Kennedy-Johnson allegiance
Was strictly a marriage of convenience!
Would Lyndon Johnson be integrated –
Or would he soon be castigated?

For a while the bid for the Presidency
Resolved their mutual animosity –
"Let's bury the hatchet!" they said –
But did they bury it in Kennedy's head?

Bobby Kennedy couldn't hide his contempt
For the traditional Southern establishment!
Instead, he would bear his legal claws
To fight against the Southern cause!

Soon after the meeting at Murchison's house
LBJ told Madeleine, "You'll see, I'm no slouch!
After tomorrow I vow those Kennedys
Will never again embarrass me!"

Sam Giancana was the Chicago boss
Who felt that he'd been double-crossed –
"I helped Kennedy win the Illinois race –
Now he's trying to send me to Joliet State!"

THE MEETING AT MURCHISON'S

John McCloy

John McCloy and the Eastern bankers did dread
John Kennedy would ruin the power of the Fed!
If U.S. Notes were backed by the Treasury
The Federal Reserve would have to end its' usury!

Thus multiple forces agreed to combine –
"JFK's not our man!" they together opined!
"It's for the good of the nation," they rationalized –
"Why, the oil companies he's threatened to nationalize!"

The CIA, the Cubans, the Mafia and the bankers
Were all filled with contempt, distrust, and anger!
The Texas businessmen were in a stew –
John Kennedy, they said, would never do!

Your political future is about to crumble –
The President's brother is making rumbles!
Your closest allies are going to jail –
Can you really Lyndon assail?

"I've got plenty of enemies –
Just like politicians for centuries!
But when they try to end your career
They're going to take it in the rear!"

*"I'm not going to lay down and die –
And let them bury me alive!
I've drawn a line in the sand –
Yes, I'm going to make my stand!"*

*"There's an instinct for survival
That warns me of my rivals –
Trust them in everything
And you will hear the jailhouse ring!"*

*"It's tough to be a conformer
When you're backed into a corner!
When they take you for a fool –
You have to break the rules!"*

*Is there heaven and hell behind every wall?
Can a great leader foresee his fall?
Are there demons and jackals who lie in wait –
Will the archangels come to spare his fate?*

*Assassinations are a reality
That remind us of our mortality!
Just when things seem right
The world could end tonight!*

Carlos Marcello (2nd from left), Santos Trafficante, Frank Ragano

CUTLER MAP OF DEALEY PLAZA

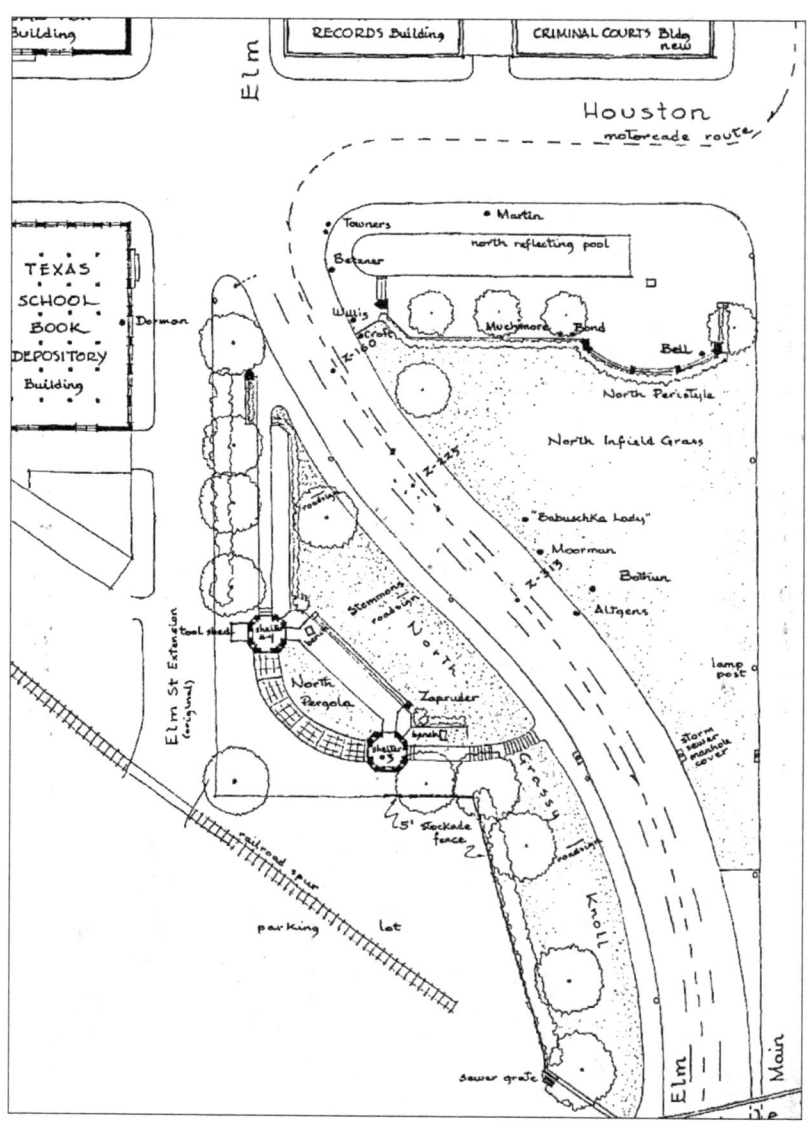

You play the game like there is no end –
Ignoring life's final bend!
And when you finally descend down Elm –
The Lord will come and take the helm!

NEW ORLEANS, DALLAS, AND LAS VEGAS

Dr. Alton Ochsner was an interesting man –
His Ochsner Clinic was the best in the land!
He carried out studies with apes and white mice –
A cure for cancer was in his sights!

Ochsner was best friends with spy chief Bill Donovan –
The two hung together and had a lot of fun!
Ochsner was president of the International House
And Clay Shaw was director against the communist louts!

Ochsner founded Information Council of the Americas
And was a distinguished Tulane Professor Emeritus!
He disliked communists, there's no doubt
And talked one day of a Castro rout!

Communism was perceived
Just like a disease –
You had to root it out
Before it spread about!

Now, is it really critical
For a surgeon to be that political?
Did Alton Ochsner become too addicted
To solving all of man's afflictions?

Dr. Ochsner was a superhuman sort
With doctors and politicians he did cavort –
Surgeons and world leaders found a star
But sometimes, you can go too far!

Was Dr. Ochsner an innocent victim
Of the people who hung with him?
Or did he spend too much time
With the oilmen, the politicians and the spies?

Dr. Alton Ochsner

It's great to be a doctor and surgeon –
To find cures for diseases that burden--
But too much dabbling in affairs internal
Can lead you down a road infernal!

Dr. Ochsner was a major force
In New Orleans political discourse –
But no one has a genuine proclivity
To discuss Dr. Ochsner's political activity!

Dr. Mary Sherman was in his crew
She worked with David Ferrie, too!
They radiated cells in a linear accelerator –
The cancers grew even greater and greater!

Dr. Alton Ochsner was a driven man –
In science and politics he did command!
His projects would try to cure disease –
And put the communists ill at ease!

Some say there was a darker side
With projects he would try to hide!
Does it matter how a leader passes –
If it's for the good of all the masses!

THE QUATRAINS OF CAMELOT

Oswald's girlfriend was Judyth Vary
He introduced her to Bannister and Ferrie –
Dr. Ochsner introduced her to Dr. Sherman –
They worked with hundreds of laboratory vermin!

Oswald traveled to Clinton, it's not sure why
And entered a voter registration drive –
He applied for a hospital job at nearby Jackson
But nobody knows his real action!

Could cancer be used as a bioweapon?
Inject the cells and see what happened?
Were the Cuban prisoners in a Jackson town
Injected with some toxins found?

Oswald had a medical library card
That could have led to the cancer Czar!
David Ferrie searched high and low –
"There are things the people must not know!"

Thus the mystery does continue
What was Oswald's real venue?
He worked for the CIA and the FBI
Was he a traitor or a spy?

Nicolai Ceausescu of Romania did threaten
To use cancer as a bioweapon –
Political opponents were given a radioactive drink
And in six months from cancer they were extinct!

The Russian KGB
Fed thallium salts to their enemy!
If you called the government crazy –
You'd soon be pushing up daisies!

Governments don't run like the Wizard of Oz
With one man in the sky who controls all the shots
It's more like a Casa Blanca story –
With all different groups fighting for glory!

"Wild"
Bill Donovan

John Kennedy was quite the cad –
He'd steal out of the White House in a cab!
But the FBI bugged all of his mistress's pitfalls
And sent the Secret Service with the nuclear football!

Are we victims of our hormones –
With actions really not our own?
Are we heeding nature's call
When we break the moral law?

Now, if you're not acting Presidential
Others may become resentful –
If they hear word of a coup
They may not be true to you!

Dr. Max Jacobsen gave Kennedy injections
Of amphetamines and other confections!
Kennedy said it made him feel alive
But the doctor lost his license in '75!

John cavorted with Mary Pinchot
She was an accomplished artist and quite a pistol!
She said they dabbled in some LSD
From Dr. Timothy O'Leary's pharmacy!

Mary had a meeting with Che Guevara
And talked of peace instead of sayonara!
But she talked of CIA involvement with Kennedy's death
And died on a Chesapeake towpath – a bullet in her head!

THE QUATRAINS OF CAMELOT

Mary Pinchot Meyer

*Now her ex-husband went to Mary's house
And found the CIA's James Angleton snooping about!
He was looking for Mary's secret diary
Which talked of JFK and a romance fiery!*

*It turns out there was a C-Day plan
To invade Fidel's Cuban land!
Che Guevara would lead the way –
Was Mary Pinchot working with the CIA?*

*Castro later arrested Che Guevara
And from the Cuban isle he soon departed –
He went to Bolivia to lead a revolution
Where the CIA arranged his execution!*

*After the Bay of Pigs, John became disenchanted –
Against the CIA he raved and ranted!
"I'll splinter the CIA into a thousand pieces –
I'll run things myself!" was the Kennedy thesis*

*John met Judith Exner through Frank Sinatra
She was also friends with Sam Giancana!
Judith carried envelopes to and fro
That dealt with plans against Fidel Castro!*

J. Edgar Hoover then talked to John Kennedy
And said, "For Judith Exner you must find a remedy!
You must not associate with Mafia friends
Or your Presidential reputation will come to an end!"

Frank Sinatra had built a helicopter pad
For the arrival of the Kennedy clan –
But Peter Lawford phoned Frank Sinatra
And told him he was persona non grata!

Frank then became quite enraged –
Some said he was even fit to be caged!
He was so mad that he stuttered and stammered
And tore up the pad with a giant sledgehammer!

Was there a Lilith who stole the light –
A beautiful dessert Queen of the night?
A seductress who would take away
The life of all who came to play?

Lilith
by John Collier

Then there's the story of the singer, Dean Martin
Who was so handsome, he left all the girls a smartin'!
He ran around with Sinatra's Rat Pack –
Sammy Davis and Shirley MacLaine, the first Rat Brat!

Now, in his final days, Dean Martin was sober
With the loss of son, Dino, he couldn't get over –
Like the American people, with the loss of their son,
Things are never the same when you've lost a loved one!

Jackie had problems with John's roving eye –
But they both cried together when little Patrick died!
They renewed their marriage and vowed not to quit
And Jackie joined John for the brief Dallas trip!

Sinatra was close friends with Sam Giancana –
Their lives twisted together like a giant anaconda!
But when John Kennedy's life did end –
Frank spoke to Giancana never again!

THE QUATRAINS OF CAMELOT

"I loved John Kennedy!" Sinatra exclaimed
"When he died, I felt sorrow and pain!"
Frank briefly dated Jacqueline Kennedy
But Robert Kennedy would soon intercede!

Jackie dated Sinatra just one time –
Frank said the experience was truly sublime--
But did Jackie pump Frank for some inside information
About the John Kennedy assassination?

Jackie believed there was a conspiracy
To end the Kennedy dynasty –
She feared that her children were not safe
As long as the conspirators roamed the state!

There was a hotel in Miami named the Fontainebleau
Where mobsters and spies would often accrue –
Nearby was a restaurant named Sloppy Joe's
Where the darkest of plans were often proposed!

Now in order to understand the Kennedy assassination
You can't look at things in isolation!
The CIA and Mafia each have a role
And at times work together for a mutual goal!

The assassination was planned first in Chicago
But rifles were found in one Cuban's cargo!
A black Secret Service agent named Abraham Bolden
Told the Warren Commission, but received a scolding!

They arrested Abraham quickly, before he could talk –
He spent three years in jail before he could walk!
Sometimes you can get in quite a thistle –
If you try to blow the proverbial whistle!

The assassination in Chicago was planned near Hillside
Where Kennedy along the expressway would ride –
But two Cubans were arrested with rifles in their trunk
And the Chicago assassination was soon defunct!

The President was planning to entertain
At an Army-Air Force football game –
But the President's trip was spoiled
When a Cuban plot was foiled!

The car for the Chicago raid
Was registered in another's name!
The Secret Service was quite appalled –
When they saw the name – Lee Harvey Oswald!

JFK with Secret Service Agent Abraham Bolden

Abraham Bolden was a true American hero
They should put his name on the FBI bureau!
One of the greatest Americans in our nation –
He spared Chicago from a JFK assassination!

If you don't believe in the Lone Gunman
You're bound to become a target for someone!
It's important not to fall from grace
When the government's trying to save its face!

The assassination was next planned for Tampa
With the approval of Santos Trafficante!
But Tampa police learned of the intended crime
And the plans were canceled just in time!

THE QUATRAINS OF CAMELOT

The assassination was next planned for Dallas
Where Kennedy in a crossfire would die with malice!
With tall buildings and a sharp turn from Houston to Elm
Dealey Plaza was the perfect assassination realm!

Thirty two years later, in 1995
The Secret Service decided it was time –
Chicago and Tampa assassination records were spoiled
And conspiracy theorists were once again foiled!

Now LBJ was a Vice President
Who set a dangerous precedent –
In order to avoid a dangerous coup
The Vice President must to his leader be true!

This may be idle speculation
But since the Kennedy assassination
Vice Presidents chosen have all been weak –
No threat do they offer to their Chief!

There was a labor camp named Atchafalaya
Near Morgan City down by the Louisiana bayou –
Where Chauncey Holt sent the Oswald leaflets
From Philip Twombly, who was the CIA secret!

On Canal Street in front of McCrory's store –
Lee Oswald was handing out leaflets galore
Labeled "Fair Play for Cuba" – New Orleans Chapter –
Was Oswald a communist or just a play actor?

David Ferrie and Guy Bannister heard Oswald rant
At Bannister's office on 544 Camp –
But the "Fair Play for Cuba" leaflets Oswald passed out
Were stamped with the same address as Bannister's louts!

Bill McLaney owned land near Lake Pontchartrain
Where anti-Castro Cuban exiles worked and trained!
In the film viewed by the House Select Committee
Were Guy Bannister, Lee Oswald, and David Atlee!

Joe West was a Baptist minister
Who suspected a plot quite sinister!
He interviewed James Files as a private eye –
The Grassy Knoll shooter when Kennedy died!

Joe West deserves the credit
For detective work of merit!
His tireless work and investigation
Helped solve the riddle of the JFK assassination!

James Files, with his 0.222 Remington Fireball
Claimed he fired one shot from the Grassy Knoll!
Ed Hoffman watched from the overpass
As the gunman reversed his coat and put on his hat!

James fired an exploding mercury round
That lifted up skin flaps wherever it found!
One flap was raised in front of the right ear
Before the bullet exited the right rear!

The mercury went in multiple directions –
Which created multiple imperfections!
The bullet exploded – that was clear –
And sent fragments of bone flying left and rear!

James bit the spent shell and put it on the picket fence –
Such was the young man's unbridled arrogance!
As he sits in federal prison for a framed-up crime
He questions his deed, as he puts in his time!

"I did what I was asked to do –
I worked for the Mafia and CIA, too!
At the Bay of Pigs we all felt thwarted
When Kennedy had the mission aborted!"

Twenty four years later –
A gardener named James Rademacher
Went digging near the picket fence
And found a .222 casing bent!

THE QUATRAINS OF CAMELOT

James Files

Grassy Knoll Shooter?

*James Files says he bit the shell –
And tooth marks you could plainly tell –
But to this day the FBI riles –
And won't release James' dental files!*

*Malcolm Summers saw a man on the Knoll
With a gun he described as a long pistol –
He identified the gun as a Remington Fireball –
The same gun that Files from Chicago did haul!*

*"I wasn't the only shooter that day –
Chuck Niccoletti fired from a Dal-Tex bay!
Lee Oswald was a shooter not –
He took the blame for my final shot!"*

*"I never knew Ozzie was the sacrificial lamb
As part of the lone gunman scam!"
He was really a very dedicated spy
And worked as an informant for the FBI!*

*Was Marshall Caifano the third man –
A shooter from Chicagoland –
Who, with Niccoletti and Files
Ended the life of the Camelot child?*

*Now, Oswald thought he was infiltrating the group
That was planning the assassination coup –
Oswald gave a note to FBI Agent James Hosty –
Who was ordered by Hoover to make it toasty!*

But, just what was in the Hosty note?
John Judge says Hosty's daughter had a vote –
She said Oswald warned the FBI
Of a JFK assassination try!

That morning when Oswald woke up
He left his wedding ring in a cup –
Some say this proves with simplicity
Oswald's lone gunman complicity!

It's fair to say Oswald knew of the plan
But was he trying to stop it before it began?
Oswald knew that something big would happen
But could he really stop the action?

When Oswald reported to work that day
He heard the shooters had walked away –
Was he sipping a Coke on the second floor
When the Mafia team slipped in the back door?

In a world of smoke and mirrors
The first team shooters disappear –
Everybody then relaxes
And the second team slips into action!

Of course it wasn't meant that way
But Giancana ruled the day –
If the CIA won't do the deed
The Mafia will their leader heed!

Now, did James Files really fire that shot?
Billie Sol Estes talks of a different plot!
The Texas Mafia's really to blame –
Cliff Carter, Mac Wallace and the oil patch gang!

On Grand Avenue, a restaurant named Brownie's
Was frequented often by all the local townies!
The rich, the poor, cops and robbers and whores
Were all regular customers at Brownie's front door!

THE QUATRAINS OF CAMELOT

The second floor at Brownie's was a gambling operation
With some of the richest people in the nation –
Cliff Carter, H. L. Hunt, W. O. Bankston, and Byrd
Planned a murder that 'round the world would be heard!

Now W. O. Bankston was the financial backer
And personal friend to Dallas County Sheriff Bill Decker!
The owner of several car dealerships –
Did he make Decker a deal he couldn't resist?

Bobby Baker had plans to build casinos
In the Dominican Republic with Rafael Trujillo –
But with Hoffa's Teamster loans through the mail
Bobby Kennedy was threatening to put them in jail!

Now Billie Sol Estes did something quite rotten –
He collected money for growing non-existent cotton!
He received federal agricultural subsidies
Until he got caught by the Kennedys!

Then there was the awarding of the TFX –
A fighter plane that had Congress vexed!
Boeing's bid was 100 million dollars less –
But General Dynamics in Texas would LBJ bless!

With the Scandals of Baker and Billie Sol Estes
There was concern that power would be lost in Texas –
The oil depletion allowance might lose in a vote
And defense contract money would go back to the coast!

At Bobby Baker's Quorum Club on Capitol Hill
Kennedy met Ellen Rometsch, an East German shill!
The stunning young brunette was courted for months
Until J. Edgar Hoover gave Kennedy his lumps!

Now, if a President has a wandering phallus
Should he really meet with malice?
Politicians are, after all, social beings
Who live in worlds of dreams and schemes!

NEW ORLEANS, DALLAS & LAS VEGAS

Not that I'm lacking in moral rectitude –
A President should never yield to turpitude –
It's just that if a President should dally
Is that cause for his enemies to rally?

A power shift was under way
With the Eastern Democrats holding sway –
The movement was gaining political force
And only an assassination could reverse the course!

Now they were in the middle of a five card draw
When H. L. Hunt said, "Let's go for it all!"
He put down the King right next to the Queen
And started the plans for the Dealey Plaza scene!

One million dollars was put in the pot
With political decisions made right on the spot!
Thus the plans for President Kennedy's eventual fall
Were started in Dallas at Brownie's gambling hall!

Senator George Smathers was slated for '64
And LBJ soon would be out the door!
Billie Sol asks, "Who had the most to gain
In this treacherous Presidential game?"

Payoffs were made from Las Vegas to Dallas –
Casinos had become the modern day palace!
Money and drugs were transported in a hearse
So local police wouldn't check for the purse!

Cliff Carter was Lyndon's organization man
Who initiated the assassination plan –
Carter was aware of the various forces
That disliked Kennedy's political discourses!

The CIA was having concussions
They felt Kennedy was too soft on the Russians!
And Cuban exiles were in Castro's brig
Because of the failed Bay of Pigs!

THE QUATRAINS OF CAMELOT

*Mafia members were doing time
Courtesy of Robert Kennedy's War on Crime!
And Jimmy Hoffa thought Kennedy a churl
After Kennedy told Hoffa he giggled like a girl!*

*So Cliff Carter ordered all these factions
To develop a mutual plan of action –
If they all showed up at the Dealey pulpit
How could you find the real culprit?*

Ed Tatro

*But Billie Sol said that Lyndon barked
At the thought of owing the Mafia a mark!
Let the Texas Mafia do the action
While the other groups provide distraction!*

*Ed Tatro spent his entire life
Teaching his Boston students to do what's right!
"Leave no stone unturned in your search for truth!
And many a lie you will uproot!"*

*Ed interviewed people who knew LBJ
And wandered into the Texas fray
He studied the people who at Murchison's did meet
The night before Kennedy went down Elm Street!*

Clyde Tolson and J. Edgar Hoover

And what was Hoover doing, pray tell?
When he answered the Murchison dinner bell?
Did he just happen to be passing through?
Or did he help to stir the witches' brew?

Hoover claimed to solve the Kansas City Massacre
But the fingerprint evidence was manufactured!
Pretty Boy Floyd was made to take the blame
And thus started Hoover's rise to fame!

The whole idea, don't you see
Is to provide plausible deniability!
You never know how things will go –
So put an unknown gunman at the Knoll!

It must be someone who's shot before –
Someone you can count on to make a score –
Who can look a President in the eye
Then pull the trigger and watch him die!

THE QUATRAINS OF CAMELOT

There was such a man who had the gall –
In '62 he'd taken a shot at Charles DeGaulle –
A Corsican opposed to Algerian independence
Who worked for the oilmen and French intelligence!

Now, the Grassy Knoll is quite exposed
With the greatest risk of being disclosed –
If you put a shooter at this station
Let him be from a foreign nation!

With Jan Michael Mertz you wouldn't trifle –
Involved with heroin, French spies, the CIA's ZR/Rifle!
He used frangible bullets – guaranteed to explode
Did he fire point blank from the Grassy Knoll?

Chauncey Holt was behind the picket fence –
A CIA man who helped overthrow Arbenz!
He forged the Secret Service badges
And was one of three tramps in Dealey Plaza!

Holt was part of Executive Action –
To remove foreign leaders who had become a distraction!
He provided fake ID's to Oswald with the name of Hidell
And was part of Operation Mongoose to get rid of Fidel!

Now William Harvey's Executive Action
Had specific rules for each transaction –
"Never mention the word 'assassination'
And be prepared to blame a Soviet Bloc nation!"

"No projects on paper, singleton ops –
Should look like counterespionage!
No chain of connections permitting blackmail –
Operationally competent, ruthless, and stable!"

William K. Harvey
(Photo by Driver)

William Harvey was put out
When the Bay of Pigs became a rout!
Kennedy fired him on the spot –
But William Harvey wouldn't stop!

William Harvey liked LBJ –
Together they'd go all the way!
Harvey still held onto the belief –
That he should be the next CIA chief!

Charles Harrelson, Charles Rogers, and Chauncey Holt
Were arrested by the Dallas Police in a boxcar hold –
Three "tramps" were marched to the Dallas police station –
Then released without fingerprints or photographs taken!

Three "Tramps" in Dealey Plaza

Holt was upset with Oswald's demise –
That the CIA should sacrifice one of its spies!
Oswald was malleable and trusted his boss –
Little did he know his life would be lost!

One job that Chauncey Holt did win
Was to make phony Secret Service pins –
So people like Milwaukee Phil
Could keep police from the Grassy Hill!

Now you must realize there's a drug connection –
You've got to have money to be clandestine!
The intelligence agencies took 10% off the top
To pay for gun-running and intelligence ops!

Since the Boland amendment, money was little –
For covert CIA ops, the Congress belittled!
The spies had to make money on the side
To fund the plans they wanted to hide!

THE QUATRAINS OF CAMELOT

Peter Dale Scott talked of the politics of cocaine
And how efforts to stop cocaine traffic are lame!
Drug money for over a generation
Has been used to finance clandestine operations!

Havana was an important drug connection
That the Mafia used under Batista's direction –
Heroin shipped from the Middle and Far East
Would find its way to American streets!

President Kennedy died like Julius Caesar
But no one dared to call it treason!
Each group had their ax to grind
But no one would admit the crime!

But does it really matter who pulled the trigger
Since multiple groups came in to figure?
Even though you're just a decoy
Aren't you still a part of the ploy?

Oswald wasn't meant to live
For two days after the Kennedy hit!
Some did doubt a Mafia plot
Until Jack Ruby fired his fatal shot!

LBJ helped promote the lie
By suggesting there might be a Russian tie!
He said, "We must investigate no more,
Or we might trigger a nuclear war!"

Now, was Arlen Specter genuinely convinced
That a Russian attack would definitely commence?
And that it would be guns instead of butter
If Oswald wasn't shown to be a Lone Nutter?

Some ask, "Who killed Officer Jefferson Tippit?"
The spent shells had notches from an automatic!
But no one dared dispute the verdict –
Oswald's revolver must be the culprit!

They said that the suspicious man
Said, "Poor dumb cop!" – then sort of ran –
Frank Schweihs was known to have a limp –
From a bullet he took in a Chicago hit!

Frank Schweihs was known to take no quarter
On people who wouldn't follow orders!
If you didn't do your job –
You'd take a hit from the Chicago mob!

Was Tippit to kill Lee Oswald
As a policeman answering the call?
Was the lone gunman to be the story –
Shooting from the Depository?

Did Frank Schweihs Tippit kill
When Tippit suffered a lack of will?
With Boss Giancana, a mission failed
Would cause you soon to meet travail!

The case against Oswald was circumstantial –
The evidence was not substantial!
It would never stand up in a trial –
So Oswald's murder proved quite worthwhile!

Helen Markham couldn't identify Oswald
Until the FBI paid her a house call!
"He's the one who killed Tippitt," she finally said –
Out of fear that she might turn up dead!

In England, from the County of Essex
Comes Ian Griggs, an English detective –
He says Oswald in the lineup was thwarted –
The only one with a bruise on his forehead!

Ian Griggs

Oswald was a gift from the CIA –
Someone for the assassination had to pay!
The lone gunman is a convenient explanation
If you want to avoid a serious investigation!

The government is quite upset
That people will not it's verdict accept!
They say, "Conspiracy theorists are quite outrageous!"
Yet the government keeps classified over a million pages!

"This is the worst type of speculation!"
Jack Valenti howled and gesticulated –
"People mustn't hear this conspiracy news –
It really might distort their historical views!"

The Stream

"I'm simply trying to protect and preserve
The reputation of a man under whom I served!
LBJ was, after all, our President
I do believe he was innocent!"

Lyndon picks up a stone sliver
And skips it along the Pedernales River –
Back at the Johnson City Ranch
He thinks about the days gone past

"I throw a pebble in the stream
And watch the ripples fade –
It's nice to have some time alone –
I like to get away!"

"The water rushes 'round the rocks
And churns an airy foam
As I journey through this life
I've wandered far from home!"

*"And as the circles widen
They share a common lore –
Like the friends that I have known
They touch the one before!"*

*"And though the ripples of the past
Have faded long ago –
I love to sit here by this stream
And watch the water flow!"*

*"I close my eyes and float
Along the channels of my mind –
I see the scenes of yesterday –
The people left behind!"*

*"Too bad we can't relive the past
And change what we have done –
I know I'd chart a different course
With yet another run!"*

*LBJ became quite depressed
When he was no longer President –
Was he a victim of the times?
Or was he guilty of high crimes?*

*He grew his hair long, and went into seclusion
"Was I a part of some great delusion?"
As Lyndon gazes out on the morning haze
He ruminates about those fateful days!*

*"Communism, the cold war, and racial strife
Seemed a part of daily life!
The country was in a great turmoil
The Vietnam War was about to boil!"*

*"I was worried about communism
While the hippies laughed at my patriotism!
The political candidates were out to foil
And civic leaders seemed quite disloyal!"*

THE QUATRAINS OF CAMELOT

*"He who thinks he wouldn't do
What I gave approval to –
Should think how they would react
To being stabbed right in the back!"*

*"I wasn't doing anything illegal –
Why should it create an upheaval?
To funnel business to my state
Is how a politician rates!"*

*President
Lyndon Johnson*

*"I sent contracts to Texas
And that was the real nexus!
The Kennedys funneled business to Massachusetts
And prided themselves like they were Confucius!"*

*"The Kennedys would look at a political map
And say, 'What's the harm in that?'
With little blue pins they'd mark the land
For business contracts with Uncle Sam!"*

*"What's good for the goose is good for the gander –
A good politician will gerrymander!
A worthy public servant takes care of his own –
Or the citizens will him disown!"*

"The Pentagon generals were up in arms –
They thought Kennedy would do us harm!
He lacked the will to go to war –
And send our troops to distant shores!"

"So enough of this political guilt –
I've had it to the absolute hilt!
You play the game by the rules –
Or you get kicked right out of school!"

The doctor pays Lyndon a daily call –
Was he to blame for Kennedy's fall?
Should Lyndon have blocked the oilmen and spies –
And faced his own political demise?

"I hear voices in the night
That at times do give me fright!
Do they warn of hidden danger
From some dark, concealed stranger?"

"My conscious thoughts
Push back subconscious haunts –
The light of day
Keeps the ghosts away!"

Does a maniacal urge for power
Explain ambition's hour?
Did Lyndon forego reason
To commit an act of treason?

"Did I overly rely
On my generals and spies –
That a communist persuasion
Might soon overtake the nation?"

These are questions that no one will ask –
Is anyone really up to the task
Of solving the JFK assassination –
The greatest mystery of our nation!

THE QUATRAINS OF CAMELOT

Conspiracy views are called bizarre –
"That's not the way things really are!
Let's stop this politician roast –
Never ask who gains the most!"

Let's step back and think awhile –
Why are we so easily riled?
Are fame and fortune worth the cost
Of losing friends and getting lost?

It must be nice to be so blind –
To blandly accept the party line!
To strut and fret upon the stage –
And never see the hidden rage!

The illusion of knowledge
Sends us off to college!
But can you learn the truth
From a political sleuth?

History is filled with misdirections –
Meant to cover imperfections!
Politicians try to pass the blame –
While scholars seek the truth to gain!

Immerse yourself in the destructive element –
Joseph Conrad's words are eloquent!
But don't we face an early demise –
If caution isn't exercised!

Is it serendipity
When things end happily?
Is it Divine Providence –
Or just coincidence?

Is part of the Universe missing –
With secret files in some giant listing?
Will black holes of knowledge hold the key –
To understanding reality?

Do you get a job and join the race –
Or ask the questions no one will grace?
Do you sit around and philosophize –
Or just ignore the official lies?

Certain things, it's been agreed
The public must never read!
Better to leave them in the dark –
Than hear the angry voices bark!

Do our brains constantly hash –
Trying to relive the past
Dreaming while we're still awake
With voices and visions that reality break!

Are parts of the truth forbidden
Destined to be deeply hidden –
So that a palatable explanation
Can be fed to a hungry nation?

Dealey Plaza Memorial Plaque

HUNT BLAMES JFK HIT ON LBJ

January 14, 2007 – **E. HOWARD Hunt** - the shadowy former CIA man who organized the Watergate break-in and was once eyed in the assassination of President Kennedy - bizarrely says that Lyndon Johnson could be seen as a prime suspect in the rubout.

Only the most far-out conspiracy theorists believe in scenarios like Hunt's. But in a new memoir, "American Spy: My Secret History in the CIA, Watergate & Beyond," due out in April, Hunt, 88, writes: "Having Kennedy liquidated, thus elevating himself to the presidency without having to work for it himself, could have been a very tempting and logical move on Johnson's part.

"[LBJ] had the money and the connections to manipulate the scenario in Dallas and is on record as having convinced JFK to make the appearance in the first place. He further tried unsuccessfully to engineer the passengers of each vehicle, trying to get his good buddy, Gov. [John] Connolly, to ride with him instead of in JFK's car - where . . . he would have been out of danger."

Hunt says Johnson also had easy access to CIA man William Harvey, who'd been demoted when he tried to have **Fidel Castro** poisoned in defiance of orders to drop covert operations against Cuba. Harvey was "a ruthless man who was not satisfied with his position in the CIA and its government salary," Hunt writes.

"He definitely had dreams of becoming [CIA director] and LBJ could do that for him if he were president . . . [LBJ] would have used Harvey because he was available and corrupt." Hunt denies any hand in the assassination, insisting he wasn't one of three mysterious hobos who were photographed at the scene.

THE SIMULATION

*The motorcade turned from Houston to Elm
With Secret Service driver Greer steady at the helm
As the shots rang out, Greer slowed and looked back –
And Kennedy was caught in a crossfire trap!*

*Joachim Markus created a computer simulation
And calculated the Depository angulation –
With the Secret Service Agents standing in the car behind
There was a sea of heads from the Depository blind!*

*"It would have to be a perfect shot
To kill President Kennedy from this spot!
You'd have to adjust for wind and elevation
And you'd need a tripod for stabilization!"*

*Kennedy was supposed to fall, you see
While he was in front of the Depository –
A later shot farther down the road
Brought the Secret Service men into the scope!*

*Now the government staged a simulation
Of the John Kennedy assassination –
But they moved the back wound up to the neck
In order to the lie protect!*

*You'd think if you were doing a re-creation
They'd try to duplicate the exact situation!
But instead of a Lincoln, they used a Cadillac
Which left Connally's position out of whack!*

*The Secret Service men standing on the car behind
Were blocking a shot from the Depository blind –
Now, that's a problem, so the thing to do
Is to leave them off, so they won't obstruct the view!*

Thus the Dealey Plaza simulation

THE QUATRAINS OF CAMELOT

Was yet another obfuscation!
And the supposed attempt to find the truth
Was just another political ruse!

History is but a collection
Of mankind's predilections –
Flavored just right
To the victor's delight!

Is the truth so terribly dreadful
That politicians will not level –
Tell it to the people straight
And restore honesty to the state!

Now the acoustics don't lie – of that I'm certain
Five shots were fired and three men were hurtin'!
Three shots in a group, then two at the last –
The Dealey Plaza scene left people aghast!

On the acoustic tape, the only shot from ahead
Was localized from the Grassy Knoll hedge!
The rest were fired from the rear –
Though the exact location is not clear!

"Hear no evil!" the government states –
"Don't listen to those audio tapes!"
The dictabelt locates the Grassy Knoll shot –
To within two feet of the shooter's spot!

Now the National Academy of Sciences took exception
To the Weiss and Ashkenazi acoustic detections –
But Don Thomas analyzed in greater detail
And the acoustic evidence did prevail!

D.B. Thomas says the acoustic record is clear –
One shot from the front and four from the rear!
The Grassy Knoll shot was localized –
To ten feet west of the corner picket fence line!

THE SIMULATION

Don Thomas

The shooting began with three rear shots –
With the middle being from a rogue spot!
Three men were shot in the initial burst –
First Tague, then Kennedy, then Connally worst!

Then there was a five second pause –
Before the final two shots ended the cause!
The Grassy Knoll shot was the next to hit –
Before the final shot hit Connally's right wrist!

Connally then drops his Stetson hat –
The radius bone was shattered just like that!
Fragments of bullet in his forearm and right wrist –
Meant the pristine bullet CE-399 was not the culprit!

Some people say the Depository shot was easy
But I think that's a little cheesy!
Four shots were fired from behind
But the fatal shot came from the Grassy Knoll blind!

Some argue the neck wound was so small
That an entry wound must be the call
But the skin of the neck is elastic and thin –
An exit wound it still could have been!

THE QUATRAINS OF CAMELOT 203

Traveling 12 degrees up, from his back to his neck
How can you explain such a curious event?
A metallic clank was heard by Agent Hill standing there
As it bounced off the trunk, sending sparks everywhere!

The bullet hit the trunk with a metallic clack
Then entered Kennedy at the upper back –
Kennedy grabbed his throat, as it exited his neck
And Connally turned around before he was hit!

"My God, I'm hit! Get me to the hospital!"
Those are the words that gave a chill –
Kennedy was alive and still able to talk –
But driver Greer turned back again to gawk!"

Thus one bullet couldn't have hit both men –
The reaction times were different then –
And at the risk of incurring Arlen Specter's wrath
The bullet would have to travel on a zigzag path!

Bullets don't go straight, you see
At the political university!
Bullets do just what they're told
In order to play the lone gunman role!

As a trauma surgeon, I do know
That bullet tracks are hard to probe –
The muscles fall back into place
And make a bullet hard to trace!

Though the back wound did not initially probe
That does not mean that it was a shallow hole –
A bullet can go through and through
And make the path hard to construe!

Dr. Gary Aguilar recorded a phone interview
With Dr. John Bosworth of the autopsy crew –
"A probe was passed from the back to the neck –
Which showed that the two wounds did connect!"

THE SIMULATION

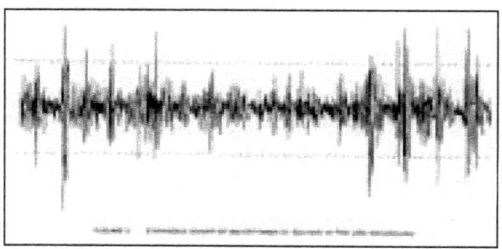

Courtesy D. B. Thomas from "Hear No Evil"

Table 1.- Synchronization of Putative Shots to Zapruder Frames

ACOUSTIC SHOT EVENT ORIGIN	TAPE TIME	TAPE-TIME INTERVAL	REAL TIME	Z-FRAME	EQUIVALENT
A	136.2	- 8.7	9.1	Z - 147	No Match
B	137.7	- 7.2	7.5	Z - 175	TSBD
C	139.2	- 5.6	5.8	Z - 204	Rogue Shot
D	140.3	- 4.6	4.8	Z - 224	TSBD
E (145.1)	144.9	0	0	Z - 312	KNOLL
F	145.6	+ 0.7	0.7	Z - 326	TSBD

Tape Times from BBN Report Table 2.
Event E time correction at 8 HSCA 115.
Tape speed correction factor 1.043 [8 HSCA 27].
Zapruder Film speed 18.3 fps.

Acoustics shows four rear shots and one frontal Knoll shot

THE QUATRAINS OF CAMELOT

A 12 degree angle is what I would trace
To bounce off the trunk and the Kennedy wounds make!
The trajectory traces back to the Depository berth
Where a shooter could fire from a hidden perch!

Can a bullet enter the back
And exit on an upward path?
If the shot was low and hit the car –
An upward path would then be par!

There's a collar on the back wound
That argues for an upward move –
And outward fibers on Kennedy's neck tie
Do an exit wound belie!

A hole in the windshield – how did it happen
With a bullet traveling in a downward fashion?
But a shot from the rear that bounced off the trunk
Goes up through Kennedy before the windshield's struck!

Computer Simulation of JFK Neck Shot From Rear
Bullet rises through Kennedy from back to front

THE SIMULATION

Computer Simulation of JFK Neck Shot Off Trunk
Sparks were seen around JFK and thought to be a firecracker

But the argument over the neck wound is moot –
The head wound ought to settle the dispute!
With a large exit wound in the back right skull
The head shot came from the right Grassy Knoll!

A conspiracy consists of two people or more
Who plan to settle some political score –
With shots fired from the front and rear
It's plain to see there's a conspiracy here!

Rose Cheramie was found by the roadside in Eunice
She'd been left on the road by two crazy Cubans!
She said, "They going to kill President Kennedy!"
But none of the doctors would listen to her plea!

Now, Rose Cheramie's reputation was tainted
But she knew Oswald and Ruby were acquainted!
She had worked in Jack Ruby's Carousal Club
But the Warren Commission gave her story the snub!

THE QUATRAINS OF CAMELOT

Rose was later found on the road near Big Sandy –
Her "accidental death" appeared mighty handy!
She had talked of Jack Ruby and gun-running and drugs
But Sheriff Decker in Dallas swept it under the rug!

Oswald was seen at Ruby's lair –
He introduced Lee to some friends of his there –
Ruby said, "This is my friend, Lee, from New Orleans –
He speaks Russian and Spanish – a former Marine!"

Now David Atlee Phillips was a CIA handler –
It was to him that Lee Oswald would answer!
Oswald was pliable, and would do what was told –
Little did he think he'd be left in the cold!

One problem with being on a need to know
Is that you don't get to see the entire show!
Your only job is to play your part –
And hope that your handler is true at heart!

A friend of mine, Dr. Robert Arnold
Stayed at the home of General Edwin Walker –
With printing presses in Turtle Creek
The house was a political place to meet!

Robert's wife was General Clyde Watts' daughter
And that's how they met General Edwin Walker –
When Dr. Arnold and his wife needed a place to stay
They would sleep at General Walker's when he was away!

Now Robert and his wife woke early one morning
To hear men below who were fighting and storming!
Then one man, in a New Orleans drawl
Said, "I'm going to kill Kennedy, with guns for us all!"

General Walker had friends who were Minutemen –
A right wing group of radical citizens
Along with H. L. Hunt, Guy Bannister, and David Ferrie
They helped provide guns to the Cuban mercenaries!

*In the early spring of 1963
Oswald supposedly went on a shooting spree –
Did Oswald really shoot at General Walker?
Was Oswald being sheep-dipped as a communist stalker?*

*Dr. Walker kept a dressed up mannequin
That he sat in a chair in the front den
He showed Dr. Arnold the hole in the wall –
But was General Walker ever sitting there at all?*

*The assassination became a looking glass
For hidden fears in ages past –
The Syrians in Damascus blamed Zionism –
And Egyptian diplomats blamed Southern racism!*

*And what about our security?
If someone could shoot President Kennedy –
Who would be the next to light
Within the assassin's rifle sights!*

*Now General Walker had gone to Oxford, Mississippi
And was later arrested by Attorney General Kennedy!
Walker was charged with seditious conspiracy
For blocking black students at the University!*

*"I'm a political prisoner!" General Walker exclaimed
"I just want to express my rage!"
"The federal government has no right to demand
Racial equality throughout our land!"*

THE QUATRAINS OF CAMELOT

*Jean Hill and Mary Moorman with her Polaroid camera,
as JFK's limo passes directly in front*

*Oswald's close friend was George de Mohrenschildt
Who he treated as father, which caused George guilt!
Oswald was malleable and would do what was told –
So he moved to New Orleans under Bannister's fold!*

*Richard Trask published pictures of the pain
To help researchers solve the puzzle that remains!
As a child of 16, he hailed JFK's New Frontier –
And regretted our loss of innocence that year!*

*Mary Moorman took a Polaroid photo just before
The fatal headshot scattered blood, bone, and gore!
And Abraham Zapruder, from his pedestal across
Filmed the entire event of our country's great loss!*

*Now, in the Moorman photo, when it's enlarged
There's a suggestion of a policeman wearing a star –
The view of Badgeman is obscured by leaves –
Was this the man who killed John Kennedy?*

*With bone fragments flying to the left and back
It was obvious that this was a frontal attack!
But the Warren Commission told a bedtime story
And said the fatal shot came from the Depository!*

THE SIMULATION

Moorman Photo with Grassy Knoll in Background, moments before the Grassy Knoll head shot. Officer Hargis (at right) had bone fragments embedded in his vest, and thought that he had been shot.

The Select Committee conducted another investigation
And said the Warren Commission had been mistaken –
The acoustics showed a shot from the front and right
And concluded the Grassy Knoll was the obvious site!

The House Select Committee said conspiracy
Was the only conclusion they could see –
A lone gunman seems out of the question
When shots are fired from two different directions!

But the House Committee raised the possibility
Of two random shooters from two different vicinities –
But such a solution was mere mathematical fun –
For the odds of such an occurrence are a million to one!

Now some say the acoustics is kind of muddy –
The sounds and echoes are kind of fuzzy!
But the same type of triangulation scheme
Is used to locate enemy submarines!

THE QUATRAINS OF CAMELOT

George DeMohrenschildt   *Guy Bannister*

Guy Bannister worked on the sly –
Retired from the Chicago FBI –
With mobsters and spooks he did cavort
And gun-running was his major sport!

But the most interesting man was David Ferrie
He studied at St. Mary's seminary!
Then he taught at the New Orleans Civil Air Patrol
Where he met Barry Seal and Lee Harvey Oswald!

Now David Ferrie was an unusual geek
With a photographic memory, he spoke Italian and Greek!
With a doctorate in philosophy, he dabbled in science –
And, just for fun, he'd hypnotize his clients!

Was Oswald a Manchurian candidate?
Who acted under a subconscious mandate?
Did he shoot an American President
As part of a hypnotized regiment?

I personally doubt the explanation
Though it raises an interesting situation –
How well do we control our perceptions
If we are perpetually fed with lies and deceptions?

THE SIMULATION

David Ferrie ran the Civil Air Patrol –
Where young men could play a role!
Lee Oswald would train in camp –
As part of Ferrie's chicken ranch!

When young men together stay –
They think of different ways to play!
Some are natural, some are not –
Beware the teacher of the lot!

A malleable young man
Falls into the wrong hands –
Looking for a lost Father –
And becomes canon fodder!

When Carlos Marcello was by Robert Kennedy deported
To Guatemala the gangster was sported!
He was flown back the next day by a CIA mercenary –
Who happened to be none other than David Ferrie!

John Kennedy ordered a daylight raid
At a base camp near Lake Pontchartrain
Where Ferrie and Bannister trained Cuban exiles –
For another invasion of the Cuban isle!

Guy Bannister debated LSU students
On civil rights and Bay of Pigs Cubans –
It was an attempt to infiltrate the left –
And Lee Oswald was often one of the guests!

Michael Kurtz at LSU went to Mancuso's restaurant
And chatted with Oswald and Bannister having lunch!
Kurtz reported his encounter after the assassination
But the FBI categorically denied the association!

Lee was more of a theoretical man –
Who enjoyed discussing philosophical plans!
He was not a man of mechanical action –
He was in Dealey Plaza to provide a distraction!

THE QUATRAINS OF CAMELOT

Lee could argue with Bannister's crew –
And give the LSU students ideas to chew!
But while he spoke Russian and Spanish as well –
He was never part of the old college swell!

Through it all, Lee was naïve –
Looking for something he could believe!
A Don Quixote traveling with banner unfurled –
He was dangled like a puppet before the world!

Lee loves to play with the kids in the neighborhood –
A side to Lee that's often misunderstood!
He argues politics in the coffee shop –
And often makes a library stop!

Now with his wife he was quite contrary –
But Lee had a love named Judyth Vary!
Yet a loner in history he will always be –
To fulfill the lone gunman legacy!

The legend of the forsaken man –
Rejected by his clandestine clan –
Is a story you must never know –
Unless history should be retold!

The Warren Commission's end
Was to deny Oswald had any friends!
But with all these different collusions –
A lone gunman becomes an unlikely conclusion!

Ferrie experimented with laboratory rats –
His apartment was full of all the small brats!
By injecting with cancer he hoped to threaten
The use of cancer as a bioweapon!

Lee Harvey Oswald dated Judyth Vary
Who worked in the lab with David Ferrie –
She reported to Dr. Mary Sherman –
A Tulane surgeon who was later found murdered!

THE SIMULATION

The official report claimed no cause for alarm –
But Mary was burned, with the loss of her arm!
Ed Haslam researched the entire event –
And found Mary's death was no accident!

Judyth relates that Oswald's plan
Was to transport toxins to the Cuban land –
But when Oswald got to Mexico City
To get a Cuban visa, he wasn't privy!

Linear Accelerator
1960's Era

Is it wrong for science to develop a strain
That could be injected into an opponent's vein?
Should science be used against political opponents
Or must we limit ourselves to bullets and blow-ups?

Does the world know what secret labs explore
That operate underground, behind closed doors?
What concoctions must they germinate
To do away with heads of state?

And what became of Judyth Vary –
The girlfriend who with Lee did tarry?
After 30 years she tells the story
Of how Lee ended up at the Depository!

"I was in love with Lee –
We had a romance that wasn't to be!
We talked of religion and politics and art –
And vowed that we would never part!"

"We worked at Reilly Coffee on Magazine –
But we were both working behind the scenes!
We'd take the bus to Audubon Park –
And roll down Monkey Hill in the dark!"

"We'd hang out around Lafayette Square –
Thompson's Restaurant was our favorite lair!
Anna Lewis would serve us our food –
Her husband, David, worked for Bannister's brood!"

THE QUATRAINS OF CAMELOT

Shackelford, Judyth Baker, Anna Lewis, Platzman

*"Stay close –
Put your arms around me tight!
Save me
From the gremlins of the night!"*

*"Take me
To your lovely home!
Keep me
From being all alone!"*

*"Tell me
The words I want to hear –
Spare me
From all the things I fear!"*

*"Kiss me!
And show me that you care!
Teach me –
All the things you dare!"*

*"We live between disasters –
Love is all that matters!
Trying to make our way
In a world of dismay!"*

"Dr. Alton Ochsner worked at Charity
And believed in freedom from the communist creed!
Would you kill Castro with a cancer seed
If it might help prevent World War III.?"

"But politics would interfere
With a love that we both held dear!
I was told it was for the good of the nation
That Lee and I endure a separation!"

"I left Lee with a tear in my eye –
It's not easy to say goodbye!
Little did we for one moment suspect
That Lee would take the heat for all the rest!"

"I talked with Lee by telephone
The night before the President rode –
He didn't know the real story
Of why they wanted him at the Depository!"

"He was told to follow the crew
And report what they intended to do –
But why not just arrest the bunch
Before they pulled their nasty punch?"

"I was forced to leave New Orleans and deny
That Lee had ever been a spy!
With Lee's death, there could be no trial –
So the CIA issued an official denial!"

"We never heard of Lee Oswald –
He was never at our beck and call!"
And so, with great agility
The CIA maintained plausible deniability!

"I was told to never talk
Of when Lee and I together walked –
The good times that we shared together
Were in the Land of Never Never!"

THE QUATRAINS OF CAMELOT

*"How will I remember
The good times that we shared?
Why do things we cherish most
Vanish in the air?"*

*"I've gathered all your pictures –
I've got your Valentine!
Remember when we had a love
That conquered space and time!"*

*"It truly is a paradox
That nature does create –
The perfect shapes and perfect forms
That soon evaporate!"*

*"They say that time will heal all wounds –
The pain soon disappears!
But every time I think of you
I see you through my tears!"*

*So Lee knew Ferrie and Ruby, too
As well as Bannister and his crew –
What was Lee doing with all these front men
If he truly acted as a lone gunman?*

*David Ferrie, Mary Sherman and Judyth Baker
All participated in the cancer caper!
Should cancer be used as a bioweapon –
When prominent leaders it could threaten?*

*Jack Ruby ran the Carousel Club –
It was a politician and spy and Mafia hub!
A steel guitarist who played there told me –
"You have ears that don't hear, and eyes that don't see!"*

*"For a little cerebral stimulation
A man will risk his entire reputation!
Thus I live off man's corruption –
Or is it simply reproduction?"*

Jack Ruby and the Carousel Club

Now Jack Ruby had an admission
He tried to tell the Warren Commission
"There's more to this tale than the eyes do see –
Let me tell you of conspiracy!"

"Dallas is a dangerous place –
I'd like a chance to plead my case!
Transfer me to Washington –
And I'll talk about the deed that's done!"

But the Commission members wouldn't hear
They looked at Ruby with a sneer –
"This is a man we cannot trust –
His admission's not worth a grain of dust!"

So Jack Ruby was tried and sentenced to jail
Where he looked out over the motorcade trail!
"A new form of government is going to replace –
The democracy we know might soon be erased!"

"In order to have a true perception
You must disregard your preconceptions!
Prepare for your world view to be shattered
If your search for truth is all that matters!"

THE QUATRAINS OF CAMELOT

*"We live in an artificial world
With candy canes and sugar swirls!
If the truth should perchance alight –
It would surely give us fright!"*

*Jack Ruby in jail talked to journalist Dorothy Kilgallen
With information that would send the CIA scowling!
She said Ruby and Tippit at the Carousal Club fiddled –
And in five days she'd solve the JFK riddle!*

*One of Dorothy's best friends was Florence Pritchett
Who had a romance with Kennedy – almost hitched him!
Dorothy gave her notes to Florence in case of things dire
But by the next week, both women had expired!*

*We must not forget Sherman Skolnick, the Sleuth –
A paraplegic man from Chicago on a search for the truth –
He talked of gangsters and foreign agents in high places
Who wheeled and dealed without any traces!*

*John Kennedy fired Allen Dulles from the CIA
Yet he was appointed to the Warren Commission by LBJ!
Was the Warren Commission guilty of corruption?
Or did they just make a faulty lone gunman deduction?*

*Now the Warren Commission was in a box
To explain the assassination with just three shots –
They pondered and pondered, then announced with glee –
We'll have one bullet do the work of three!*

*The bullet first enters President Kennedy's back
Then exits outward through his neck –
Then it pauses, and on a zigzag track
Enters Governor Connally in the back!*

*The bullet then exits Connally's chest,
And shatters bones in his right wrist!
Yet Connally holds on to his Stetson hat
As the bullet continues on its wayward path!*

THE SIMULATION

The bullet finally stops in Connally's left thigh
With several small pieces that the X-Ray spies –
But the pristine bullet seems an unlikely fit
With several large pieces in Connally's right wrist!

The bullet must remain intact
As it travels on its zigzag path –
And in order to satisfy the Warren Commission
It must retain 99% of its original condition!

According to the physical arts
A bullet can't be more than the sum of its parts!
But with several large fragments from Connally's wrist
You need one and a half bullets to do the trick!

Now, Einstein's theory of relativity
Must be viewed with certain specificity –
Unless the bullet nears the speed of light
It can't gain mass during normal flight!

The laws of physics are fairly firm
Until the politicians take their turn –
A bullet can't violate the laws of physics
Unless it's part of doing business!

Senator Hale Boggs sat on the Warren Commission –
But he later had doubts and claimed sins of omission!
He had startling revelations about the JFK assassination –
But his plane crashed in Alaska with no obvious explanation!

Now Hale Boggs called for Hoover's resignation –
And threatened more Watergate revelations!
He called for an inquiry into JFK's death –
Which helped to hasten his final breath!

What happened to Congressmen Hale Boggs?
His plane went down in the Alaskan fog!
But warm bodies on the infrared photos –
Went the way of the Mauritius dodos!

*Then the FBI made an appearance
At the Tulane University library entrance!
They confiscated Hale Boggs' Oswald files –
But said there was nothing there worthwhile!*

*"It's an ongoing investigation!" –
That's the official explanation –
For why the facts can't be revealed –
And why the records must be sealed!*

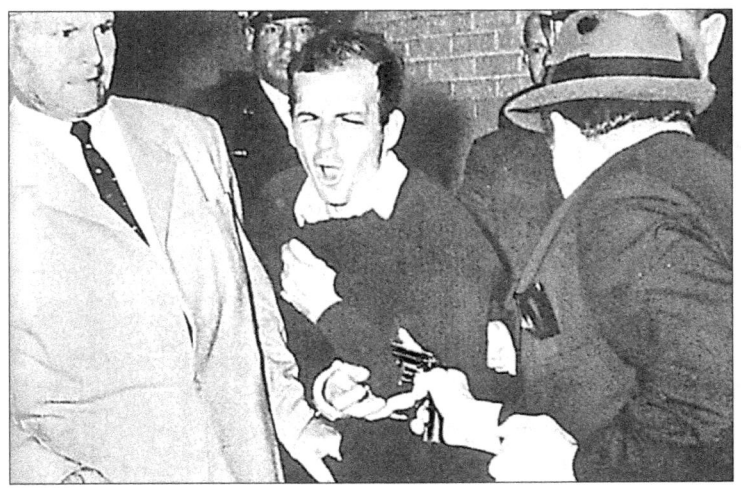

Jack Ruby shoots Lee Harvey Oswald   (AP Photo)

*Governments create their own reality –
Truth is what they want you to see!
Conspiracies are a myth, you know –
When framed lone gunmen take the blow!*

*The JFK Records Act
Sought to release the facts!
But "Denied in Full"
Became the CIA bull!*

*Are there places you can't go –
Like entering a black hole?
Is our civilization in retreat
From forces we can't beat?*

THE SIMULATION

Is history a contact sport –
Is physical violence our resort?
Does the roughest, toughest team of all
Get to make the final call?

What do you do when it's time to die?
Fold your hands and prepare to fly!
Let your shackled soul flee from its' berth –
And await its' chance for a new rebirth!

Is God a spectator?
Some sort of moderator –
Who observes the various factions –
But rarely takes any action?

Does God move through Nature's laws –
Does natural selection give Him pause?
Or can God break all the rules –
And throw the scientist out of school?

Are we predestined to be good or evil –
Or does free choice create upheavals?
Does God allow us to choose our path –
And help us to avoid His wrath?

Are you waiting for Jesus' return –
Who will live and who will burn?
Will there be a final judgment –
Or simply more and more begrudgement?

Does God get mad
And punish the bad?
Or is our malady
Just part of reality?

Will there be an Epiphany –
To solve this mystery?
Or must inspired revelation
Be labeled speculation?

JIM GARRISON

District Attorney Jim Garrison

*Now Jim Garrison did enter the scene
As the District Attorney of New Orleans –
With a law degree from Tulane University
He tried to solve the JFK adversity!*

*Clay Shaw was head of the International Trade Mart
And with Oswald and Ferrie he played his part!
Clay traveled with Oswald to Clinton and Jackson –
At Ferrie's abode, they mapped out their action!*

*Clay Shaw tried to mine Cuban nickel –
But Castro's regime put his plans in a pickle!
They planned to refine the ore in Braithwaite
But the Freeport Sulfur Project would have to wait!*

*Garrison linked Clay Shaw to the CIA
But the proof would wait for another day –
Richard Helms would later testify
That Clay Shaw, under oath, had lied!*

JIM GARRISON

Clay Shaw claimed he was persecuted –
But the only man to be prosecuted
For the murder of the President –
Was part of the CIA's QKENCHANT!

Clay Shaw deserves much more attention –
A war hero who practiced intervention!
Permindex had the money and means
To carry out illegal schemes!

Clay Shaw

Then Garrison turned to David Ferrie
Who he said was a CIA mercenary!
But Ferrie would never the subpoena heed –
He died the next day of a cerebral bleed!

When David Ferrie was subpoenaed by Jim Garrison
He knew that soon his life would end!
"I'm a walking dead man!" he confided –
"Before long, I'll be suicided!"

"I attended St. Charles Catholic Seminary –
My three years in Carthagena leave a memory!
I had to drop out due to nervous stress –
But I excelled in my studies, nevertheless!"

"I enjoyed talking to students –
About the various religious movements –
I may be a little eccentric –
But my views are still theocentric!"

"You know, I was never a family man
But I could do things few others can!
Like fly to Cuba at the drop of a hat –
And drop guns and ammunition to the rebel clans!"

"Lee Oswald and I would often debate
On various nefarious affairs of state –
He was a lot smarter than most people know –
Before he was cast in the Lone Gunman role!"

David Ferrie at St. Charles Seminary in Carthagena, Ohio

*"Does original sin
Explain the shape I'm in?
What law did I violate
To deserve such a fate?"*

*"It's not fair to blame me
For the murder of John Kennedy –
I know that I was in a group
Who thought that he should get the boot!"*

*"One way to alter the course of a nation
Is through a domestic assassination!
Ninety nine will accept the change
If the Lone Gunman gets the blame!"*

*"Is there a fine line between sanity and insanity?
Does it all depend on one leader's vanity?
One minute you're smiling and nice –
The next you're ordered to take someone's life!"*

"But the decision was made by the Chiefs of Staff –
I'm not the one who should take the wrap!
The Generals at the top decide –
While little fish like me are fried!"

"Now, what do you do in your final days
When you know life's in its terminal phase?
So many things I never tried –
I still say I'm too young to die!"

"A warrior whose time is done
Is like a spring that has been sprung!
Though they greet with quiet adulation –
Their thoughts turn to the next generation!"

"Our country has a certain pride
That suffered when John Kennedy died –
It violates our Constitution
And cries out for retribution!"

I gaze out of my window at the frenetic pace below –
Everyone's in a hurry with no particular place to go!
I wish I had more time to live out my days –
I'd really like a chance to rectify my ways!"

"I don't want to die!
I'd like to spread my wings and fly!
Too short is our mortal visitation –
I'd like to see all of God's creation!"

"Chasing a career
Is something we hold dear!
We work like devils 'til we die –
And never know the reason why!"

"Religion and politics intermix –
The gods of heaven and earth do both assist!
We pray to God for world peace –
But will the killing ever cease?"

*"Will I find some eternal hell
Where all the evil spirits dwell?
Do eternal fires of damnation
Await those who practice assassination?"*

*"Will I feel the sting of conscience old
That will never my soul repose!
Or will I live in limbo, my soul aghast
Knowing only the future and the past?"*

*"In what circle of hell will I reside –
Will I see where Satan's tied?
Will I drown in a river of boiling blood
Or get bit by snakes in a giant flood?"*

*"Or will I find some celestial sphere
Like Mars, where all the warriors cheer!
Did I do good or did I do evil
In trying to stop a communist upheaval?"*

*"Is there some undiscovered orifice
That leads to a world serene and glorious?
Or will we forever dwell
In our own self-constructed hell?"*

*"Will there be a battle of Armageddon –
And will the good be safe in heaven?
Will all bodies rise from the graves –
Both the heroes and the knaves!"*

*"Will the Har Megiddo
Be the site of further evil?
Will Christ destroy the Seven-Headed Serpent
And answer prayers so long and fervent?"*

*"Will the world end
When the Red Horseman rides again?
Or will pestilence spell our demise –
With diseases and locusts and flies?"*

*"Did the Four Horsemen ride
On the day John Kennedy died?
Did the anti-Christ ride the white steed
Because the world failed to take heed?"*

*"Will there be a false religion
Riding a White Horse contingent?
Will mankind fall from grace
And lose the Holy Place?"*

*"Will there be a Divine Rapture
In the words of Cotton Mather?
Will the Millerites return –
And watch the world burn?"*

*"Are wars and great destruction
A giant Satanic construction?
Or does the suffering we bear
Arise from lack of prayer?"*

*"Will I see Shiva, God of death
As I take my final breath?
Was that rainbow in the early morn
A sign of Shiva's wrath and scorn!"*

*"Does the water turn into wine –
When Jesus takes the time?
Or is transubstantiation
Just a figment our imagination?"*

*"They'll label me a suicidal mess –
Who couldn't deal with pain or stress!
My clandestine life of daring do –
Must the public never view!"*

*"Who can you believe
When Elders do deceive?
Is scientific truth
The only Absolute?"*

*"In the deepest part of the soul
The truth will make you whole!
But if lies are all that you hear –
The truth will never be near!"*

*"I'm troubled by demons –
They never stop screamin'!
Tortured in the night
Between what's wrong and right!"*

*"I live in a distorted world
With colors and sounds and swirls –
It's a totally different reality
When you live in a duality!"*

*"We create artificial constructs
To regulate human conduct –
Religion and politics are the guide
For humans to fight and die!"*

*"Am I trapped within myself –
Trying to get out?
Looking for a way
To let my spirit play?"*

*"The unjustified dead
Raise up their heads
And come back to scream
In the conspirator's dreams!"*

*"Do we fear death –
Putting off that final breath?
By living as long as we can –
Do we delay God's final plan?"*

*"Why do I dream of danger
From a surreptitious stranger?
Do the gods warn me at night
Of an unexpected fright?"*

*"We struggle to survive
And keep ourselves alive!
Fighting each day
The forces of decay!"*

*"When your dreams go away
And turn into clay –
Do the best you can
And play the bad hand!"*

*"We all seek pleasure –
Like some hidden treasure!
Trying to make whole
The gaps within our soul!"*

*"Do the military and religion
Create an artificial condition
That prepares people to fight
For what they think is right?"*

*"We fill the empty spaces
That tragedy embraces –
Looking for a way
To keep the pain at bay!"*

*"We live imperfect lives –
Not the ones we fantasize!
Hoping that one happy day
All our dreams will come to play!"*

*"I hear a noise outside –
Should I run and hide?
Beware the lifelong friend
Who comes your life to end!"*

*"But I guess it's time to accept my fate –
We throw the dice and then we wait!
Life is nothing but a series of chances –
I can't afford the backward glances!"*

*"I'll say goodbye to all my friends
And act like I'll see them soon again –
It's too painful to make a final goodbye –
I'll walk away and silently cry!"*

*"What if you knew the day of your death –
The moment you'd take your final breath?
Would you be kinder to the people you see –
And help them with their infirmity?"*

*"There is an impermanence to all we see –
Like ships upon a swirling sea!
The frigates appear quite solid and strong –
But blink your eyes and they're all gone!"*

*"We are damaged in ways we cannot see
Living in a false reality!
Trying to mingle with the crowd –
Afraid that they might laugh out loud!"*

*"I help people find their way –
Through clouds of smoke and clouds of gray!
When ill winds blow with force –
I keep them on life's course!"*

*"Is there a life beyond the grave –
A place that rewards the humble and brave?
Where life begins fresh and new –
Without the hatred that we once knew!"*

*"Will I cross the Chinvat bridge –
That trail of judgment across the ridge?
Or will my soul to darkness fall –
And await the Good Lord's final call?"*

*"It all disappears in a cloud of light –
That pretty world that shines so bright!
We live in a world of tranquility –
Until the beginning of hostilities!"*

*"Ambition is a healthy trait –
It forces you to concentrate!
But focusing on your own concerns –
Can blind you to another's burns!"*

*What fine line separates us
From a world of turmoil and mistrust!
Beneath the thin veneer of sanity
Lies a world of greed and vanity!*

*"How do I contemplate my approaching demise?
The end of a life with mobsters and spies!
You risk your life in offshore revolutions –
Then they arrange for your execution!"*

*"As I await my death I ponder –
What's in the wild blue yonder?
Will mankind continue to thrive –
Or will he be burned alive?"*

*"Many problems we ignore –
Until they arrive on our front door!
Does the material life we lead
Blind us to the real needs?"*

*"Does the ascetic know the path
To save mankind from his wrath?
Perhaps if we all could share –
We all might learn how to care!"*

*"Or perhaps the way of the glutton
Will save us from our destruction!
Pursue the pleasures of life –
And not what leads to strife!"*

Medieval Hellmouth

*"Will God in all his wisdom
Save us from perdition?
And will mankind do his part
To practice the holy art?"*

THE QUATRAINS OF CAMELOT

"Is there a Hellmouth
That devours the less devout?
And opens the gates of hell
To the stubborn infidel!"

"Will science lead the way –
And teach us not to stray?
Or will science create the button
That leads to our destruction!"

"Will politicians unite us all
In one giant cattle call?
Or will each different solution
Only add to our pollution?"

"Did the devil fall out of heaven
Like a beast with heads of seven?
Is evil a primal force
That alters Nature's course?

"When the common folk believe
That the rich do them deceive –
There comes a devolution –
With another revolution!"

"My thoughts do wander far –
But I leave the door ajar –
To anyone who writes the song –
For all the people to get along!"

"Were I born a handsome lad
I might not think the world so bad!
But worldly charms do realign –
Thanks to good old Mother Time!"

"We are silly, eccentric creatures –
Not understanding our earthly features!
Frolicking in the sun
Until our day is done!"

*"I feel sorry for human beings –
They keep trying to chase their dreams!
But each time there's a higher step –
That makes you wonder what comes next!"*

*"Can't we be content –
With what the Lord has meant?
Or must we continually climb
The twisted financial vine?"*

*So jump on the merry-go-round
And take a spin around –
Make a few friends
Before your life ends!*

*"Like animals in a zoo –
We keep wondering what to do!
Living a daily life
Of heartache and physical strife!"*

*"We see a world beyond the bars –
Watching all the movie stars!
They dance and frolic on the stage –
But rarely show their hidden rage!"*

*"Nature wizens us like old, dried fruit –
With wrinkles and calluses to boot!
We steadily shrink in size and stature –
As we get turned out to pasture!"*

*"Guilt is such a terrible strain –
It fills my life with grief and pain!
Nightmares haunt me as I sleep
I give the Lord my soul to keep!"*

*Does God take revenge
If we don't make amends –
Do we go in the wrong direction
If we fail to make confession?*

"Is the Ganges River a solution –
Will my sins receive ablution?
Thousands of Pilgrims immerse each day –
Praying their sins will wash away!"

"Will the different Gods fight –
To determine who is right?
Or will the desire for domination
Lead to total subjugation?"

"Is there a primordial anger
That would keep us ever strangers?
Something in our behavior
That would make us kill our Savior!"

"Did Moses write the Pentateuch –
Or were there others in a group?
How much history do we know –
When we don't have the written scrolls?"

"My friends come to say good-by –
They know it's for the final time!
I've lived a life of dark adventure –
I guess it's time to have me censured!"

"One night as I meditate
I pretend to levitate –
I float above the frozen ground –
I can see for miles around!"

"The ice storm petrifies the leaves –
The little birds hide from the breeze!
The nights are cold as winter drones
And people huddle in their homes!"

"And as I leave the city's light
The stars above shine oh so bright!
I look above the virgin earth
And think about our planet's birth!"

*"I see no boundaries down below –
All the earth is one big globe!
If man could somehow stop his fight –
Perhaps the world would then unite!"*

*"Then I see small puffs of smoke
Where battles rage that men provoke –
Each one tries to claim the land
And take it from the other's hand!"*

*"As I come down from the air
I see small steeples everywhere!
People there inside do pray
And hope that peace will come some day!"*

*"I wake up – the room is cold
I put a log upon the stove –
If I could a spark ignite
The flame of peace would burn so bright!"*

The coroner ruled Ferrie's death accidental –
Garrison's subpoena was merely coincidental!
But James Files tells of a different fate –
A nail file through the soft palate to the cribriform plate!

The official report was a ruptured berry aneurysm –
From a blood vessel that sits above the optic chiasm!
Little did the doctors suspect –
An assassin could hide the event!

Now hitmen aren't supposed to know anatomy –
At least, that's the coroner's working strategy!
But a bruise on Ferrie's lower inner lip
Was the only clue to a Mafia hit!

Eladio del Valle was a wealthy Cuban exile
Who Garrison next decided to profile –
Though arms to Cuba Eladio did carry
He was murdered the same night as David Ferrie!

THE QUATRAINS OF CAMELOT

Now James Garrison issued subpoenas out of state
For witnesses that to the assassination relate –
But for the first time in our country's history
The District Attorneys refused the inquiries!

Thus James Garrison's investigation
Met with defeat and news media defamation!
But his memory was preserved in a grateful way
When Oliver Stone released, "JFK"!

Barry Seal was worried about Jim Garrison
And requested that he to Canada be garrisoned!
A member of the CIA's Operation 40 –
Barry and the boys would be drugs transporting!

Now Barry Seal was an interesting guy
From the Bay of Pigs to Dealey Plaza to Mena he'd fly!
Scheduled in '86 to testify about all that he knew –
He died in a hail of bullets in Baton Rouge!

One thing Barry Seal would say
That relates to how the agencies play –
"In this type of intelligence spar
People never are who they say they are!"

When Harry Connick Sr. became District Attorney
He tried to burn the transcripts of Garrison's Grand Jury!
But a young policeman provoked Connick's ire –
When he spared the transcripts from the proverbial fire!

Now Penn Jones was becoming suspicious
About all these deaths so inauspicious!
Writing in the Midlothian Mirror –
He saw too many witnesses disappear!

Penn talked about the actress, Karyn Kupcinet
Who, he claimed, tried to warn the President!
Karyn's father, Irv, knew Presidents and mobsters –
Was Karyn's murder meant to silence her Father?

JIM GARRISON

Professor Jim Marrs

*My favorite researcher is Professor Jim Marrs –
He's an accomplished, erudite history star!
When he follows the evidence, no stone is unturned
In hopes that his students true history will learn!*

*Professor Marrs researched James Files
And found his story quite worthwhile –
Files worked with CIA Cubans at No Name Key –
And was the Grassy Knoll shooter of John Kennedy!*

*The Frank Church Committee of '75
Called mobster Johnny Roselli to testify –
Johnny then proceeded to tell
Of mobster plans to kill Fidel!*

*Cuban exiles were recruited and trained
With Bannister and his team at Lake Pontchartrain!
David Ferrie would fly into Cuba at night
And drop off supplies for the brave exiles' fight!*

*Now Sheffield Edwards was the CIA's man
Who contacted Bob Maheu for the assassination plan –
Bob Maheu would later come into public view
As the personal assistant to Howard Hughes!*

THE QUATRAINS OF CAMELOT

But before Bob Maheu there was another one
Who acted as the CIA-mobster liaison –
With Cuban casinos owned by Lansky and Giancana
Their Havana connection was James Riddle Hoffa!

The Pentagon called it Operation Mongoose –
A plan to turn the Cuban exiles loose!
In hopes that they could eliminate Castro –
And spare the Cubans from a communist fiasco!

Maheu contacted Johnny Roselli –
Who acted as contact for all the consiglieri –
"We'd like you to help us eliminate Fidel
But you have to promise that you'll never tell!"

Now how much did Maheu know about Lee?
In a radio interview, he called him 'Ozzie'!
Did Maheu personally know each player?
And was Oswald really JFK's slayer?

Now Generals Lemnitzer and Edwin Lansdale
Wanted a Cuban invasion that was full scale –
Even if it required a tiny trick
To convince the trusting electorate!

General Lyman Lemnitzer had a plan
To pressure Cuba into an aggressive stand –
"Operation Northwoods" involved "pretext" operations
Designed to provoke a Cuban invasion!

"Will the jarring gong of self-preservation
Finally awaken a resting nation?
The words of Churchill still echo today –
We must act before they blow us away!"

"How much freedom can society tolerate?
Is there a limit to the protest you generate?
With multiple groups pulling multiple ways –
Will our society disappear back into the haze?"

*"Dare we raise the specter of our own extinction
Will we be able to make the distinction –
Between foreign foes who mean us harm
And domestic foes who would disarm?"*

*"Will nuclear missiles on Cuban shores
Provide a threat we can easily ignore?
The Russians don't seem to care
If nuclear missiles are everywhere!"*

*The Joint Chiefs considered then
To blow up the rocket carrying John Glenn!
They would manufacture electronic evidence
That would imply Cuban interference!*

*They even considered one day
To blow up a ship in Guantanamo Bay!
Like the explosion aboard the battleship Maine –
To the Cubans you could affix the blame!*

*These plans from the Joint Chiefs of Staff
Did nothing but incur Kennedy's wrath!
Senator Gore called for Lemnitzer's head –
But the Joint Chiefs continued full speed ahead!*

*One plan was to invade the Jamaican nation
And blame it on a Cuban invasion!
Cuban exiles would hit the beach
Dressed as Castro's military elite!*

*Another plan was to bribe Cuban commandos
To attack the Naval base at Guantanamo!
U.S. forces would repel the incursion –
And justify a U.S. military excursion!*

*When the Joint Chiefs take action
There's no need for a retraction –
If you need a change, then don't procrastinate –
Get out the guns – it's time to assassinate!*

THE QUATRAINS OF CAMELOT

Now is assassination always bad?
Could we have avoided Hitler's wrath?
What if an assassin with rifle in hand
Had put an early end to the Nazi plans?

In which circle of hell
Will an assassin finally dwell?
If his motive is perceived as good
Will he ever be understood?

What happens to the entity
In the event of a tragedy?
Does the soul fly from within –
Do we pay penance for our sins?

Where's the line between good and evil
When you trigger an upheaval?
History will applaud the victor –
Right or wrong's not in the picture!

Timely international intervention
May be an unpopular contention –
But often greater storms
Are from domestic forces born!

Only a handful at the top
Control the entire lot!
Like a shepherd to the sheep
The government will us keep!

Thus momentous decisions
May stem from a foolish derision –
As each side tries to bluff
And to the world be tough!

It seemed that the Generals were out of control
In their desire to eliminate Fidel Castro!
They presented their plans to McNamara –
And were told that Kennedy did not share them!

Another CIA player was Frank Sturgis
Who personally knew Castro's ultimate purpose!
He saw two young men leave a Russian submarine
Off Oriente Province – they were both KGB!

The KGB deserves some blame –
They forged a note in Oswald's name!
They tried to embarrass Mr. Hunt of the CIA
But there was also a Hunt of oil patch fame!

And so one of the great mysteries
Was which Mr. Hunt did the Oswald note mean?
Then one day the mystery finally broke –
When the Russians admitted they forged the note!

Thus Oswald was used by two different nations
As they battled each other for world domination!
Each side created dirty little lies
As the nuclear weapons multiplied!

It's clear that the Russians had Cuban designs
And with Fidel Castro would soon treaties sign!
The Russians declared, "We're just here to assist!"
And Fidel could not the Russians resist!

Finally, there was the creation of Operation Zipper –
With the assistance of General Lyman Lemnitzer –
If John Kennedy would not the CIA heed
Crowley and Angleton would make him bleed!

The people thought Kennedy was the greatest –
But the Generals claimed he was full of flatus!
No matter what your point of view –
Controversy was in the brew!

Operation Zipper called for a plan of action
That involved the union of several factions –
The CIA and the Mafia along with LBJ –
With J. Edgar Hoover looking the other way!

THE QUATRAINS OF CAMELOT

*Such a plan was born out of frustration
That Kennedy was not properly leading the nation!
The Joint Chiefs thought they were patriotic –
And that Kennedy's policies were idiotic!*

*There was a fatal fracture of trust
Between Kennedy and the intelligence buffs!
They felt Kennedy's policies were misconstrued
And that it was high time for a government coup!*

*General Curtis LeMay
Had to be kept at bay!
His simple construction
Was total destruction!'*

*The Russians were a menace –
They had to do their penance!
But a pre-emptive nuclear strike
Was not the way to fight!*

*Who gets to play God –
And give the orders for a job?
In order for the King to kill
The underlings must have the will!*

*The Greek stand at Thermopylae was brave –
As the ancient warriors went to their grave!
"We'll fight in the shade!" Leonidas declared –
As Xerxes' arrows filled the air!*

*Would we could fight with arrows and spears –
And limit the damage from weapons we fear!
"We'll burn Athens for Sardis!" Xerxes decreed –
Will we trade cities today for some nuclear creed?*

*The battle continues between hawks and doves –
Do you conquer with force or win them with love!
But as the nuclear stockpiles grow –
Must we still go toe to toe?*

Must man forever be plagued
By revenge and greed and alliances made?
Do leaders use the historical past
To justify yet another attack?

The whole idea of a government coup
Is that someone thinks he can better do!
For the man who speaks the people's voice
May not reflect the wisest choice!

Did forces beyond control
Compel Kennedy down this road?
Or could he have broken this curse –
And dodged the early hearse?

If it had kept raining that day –
The shooters would have gone away!
The bubble top would be up –
And the shooters out of luck!

But Nature chose to stay the rain –
And bring the Sun back out again!
I wonder how many calamities
Rely on Nature's vagaries!

In times of peace, there is no stress
And it matters not who is the best!
But when war clouds loom upon the shore
The Generals might the King deplore!

The Motorcade
on Houston Street
(Altgens – AP)

THE QUATRAINS OF CAMELOT

FAMOUS "LONE GUNMEN" IN U.S. HISTORY

ACCUSED GUNMAN	INTENDED VICTIM	YEAR/ ELECTION?	ADVANCE KNOWLEDGE?	FIRED SHOTS?	FIRED FATAL SHOTS?	COMMENTS/ INVOLVEMENT
John Wilkes Booth	Abraham Lincoln	1865 Yes	Yes	Yes	Yes	"Lax" Security Guard; Possessed rare Spy decoder; Held meetings in Canada Vice Pres., Sec. Of State also targeted
1935–SENATOR HUEY LONG ANNOUNCES HE WILL RUN FOR PRESIDENT AGAINST FDR						
Dr. Carl Weiss	Senator Huey Long	1935 Yes	Yes	Maybe	No	Used as Patsy and Decoy; Shot by own Security Guards; Mafia, U.S. Gov.?
Joseph Zangara	Mayor Anton Cermak/FDR?	1933	Yes	Yes	No	Used as Patsy and Decoy; Chicago's Mayor Anton Cermak was Mafia target
1961–USING SPECIAL RIFLES, CIA-MAFIA HIT TEAM TRIES TO TAKE OUT FIDEL CASTRO						
"Suicide"	Marilyn Monroe	1962	(Stomach empty; fatal suppository fools LA coroner)			Mafia hit designed to end RFK's career
1962–JFK DECLARES WAR ON ORGANIZED CRIME/SAYS HE'LL BREAK THE CIA INTO 1,000 PIECES						
Lee Harvey Oswald	President John Kennedy	1963 Yes	Yes	No	No	Oswald was a CIA agent used as Patsy; Was to have been killed Nov. 22; CIA, Mafia, FBI, Secret Service, LBJ
Jack Ruby	Lee Harvey Oswald	1963 Yes	Yes	Yes	Yes	Ruby assigned to kill LHO after mixup; Ruby knew LHO; CIA, Mafia plan
1968–MARTIN LUTHER KING ANNOUNCES HIS OPPOSITION TO THE VIET NAM WAR						
James Earl Ray	Martin Luther King	1968 Yes	No	No	No	A true Patsy; 111th M.I.G. involved; FBI, CIA, Mafia (Marcello)
1968–RFK PROMISES AS PRESIDENT TO RESUME WAR ON CRIME AND REOPEN JFK ASSASSINATION						
Sirhan Sirhan	Senator Robert Kennedy	1968 Yes	Yes	Yes	No	Used as Patsy and Decoy; L.A. Police Lose Evidence, apologize; RFK killed by corrupt Mafia Security Guard
1985 IRAN-CONTRA—THE CIA AND MAFIA TRADE GUNS FOR DRUGS TO HELP FIGHT COMMUNISTS						

THE RIFLE

Lee Oswald with Rifle – real or fake?

*There's a back yard picture of Oswald holding a rifle –
Researcher Jack White says it's been altered a trifle!
The shadow under the nose doesn't match the body –
The photographic masking was really quite shoddy!*

*The Dallas Police showed Oswald the picture –
He said it was obviously two photos configured!
The Warren Commission hired a photographic ace
But they published a picture without any face!*

*Oswald said he never saw the rifle before –
It was ordered from a mail order store –
But it was ordered under a different name
Than Oswald's mail box did entertain!*

*So we're left with an old rifle from ancient times
With a scope that doesn't fit and is misaligned –
With old ammunition that often misfires
And when Oswald denies it, they call him a liar!*

THE QUATRAINS OF CAMELOT

*One interesting thing about the scope
Is that it's poorly aligned and offers no hope –
Oswald, you see, shot from the right
But the scope was set up with a left-handed sight!*

*When the best shooters try to simulate the shot
They find they hit the target not!
One shot is especially hard to believe –
It must be fired through the leaves!*

*Other rifles are removed from the Depository –
Researcher Jack White keeps the inventory!
But they soon disappear and the records are stifled –
Because a Lone Gunman needs only a single rifle!*

*The experts conclude that the lead content
Is consistent with the bullets that Oswald spent –
But further investigation of the isotopes
Said such conclusions were beyond the scope!*

*Johnny Roselli went on and discerned
How the Cuban-CIA-Mafia team would turn –
The assassination team became disenchanted,
Against Kennedy they raved and ranted!*

*The assassination team traveled to the Cuban Isle
With guns and grenades they entered with guile!
But with KGB teams and counterspies galore –
They were captured before they could settle the score!*

*Roselli then claimed that Fidel Castro held sway
And ordered the team to make Kennedy pay!
Thus Roselli tried to pass the blame
To Fidel Castro and his communist gang!*

*The question arises, were the Cubans used
To promote an anti-Castro ruse –
To blame the assassination on the Cuban exiles
And stop a search through the domestic files!*

THE RIFLE

Los tres amigos leales de los Cubanos y de la causa de "Bahia de Cochinos", Bisell, Burke y Bundy, quienes defendieron como cosa propia el éxito de aquel plan, que al fracasar resultó el afianzamiento del castrocomunismo y el peor bochorno para los Estados Unidos, su Gobierno y su pueblo.

Three Loyal Friends of the Cubans: Bissell, Bundy, and Burke

Now Johnny Roselli would be dismembered
For talking to Church Committee members!
Fourteen months later, Roselli would pay –
Found floating in an oil drum off Dumfounding Bay!

Allen Dulles and Richard Bissell
Were CIA agents in quite a thistle!
Kennedy blamed them for the Bay of Pigs fiasco –
But with President Kennedy they were in a hassle!

Now Richard Bissell was a talented man
Who helped conceive U-2 and SR-71 spy plane plans –
He helped with Arbenz and the Guatemala coup
He took action whenever he thought it was due!

Did Bissell feel betrayed at the Bay of Pigs
When Kennedy refused to land the ships?
Did Bissell sign on to the assassination plans –
Over Kennedy's weak anti-communist stance?

Kennedy had the cahones to date all the girls –
But he refused to attack the communist churls!
He would pay the price for his lack of stiffness
Against the international communist resistance!

THE QUATRAINS OF CAMELOT

Was this a test of Kennedy's manhood?
To invade Cuba and prove his fortitude?
Sometimes you take the bigger stance –
If you fold your cards and skip the dance!

Now spies are an interesting breed –
When things go well, they're rarely seen!
But if things go badly, they must take the blame –
That's how you play this political game!

Ever since World War II.
The spy agencies took a different view –
"We must stop future Hitlers before they arise!
Aggressive intervention will spell their demise!"

And so every now and then
A world leader would meet his end!
"'Twas an accident!" the papers would say –
But others suspected the CIA!

Thus it remains an enigma
That spy agencies get the stigma!
You intervene and get labeled a meanie –
But you don't intervene and get labeled a weenie!

It was really a noble construction
That mankind could avoid destruction –
By manipulating governments here and there
As long as no one seemed to care!

Now the purpose was to stop communism –
But others did suspect a schism!
Corporate interests came to play a role
And foreign leaders were on the dole!

One of the problems is all these lawyers –
They force people to be paper destroyers!
As a spy, what you put down in writing
Ends up fair game in court to be fighting!

THE RIFLE

Senator Frank Church

The Church Committee sought to find the guilt –
They called Hoffa, Giancana, and de Mohrenschildt!
But each one proceeded to die
Just before they could testify!

"'Tis a strange thing," the Senators said
"Each one we subpoena turns up dead!"
Were these all men of consequence?
Or were their deaths just coincidence?"

Senator Frank Church was quite eloquent –
He called the CIA a rogue elephant!
With Golden Triangle drug smuggling, the CIA rules –
He uncovered covert actions, dubbed the "family jewels!"

Now family jewels should be kept discreet –
They're not for human eyes to meet!
There are certain things that should not be shown –
That would force the government to disown!

Are all these names beginning to sound familiar?
From the CIA to the Mob to the government – go figure!
These men of action are small in number
But the deeds they perform will echo like thunder!

THE QUATRAINS OF CAMELOT 251

Joseph Kennedy said fifty people run the nation –
And even that was an exaggeration!
Are democracies just a proletariat sop?
While men of influence call the shots!

This is the biggest whitewash in history
From a government that denies reality!
By offering lame explanations
To avoid serious investigation!

The House Select Committee in '78
Gathered a group to pontificate!
They concluded a small hole in Kennedy's head
Was what the Bethesda doctors had said!

Now is a House Intelligence Committee an oxymoron?
It's a group of Congressmen who aren't really morons –
But when they say a large hole is small
Do they have any intelligence at all?

Then came Dr. Gary Aguilar –
He's a bonified superstar!
Under the Freedom of Information Act,
He got the government to release more facts!

The official reports then revealed
What the House Select Committee had concealed –
A large hole was seen in the back of the head
"More like an exit wound," the doctors had said!

But Robert Blakey and the Committee of '78
Did one thing that was really great –
Acoustic experts the Committee hired
Determined how many shots had been fired!

Police Officer J.B. Mclain left the switch turned on –
His motorcycle microphone did respond –
It recorded the sounds on a police dictabelt tape
That audio experts could discriminate!

THE MYTH OF THE LONE GUNMAN

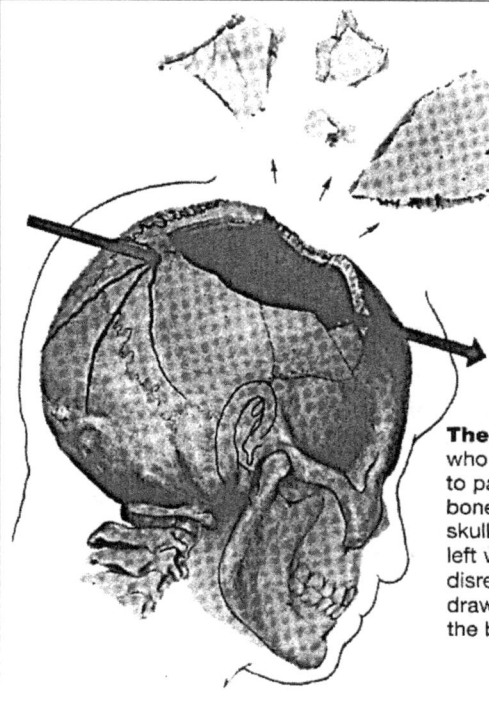

The Myth: Rydberg diagram, drawn by artist who was not present at the autopsy. According to pathologist John Boswell, large pieces of bone were blown off the back of Kennedy's skull and were replaced before the diagram at left was drawn. The Warren Commission disregarded Parkland witnesses, and used this drawing, which argued for a small entry hole in the back of Kennedy's Head.

The Reality: Twenty-six Parkland Hospital witnesses, including the chief of neurosurgery, Dr. Kemp Clark, and 24 Bethesda Hospital witnesses observe a large hole in the back of Kennedy's head. Trauma surgeon, Dr. Charles Crenshaw observed a small entry hole in Kennedy's right sideburn, and a "baseball-sized hole" in the back of Kennedy's skull. If you believe in the "lone gunman theory," this large hole must be an entry wound.

If you believe in common sense, this large hole is an exit wound from a second gunman to Kennedy's front and right. Congratulations! You have now become a "conspiracy theorist!"

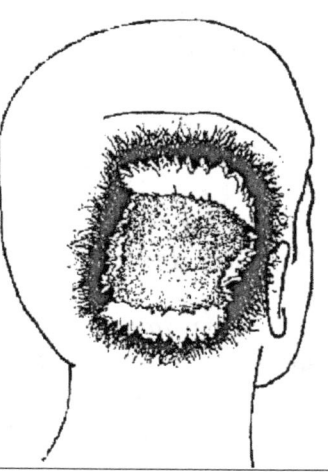

The House committee concluded at least four shots
Had been fired during the assassination plot!
At least three shots fired from behind –
And one shot fired from the Grassy Knoll blind!

THE QUATRAINS OF CAMELOT

Now the Politburo was quite surprised –
Was the KGB involved in Kennedy's demise?
But Shevchenko relieved their immediate concerns
It was the Texas oilmen and Mafia they quickly learned!

But if the KGB knew all of this
Couldn't they interfere before the hit?
"Many people knew the plans that day –
Not just the Mafia and the CIA!"

Dick Russell talks of Richard Case Nagel
Who the Soviets paid to follow Oswald's trail!
Nagel begged the CIA and FBI to explore –
But yet another warning went ignored!

Then the Russians asked Richard Case Nagel
To kill Oswald before his Dallas travail!
As a shooter Oswald was lame –
But as a patsy he was fair game!

Even the Israeli Mossad
Had contacts with the CIA squad –
But while they had no part to play
Did they agree to look the other way?

Now if the plans were widely known
Why not interfere before they were sown?
Kennedy had no friends that day –
And with his life he would have to pay!

Yuri Nosenko defected from the KGB
But James Jesus Angleton denied reality!
Nosenko had read Oswald's KGB files
And said there was nothing there worthwhile!

Nosenko said Oswald was never a Russian agent –
He was followed in Minsk by the KGB station!
But Angleton, never known for refinement
Had Nosenko tortured and put in solitary confinement!

Nosenko testified before the Church Committee
But Angleton said that was really a pity!
"Nosenko's a double agent, that's what I fear!
It's all just become a wilderness of mirrors!"

And how many Oswald's did really exist?
Tales of Oswald imposters continue to persist!
Was the CIA busy laying false trails –
So the Warren Commission would meet with travail?

But Angleton was hardly a neutral bystander
Would the CIA ever be made to answer?
And why was Edward Lansdale of the CIA
Walking with the three tramps on that fateful day?

Now Robert Kennedy helped plan an invasion
For the first of December against the Cuban nation!
Called C-Day in the archive files
It was a plan to reclaim the Cuban isle!

But after the assassination LBJ took charge
And cancelled the C-Day plans at large –
Did Robert Kennedy block the JFK investigation
To keep secret his involvement in the Cuban invasion?

And through it all, there remains one Mover
Who headed the FBI, by the name of J. Edgar Hoover –
From Huey Long to FDR to JFK and King
The Man had foreknowledge of everything!

Now J. Edgar Hoover was compromised –
Though he kept files on everyone's lives!
The Mafia caught him in a position twisted –
So he claimed the Mafia never existed!

But Hoover had connections at every level –
He'd get hot tips from columnist Walter Winchell!
Edgar went to the race track every week –
And bet on a horse that couldn't be beat!

THE QUATRAINS OF CAMELOT

So could Hoover, with all his machinations
Have been able to stop the Kennedy assassination?
The fix was in, I do believe –
And LBJ would take the lead!

For who else would stand up to the Russians?
And give the Cubans their come-uppance?
Who else would prosecute the war –
And keep the communists from our shores?

The perception was that LBJ had a plan
And that Kennedy wasn't quite the man!
A strong leader would show the way –
Keeping Khrushchev, Castro and the communists at bay!

Will the people have more trust
In a government that covers up?
Or one that has the cojones
To stop with all the baloney!

Left/Above/Right: The myth that Ferrie and Lee had never met was exploded when witnesses who were with them both at the same time came forward in 1992. This amazing photograph presented by John Ciravolo shows Ferrie on the left and Lee on the right. They were at a Civil Air Patrol picnic in 1955 when the picture was taken.

David Ferrie and Lee Oswald at New Orleans Civil Air Patrol in 1955
(Photo courtesy Robert Groden)

CONTEMPLATIONS

*Like the Wizard of Oz in the Emerald City
Do we live in a world of passion and pity?
Where one man rules, and controls all the force –
And occasional lone gunmen change history's course?*

*Or do we live in a Casa Blanca world?
Where all different forces rotate and swirl –
And the destiny of millions who hope to prevail
Is determined by dark forces yet to unveil?*

*Is all that happens part of God's divine plan?
That we must accept, however we can?
Is man able to control his fate?
Or can we only contemplate?*

*We all get shot one way or another –
But we always hope to recover!
You pray that you will jump right back –
But sometimes you just get laid out flat!*

*I'd like to think that by our actions
We can control our disparate factions!
If we could only find the truth
Then treachery we might one day uproot!*

*But perhaps we are all mistaken –
Are democracies our safest haven?
Do the people always know what's right?
Or must unseen forces rule the night?*

*Can a democracy survive
When all different viewpoints collide?
Or will it fragment into pieces
As each side promotes its thesis?*

THE QUATRAINS OF CAMELOT

A unified front helps win a war
That's where dictatorships can score!
But unless the various factions unite –
Democracies won't win a fight!

If a strain of killer bees
Lurks within the distant trees –
Can a killer force be mounted
Or will the victims be surmounted?

Is there a virulent strain of behavior
That would claim to be our Savior –
Which would offer a plan of construction
That could lead to our destruction?

The irony of the whole situation
Is that in order to save a nation –
Popular dissent must be controlled
Or the democracy will have to fold!

But dictatorships can be quite evil –
And lead to even greater upheaval!
For without the natural human ply –
A dictatorship oft' goes awry!

Thus you need the military
To save us from the vagary
Of dictators who run nations
Seeking world domination!

Does religion really provide the solution?
Do we all just need a little ablution?
Will religion help us find the door?
Or provide another cause for war?

Muslims, Buddhists, Christians, and Jews –
Each religion has its different views!
But please do not incur their wrath –
For each one claims the One True Path!

*Is there one religion for all man –
And all the others just a sham?
Just one path where God does dwell –
While all the others lead to hell?*

*Are matters only black or white –
Always wrong or always right?
Or like the many grains of sand
Can truth be gray or brown or tan?*

*Must everything be absolute –
Each tribe with its sacred root?
If differences we underscore –
Surely they will lead to war!*

*It's nice to have one point of view –
That keeps life simple, straight and true!
But I think that real peace is found
If we but search for Common Ground!*

*Are we doomed to mass extinction
If we fail to make distinction
Between religion and politics –
Can there be a happy mix?*

*Is there a primordial anger
That would keep us perfect strangers –
A fury against Almighty God
That surely would our reason prod?*

*With twenty different religions –
Each one claiming its dominion –
Can people ever get along
If politicians preach a religious song?*

*The key to our survival
Will not be a religious revival –
Unless we preach tolerance for all
Regardless of their religious call!*

THE QUATRAINS OF CAMELOT

We need a paradigm shift –
A way to make all people fit!
Instead of competing for domination
Let's strive for mutual integration!

There are different ways to communicate –
Dropping bombs or negotiate!
But as the bombs get ever bigger –
We get closer to that nuclear trigger!

Did God create Holy Land
For religious groups to make a stand?
Should we combat one another –
Or learn to love our fellow brother?

It's always nice to pontificate
About our various affairs of state –
But the real crux of our survival
Is making peace with all our rivals!

The JFK assassination was the perfect storm
Where rival forces did conform –
They joined to form the perfect coup
That, in their minds, was overdue!

Thus life remains a mystery
That's still unsolved by history!
I sit back down in Dealey Plaza
As tourists look to see what happened!

Do we enter a time warp
At the Dealey Plaza court –
When we go back in time
To relive a heinous crime?

The Depository faces a red brick road
That hails to many years ago –
When horse drawn carriages plied the street
To the clickety-clack of horse's feet!

Now there is a railway station –
A real sign of modernization –
The trains now go clickety-clack
As they ply the railroad track!

So young and old together meet
As you walk the Dealey streets –
You can't help but relive the past
As you walk along the Dealey paths!

The railway tower austerely stands
And looks down upon the Dealey land –
What trickery did the tower see
As it looked down at Kennedy?

Would that brick and steel could talk
As we take our Dealey walk!
For surely they could tell a tale
That no human has yet regaled!

The brain remembers by location
So examine the Dealey Plaza Station!
Fix the landmarks in your mind –
That take you to another time!

Remember what happened here –
Though the events won't give you cheer –
There's a lesson here for all to learn –
That violent means must be deterred!

THE QUATRAINS OF CAMELOT

There are three types of people in all –
The sheep, the wolves, and the sheepdog!
The government must protect the sheep –
To keep the wolves from striking deep!

They come from all around the world
With cameras and maps that they unfurl –
"Do you know the assassination story?
And just where is the School Depository?"

"Can you tell me, where's the Grassy Knoll?"
As with their friends they slowly stroll
Down Elm Street toward the North Pergola
"Is there any Coca-Cola?"

They peer from behind the picket fence
And try to figure out from whence
The fatal shot was really fired –
"Can you tell me what transpired?"

"This would be an easy shot
If a shooter fired from this spot!
A gunman at this Grassy Hill
Could easily make a fatal kill!"

Most of the spectators stand in awe
Of a place in history where a President did fall!
They imagine the motorcade as it traveled
Where American history became unraveled!

They mark Elm Street with an "X" –
As if that spot were surely hexed!
They stand upon the Elm Street line
And try to travel back in time!

People stand in the middle of the street –
Oblivious to the traffic they meet!
Trying to capture a moment in space
That time has been unable to erase!

View from behind picket fence at Grassy Knoll

Teacher instructs his class about the JFK assassination

THE QUATRAINS OF CAMELOT

They take pictures along Elm Street and the Knoll
And pose with friends as the tale is told –
Of a King who once traveled down this street
With his Queen at his side did the people greet!

The King and Queen of Camelot
Which ended at this very spot
Must wonder what otherwise might be
Without this day in history!

Is mankind doomed to go to war
In order to settle a political score?
Will avarice and power rule the day?
Or can we find another way?

Larry Hancock

"Why don't they re-route the traffic
Around this site that is so tragic?
A quiet park would provide a place
Where people could sit and contemplate!"

Ed Sherry, known as the Tree Frog
Will give you facts until your memory bogs!
He keeps track of each and every one
And never quits until his work is done!

Ken Holmes Jr. gives a historical ride
As your Dealey Plaza travel guide!
From Ruby's apartment to the Texas Theatre spot –
To 10th and Patton where Officer J.D. Tippit was shot!

Ken drives by General Edwin Walker's residence –
And the Dallas City Hall, where Oswald was resident!
Then to Parkland Hospital you will start –
As you pass by the Dallas Trade Mart!

There's a common bond, when all is said and done
That unites each and everyone!
We all eat the same food and drink the same water –
Can't we just find a way to end all this slaughter ?

Ed Sherry

Ken Holmes, Jr.

*We evolved by Nature through competition
Animals kill for their nutrition!
But if we kill from our evolution
We must find another solution!*

*What is the genesis of our ways?
Did we arise from primordial haze?
Are all the actions that we weigh
Written in our DNA?*

*Will a nuclear conflagration
Destroy the warring nations?
Will a giant mushroom cloud
Soon mankind enshroud?*

*John Kennedy preached that negotiation
Was the key to our salvation –
If all sides could put down their swords
We might avoid a nuclear war!*

*Kennedy then signed a test ban treaty
That made the generals a little uneasy!
The defense industries were aghast –
Were we prepared for a nuclear attack?*

THE QUATRAINS OF CAMELOT

At that time the official view
Was that nuclear weapons would war preclude!
The real thought construction
Was Mutually Assured Destruction!

One part of the Atomic Energy Act
Allowed measures to protect the pact –
The Oak Ridge group was hopping mad –
That Kennedy might nuclear weapons ban!

Later there arose a real question
Over Ft. Dietrich biological weapons –
Then President Nixon had the answer –
He made them part of his War on Cancer!

Mary Ferrell continues the research
As new revelations she strives to unearth!
And Andy at the Last Hurrah Bookshop tarries
With the books that no one else will carry!

Now just what is the legacy
Of this murder mystery?
Vince Foster's suicide note was forged –
And Ron Brown's skull X-Rays went out the door!

There were two explosions in Oklahoma City that morn –
The witnesses did them both report!
My broker under the table did duck –
Before the second explosion did erupt!

If we continue to allow a pattern of deception
Then we will never see a true correction –
If these deaths aren't properly investigated
People will continue to be terminated!

Of course, it's an inside game –
The politicians know the explanations are lame!
But in order to protect their legacy
To doubt the lone gunman is pure heresy!

Mary Ferrell

Andy Winiarczyk

They'll never change the history books –
A lot, you know, depends on looks!
One way to keep the people's trust
Is tell them only what you must!

So, who was the man at the Grassy Knoll?
Was it the Badgeman, a mobster, or a CIA mole?
It really doesn't matter, when all is said and done –
They all acted together, as if they were one!

John Judge at
the Dealey Plaza Pulpit

THE QUATRAINS OF CAMELOT

*Now, with Jim Marrs' conclusions, I wouldn't trifle –
A man reversed his plaid coat and packed up his rifle!
This description most closely matches James Files
Who used a .222 exploding projectile!*

*John Judge heads a Coalition On Political Assassinations
For 40 years he keeps looking for logical explanations!
Did both Kennedys and Reverend King really die
At the hands of lone gunmen – that's the official lie!*

*Debra Conway of JFK Lancer
Says, "Won't you help us find the answer –
To who, in Dealey Plaza, did fiddle?
Won't you help us solve this JFK riddle!"*

*As each anniversary takes its toll
They place a pulpit at the Knoll
And quietly say a prayer for John –
A tribute to the work he's done!*

*The mysterious force of a fragment of a moment
Draws us back to this place so potent!
Can anyone explain what happened here –
Do we treat it with sadness or face it with fear?*

*Peter Dale Scott talks of meta-history –
Hidden events that remain a mystery!
To preserve the Continuity of Government –
Certain things are not discover meant!*

*Was John Kennedy a living sacrifice
Who provided atonement for our sins and vice?
Is there a lesson to accrue
So our government can begin anew?*

*Is sin just missing the mark?
Just a shade off the truth, is it dark?
Are actions only black or white –
Always wrong or always right?*

Peter Dale Scott and Debra Conway at JFK Lancer Meeting

*"Why must people say goodbye
Instead of just hello?
Wouldn't this be a nicer place
If no one had to go?"*

*"Why do people die?
It doesn't seem quite fair!
Why do we grow old and gray
And vanish in the air?"*

*"The Lord must have his reasons
For this changing of the guard –
Evil ones are laid to rest
But good folks still die hard!"*

*"I'm sure this is a better world
With new replacing old –
But if we never said goodbye
It might not be so cold!"*

THE QUATRAINS OF CAMELOT

Are we a materialistic society
That has also lost it's sobriety?
Do we strive for the measure
Of a moment's pleasure?

When we give in to our inner greed
In order to find the pleasure we need –
And we satisfy our lusty ambitions
Are we condemned to a bottomless perdition?

Are we mere lumps of protoplasm
Struggling between orgasms?
Or is there something more that we
Inherited through our pedigree!

With tingles of delight –
We keep away the fright!
Trying to ease the pain
Of a life full of rain!

Primitive nations practiced human sacrifice
Hoping their gods they could entice!
Are modern day assassinations
Merely primitive ruminations?

Do we kill our leaders as a sacrifice
To the gods of money and power and vice?
Are today's practices of elimination
Inherited from previous civilizations?

Can it really be?
That a government can change reality?
Create false fronts and with deception
Alter an entire country's perception?

In ages past, the people swooned
When their rulers took away the moon!
But no more – the secret's quit –
Today it's called a lunar eclipse!

Adam and Eve at Indiana University

The Dealey Plaza garden scene
Like the Garden of Eden can be seen
As the day we lost our innocence
And man realized his true intents!

When Cain slew Able, the world changed
And our new-born world was re-arranged!
Rivalries developed between the brothers –
People stopped trusting one another!

And Robert Groden, like a watchful sentry
Hands out leaflets to the gentry –
Forty years he's been in Dealey Square
He tells the history to all who care!

"Oswald never fired a shot –
This you will remember not!
The world's not what it seems to be
Believe not all that you may read!"

THE QUATRAINS OF CAMELOT

The children take their Dealey Plaza retreat
With box lunches do they sit and eat –
The teacher talks of rivalry and ambition
With eyes wide open, they sit and listen!

In order to perpetuate the truth
We must explain it to our youth!
It may be ugly and make us cry –
But that's no reason not to try!

Was it three shooters or one
Who fired in the Dealey sun –
An unholy Trinity
Or a lone blasphemy?

One child raises his little hand –
He still doesn't understand –
Why did someone shoot John Kennedy?
Was that really the only remedy?

The teacher looks down with a sigh
As tears well up in both her eyes –
"That's a good question that you raise –
Perhaps we'll know some future day!"

"Some things, you see, were meant to be –
We cannot change reality!
The best that we can pray and hope
Is that our world will learn to cope!"

Sometimes I wonder why
Things happen that make people cry!
Are the positive feelings we entertain
Just opiates synthesized by our brain?

Is this the wrath of God?
Who looks down and with a nod
Man is visited with evil –
A retribution of upheaval?

CONTEMPLATIONS

Do we exist in a universe that's friendly?
Or do we live in a world of pride and envy?
Is the world outside just frigid and cold?
Or are there outside forces that take control?

School children on a field trip to Dealey Plaza –
having lunch on the Grassy Knoll

THE QUATRAINS OF CAMELOT

And what was the original sin
That got us in the state we're in?
Did we cut a deal with the devil –
And now our leader must be leveled?

Will there be a second coming of Christ
To purge sin and eliminate vice?
Or will we forever struggle through time
To make good and evil re-align?

Do the gods of Baal and Osiris
Punish us for our mortal desires?
If we don't walk the straight and narrow –
Do we still meet with a fatal arrow?

Would Zeus seek his revenge
If we fail to make amends?
Would he strike with a lightning bolt
And forever dash our eternal hope?

Did we evolve from savage Beings
Who kill each other as a means
Of establishing their territory
And proving their superiority?

Will there be a nuclear Armageddon
Where good and evil continue to threaten –
Will pestilence, floods, hailstone and fires
Put an end to our cherished desires?

Or will the various factions come around
And try to find some Common Ground –
So the Promised One will sit and smile
And save us from a thousand year trial!

Does evolution play a role
And account for our destructive toll?
Is there a code in our DNA
That makes us want to kill our prey?

The Wailing Wall

Did we arise from some primordial stew
Of carbon molecules that were brewed
To create detailed organic instructions
That would allow us to make intelligent deductions?

Did we evolve from monkeys
Along the evolutionary tree?
Or with one creative burst
Did God create heaven and earth?

Are we responsible for our behavior
Or is this just an act of Nature?
Are all our horrible imperfections
Just products of our own conception?

Or are we made in God's own image –
Unrelated to some earlier lineage?
Free to create and free to kill –
The product of our own free will!

Do we live in a world of divine creation
With one prime mover who controls all nations?
Or do we live in a world of random chance –
As victims of pomp and circumstance?

THE QUATRAINS OF CAMELOT

Perhaps there is an outside evil
That forces us to be deceitful!
When compassion and kindness we desert –
Is it nothing more than the devil's work?

Can you hear the voice of God?
Is he trying to poke and prod
And tell us all just what to do
If only we will listen, too!

Or are these inner ruminations
Merely self-justifications
Of our sub-conscious desires
Attributed to a cause much higher?

Perhaps a more mundane explanation
Would explain the entire situation –
Was this payback for the Bay of Pigs
When Kennedy refused to send the ships?

Did they think that Kennedy was too timid?
Did he make them all a little too livid?
Was he too soft on Castro and communism?
Or did he follow too closely his catechism?

Was there some undiscovered fatal flaw
That caused our beloved leader to fall?
A weakness in his humanity –
Was it pride or was it vanity?

Every so often a cataclysmic burst
Sends shock waves ringing throughout the earth!
When the shots rang out, the people cried –
Where were you when the music died?

What are the effects of trauma on the brain?
Tragic events cause psychological pain!
Traumatic events are forever burned –
They're played over again in attempts to re-learn!

Visions in the night
Present an awful sight!
Perchance the light of day
Will make them go away!

Does the whiteness of the whale
Bring us this travail –
Is a roaming, destructive force
Part of Mother Nature's course?

And why did Kennedy's brain disappear?
What did the establishment fear?
Was there a shot from the front and right –
That had to be kept out of public sight?

Did the pigeons on the Depository roof
Sense that something was aloof?
Or did they simply stop and stare
With knowledge they could never share?

Were there others on Elm Street –
Who did the President greet –
Knowing that Kennedy would soon alight
Within the cross-haired rifle sights!

Ambition, power, greed and hate
Leave me still to contemplate –
How many times will we repeat this sin?
Can we tame the savage beast within?

Was it Oswald as a crazed Lone Nutter –
Or the military seeking guns instead of butter!
Is it a tale of conspiracy –
Or one man seeking his legacy?

It's not a matter of restitution
The people just hope for a final solution –
We just want to get the facts
So we can write the final act!

THE QUATRAINS OF CAMELOT

Some say it's really unpatriotic
To look back at the past – it's idiotic!
"Keep looking forward!" – that's what they're saying –
"And don't look back – someone might be gaining!"

Why were the burglars at the Watergate Hotel
The same ones who in Dealey Plaza dwelled?
A conspiracy would make more sense
Than calling it coincidence!

The real question we must ask –
Can we really learn from our past?
If previous errors are fully vetted –
Future debacles might be prevented!

It's not a great mystery
What happened to John Kennedy –
The simple truth is that
The government won't release the facts!

Democrats and Republicans both played the game –
So no one wants to take the blame!
"It would be an embarrassment for all to see –
People might lose their faith in democracy!"

It took 80 years for the Russians to admit
That the Bolsheviks gave orders to kill Czar Nicholas!
The royal family's death remained a mystery –
Until the KGB opened its registry!

Why was the Royal Family killed?
They posed no threat to the Bolshevik shills!
But they created a traumatic memory
That was burned in the brains of the peasantry!

Was there a Rasputin among the White House Elite –
Who sabotaged the CIA fleet?
Or was this simply JFK's hesitancy
To leave an invasion legacy?

Is there a cosmic fate
To our affairs of state?
Will we achieve a world divine
Or face the very end of time?

The goal of each generation
Is to preserve the next iteration!
To pass the truth in the night –
And never give up the fight!

There's another version of history
That remains a total mystery!
It's a world that's quite distorted –
With facts that are never reported!

Certain things must not be known –
Or the government you'll disown!
'Tis better to be innocent –
Than of the truth be cognizant!

The real question we must ask –
"Do we keep track of our past?"
Is our history so meritorious
When it's written by those victorious?

Sherman's march to the sea
Was nothing but treachery!
But they hail it in the main
As some great military campaign!

If a fact just doesn't fit
In the puzzle of life we knit –
It's easier to declare a pollution
Than come up with a new solution!

We make our exits and entrances on the stage
As each generation writes a page –
Will we write this chapter in history –
Or will it forever remain a mystery?

THE QUATRAINS OF CAMELOT

Ich bin ein Berliner – Rathaus Schöneberg

Wer hat Kennedy geschossen?
Ist die Frage sehr verboten?
Wahr ist ein Anschlag von Mehreren?
Oder die Tat eines Einzelnen?

The people in La Colonia Kennedy –
In Tegucigalpa do they grieve!
"Kennedy tried to improve our lot –
We will surely forget him not!"

Quién mató al Presidente Kennedy?
Era acto solo o de mucha gente?
Y porqué no hay resolución?
Hay miedo de una revolución?

Reveal the truth, the people cry!
Reveal the truth before I die!
But the years pass ever slowly on
And one by one, we all are gone!

Qui a tué John Kennedy?
C' est un sujet interdit?
C' était un homme ou plusieurs?
Qui est responsable de cet enfer?

CONTEMPLATIONS

Berlin: a new square

Berlin: torches in the street

Seoul: sidewalk bulletins

Tokyo: Buddhist prayers

Tokyo: silence in a department store

Paris: like other homes

Moscow: sober readers
Overleaf: torchlight procession in Berne, Switzerland

THE QUATRAINS OF CAMELOT

"Don't upset the applecart!"
Or our world will fall apart!
Keep the people uninformed –
Or revolution might be born!

Shouldn't history be apolitical –
By scholars who are analytical?
Written in a neutral cast –
So we might understand our past!

Let's start a brand new beginning –
With a whole different way of thinking!
Let's put an end to excuses lame –
Truth in politics must be the game!

Real history is bizarre –
That's just the way things are!
The official version is nice and clean –
But reality is kind of mean!

The British hired the Buccaneers
To help resolve their Spanish fears –
But was this deal with the devil
An act of good or an act of evil?

What forces blot out history
And keep us in this mystery?
Is there a conscious act of deception –
Or just a lack of basic direction?

The government gets leery
When people start to query!
So they find some way that they can diss –
By calling them "conspiracy theorists!"

It's not good to question –
That's the basic lesson!
If the explanation seems absurd –
You must accept them at their word!

Assassinations represent a loss of control
That strikes fear into every soul!
Disorder rules the day –
As the devil has his way!

Why can't we see God for certain?
Does He hide behind some gossamer curtain?
Pulling levers behind the scenes –
To help mankind fulfill his dreams?

Was there a big bang
That the universe entertained?
Or is the world in steady state –
Changing in an ordered pace?

Does political change occur slow –
With everything in ordered rows?
Or must catastrophe
Control our destiny?

Do we have an impulse for destruction –
And what are the repercussions?
Will our hormones have their way –
Or will reason rule the day?

I share in the suffering of those who grieve –
Bearing the cross of a broken dream!
It's nice to put the past behind –
But must our hearts be broke in kind!

The day the clock stopped –
People stood in shock!
Faces frozen in the night –
Nothing in the world seemed right!

Do you feel the pain
Of a life without gain?
Of dreams gone awry
In the blink of an eye?

THE QUATRAINS OF CAMELOT

*We walk a thin line –
Are the living and dead entwined?
Do ghosts tarry among the living souls –
And try to guide them in their roles?*

*Presidential deaths are a mystery –
Part of our secret history!
What would the public do –
With a Presidential coup?*

*We never know what life will bring –
A cold winter or a warm spring!
We can only hope for the best –
Fate or chance will take the rest!*

*We live our lives as damaged souls –
Trying to fill the empty holes
That pain and sadness leave behind –
In a world that's not so kind!*

*We carry the burden of those who die –
Hoping that they will death defy!
So that in one day of reparation
We'll never again face separation!*

*And the ghosts of the Kennedys and Martin Luther King
Walk hand in hand down Elm Street as the people sing!
They rejoice in the hope that the truth will be told –
And that one day the true story will unfold!*

THE QUATRAINS OF RFK

Robert Kennedy campaigning in Kansas

The year was 1968
Filled with war rallies and racial hate!
It was a time of great turmoil –
Our country was about to boil!

Along came Robert Kennedy
Who said, "I'll find a peaceful remedy!"
RFK was ahead in the polls
And anxious to assume a Presidential role!

"I vow that if I'm President
I will investigators send –
To find who killed John Kennedy
And put an end to this mystery!"

But the Generals were very sore –
Kennedy didn't support the war!
And the Mafia was not too primed
To face another War on Crime!"

THE QUATRAINS OF CAMELOT

Thus the dreadful coalition
Came again to its fruition –
The Mafia, the police, and the CIA
Had yet another role to play!

Is there a fear of the dead –
Something the living dread?
That makes it necessary to uproot
All those who seek the truth?

Martin Luther King

Now, one thing that you must recall –
The communists were a threat to all!
If Vietnam should communist go
The rest would fall like dominoes!

The primary thing you must consider
Is that the Vietnam War was bigger
Than any single candidate's platform –
We were fighting a communist firestorm!

If we were to lose in Vietnam
Then other countries would succumb!
The communists would come and rule –
And we'd speak Russian in our school!

When RFK and MLK opposed the war
Many thought we'd lose what we were fighting for!
Was there no one who could make amends?
It was time for the lone gunmen to strike again!

While in Indianapolis on a campaign fling
Robert learned of the murder of Martin Luther King!
He said, "Let us tame the savageness of man!"
But two months later he met Sirhan Sirhan!

"I, too, lost a brother," Kennedy told the crowd
"Like Martin Luther King, my brother was shot down –
We must work together and coexist
If our human race is to persist!"

Robert Kennedy speaking at Notre Dame

*Now the last stop before new security
Was the California Democratic primary –
If Kennedy won the state election
The Secret Service would provide protection!*

*But the Ambassador Hotel was Mafia rooted –
A personnel change was instituted!
The security guard would be replaced
By a man who was in the Mafia's grace!*

*And what was CIA hit man David Morales
Doing in the Hotel Ambassador palace?
A hater of the Kennedys –
Was he hunting another enemy?*

*Sirhan Sirhan was held at bay
As Roosevelt Grier kept Kennedy away –
Sirhan was to provide distraction
While the security guards went into action!*

*The Ace Guard Service had supplied three guards
But Thane Eugene Caesar was the one in charge!
He was the closest one to Robert Kennedy
Who pulled off his neck tie in the melee!*

THE QUATRAINS OF CAMELOT

Both men fired 0.22 caliber shells
That turned the kitchen into a noisy hell!
Four bullets hit Bobby and five more people fall –
Sirhan's eight-shot revolver couldn't fire them all!

Two shots one tenth of a second apart
Can only mean two guns that bark!
Despite the lone gunman push –
This was more of a kitchen putsch!

For a few brief seconds, Robert seemed alright
And he asked if friend Paul was still aright –
Then he crossed himself upon the floor
And we heard from Robert nevermore!

Special Unit Senator was formed to investigate
But their efforts were strictly second-rate –
Detectives Pena and Hernandez worked for the CIA –
Did they have a double role to play?

The bullet holes were cut out of the wall –
To save the evidence would be important to all –
But the Los Angeles Police Chief, Daryl Gates
Burned the evidence at the stake!

A college student, Scott Enyart, took camera shots –
Prime evidence to discover an assassination plot!
But, after 20 years, the Los Angeles police advised
They lost the pictures – to no one's surprise!

Then Coroner Dr. Thomas Noguchi
Said too many bullet holes do I see!
It's very evident, needless to say
That as a forensic pathologist, I suspect foul play!

Four shots did Bobby Kennedy find –
Five more victims fell in line –
Two more shots in the center post –
But Sirhan's revolver shot eight at most!

THE QUATRAINS OF RFK

*FBI Agent William Bailey did say
He saw two bullets in the center post that day –
But Police Chief Darryl Gates was appalled –
He never saw any bullets at all!*

*The center post was removed for evidence
And to the lab it was quickly sent –
But when the trial ended, Darryl Gates then spoke –
"Let's burn the center post into smoke!"*

*In order to carry out a plan
It helps to have a cover-up man!
If he plays his role just right –
The public won't suspect a mite!*

RFK June '63

*Powder burns near Kennedy's ear
Placed the gunman very near –
But Roosevelt Grier kept Sirhan at bay –
Another 0.22 caliber gun had to be in play!*

*Sirhan had worked at the Corona Ranch
As a jockey, he wasn't much of a catch!
He had gambling loans he couldn't recuse
So the Mafia made him a deal he couldn't refuse!*

*Now the CIA dealt with hypnosis and drugs
To turn regular people into downright thugs!
And the Soviet KGB created Zombie Spies
Who would forget what they did – to no one's surprise!*

*William Harvey was a pistol packing brute
Who for the CIA's MK-Ultra did recruit –
Were people recruited who could be programmed to kill?
And were Sirhan and James Earl Ray merely patsy shills?*

*Now one thing that you must realize
Is that the investigation was compromised –
The Italian Mafia really couldn't move
Unless the Texas mafia did approve!*

THE QUATRAINS OF CAMELOT

*Robert Kennedy didn't have enough friends
And that's the story in the end –
The CIA, the Texans, and the Pentagon bosses
Decided it was time to cut their losses!*

*Thus the murder of Robert Kennedy
Would go down in posterity
As the random act of a crazy man
Who was never part of a conspiracy plan!*

*"You can be whatever you want to be!"
That was the message of Robert Kennedy!
No matter the religion or race –
You still can compete in the chase!*

Katie Brumbaugh and Tara Williams. Their parents work in the Surgery Department in Oklahoma City's Baptist Medical Center.

THE QUATRAINS OF MARILYN MONROE

We live in a democracy –
That's plain for everyone to see!
It's just that every now and then
The scales are tipped by ambitious men!

Giant castles and fancy cars –
We live the life of movie stars!
But how much substance do we own –
If happiness is not at home?

We are silly human creatures –
Mounting the ones with lovely features –
Hoping for some electrical stimulation
That would provide us with some motivation!

Marilyn Monroe would be the pawn
Of a tryst with Robert that went wrong –
Marilyn was killed by the Mob that night
In hopes that Kennedy would feel the bite!

Marilyn Monroe was murdered, I believe
Because of Robert Kennedy –
John's brother led the war on crime
And Giancana was the first in line!

THE QUATRAINS OF CAMELOT

For the mobster Giancana helped John Kennedy
Win the West Virginia primary
And the vote in Illinois was very close –
Until Daley and Giancana found the votes!

Nothing is illegal, nothing is immoral
In this process they call electoral –
Who's your Daddy? No one cares –
As long as you win a Congressional chair!

But then the Mob fell out of favor –
A fact that Giancana did not savor –
"I've been double crossed!" he said
And vowed that Kennedy would soon be dead!

Giancana talked to father Joe
And tried to settle Bobby's row!
But Bobby could not be persuaded –
The War on Crime went unabated!

Marilyn called Robert, who was no stranger
And said, "My life is now in danger!"
A bitter fight then did ensue –
Captured on tape by Fred Otash's crew!

Marilyn said, "We can no longer meet –
It's not enough to be discreet –
I came up through a Mafia boss
I must be loyal at all costs!"

Bobby Kennedy broke out in anger –
"I don't accept this Mafia danger!"
He threw things about the room
And chided Marilyn's gloom and doom!

The situation is a bit more complicated
Because Marilyn had become impregnated!
Some say Marilyn refused an abortion
And turned down money from the consortium!

Was Marilyn too possessive –
Were her actions too aggressive?
Growing up in orphanages and poverty –
Did she want a child of royalty?

Now Giancana told a fib
When he said the Kennedys ordered the hit –
The trick is always to pass the blame
In this sticky political game!

If Giancana played his hand
At the behest of the Kennedy clan –
Why would he act on a night
When Marilyn and Bobby had a fight?

Remember, Marilyn's house was bugged
By Fred Otash and his Mafia thugs –
Every word that Marilyn said
Was relayed to the Mafia head!

Giancana then decided
Marilyn would be suicided –
After Kennedy left that night
The Mafia would take her life!

I'm rather of the opinion
That Giancana was the only minion –
Suiciding Marilyn at just the right time
To embarrass Robert Kennedy and his War on Crime!

"This will ruin Bobby's reputation,
And help end the conflagration
That this War on Crime has brought!"
That's what Giancana thought!

Marilyn then saw Dr. Greeson
And said with Bobby I cannot reason!
He gave her a shot of barbiturate
In hopes that this would cure her heartache!

THE QUATRAINS OF CAMELOT

The hitmen left Chicago early that morn
From the Palwaukee airport near the North Shore
They attended a party near the Los Angeles parts –
Then left late at night to perform their black arts!

Frank the German was a burglar
Whose specialty, they say, was murder –
A hitman for hire from Chicagoland
Entered with Spilotro, Niccoletti, and his Mafia clan!

Now a chemist from an Illinois university
Helped concoct a rectal suppository
That would put Marilyn fast asleep
Without the coroner saying a peep!

Marilyn was given a rectal pill
And soon began to feel the chill –
Chloral hydrate and barbiturate
Would be what sealed Marilyn's fate!

"'Tis a suicide," said pathologist Henry Lee –
But he knew that this could never be!
For Marilyn's stomach contained no drugs
'Tis true that Marilyn was killed by thugs!

But Peter Lawford and the Kennedy crew
Rushed to clean up Marilyn's room –
Her diary and her personal notes
Would go the way of the Illinois votes!

Marilyn went to the hospital twice –
The first was an attempt to save her life –
The second occurred hours later
Before she went to the undertaker!

J. Edgar Hoover then joined the race
And declared Marilyn's death a federal case!
Evidence was lost before the FBI decides
That Marilyn's death must be a suicide!

So Robert Kennedy's name was clear –
He had been voted "Family Man of the Year!"
They say Marilyn died of suicide –
After dreaming of being a Kennedy bride!

But the mobster Giancana stayed in the path
Of Robert Kennedy and his wrath!
Giancana's plan to suicide Monroe
Could not derail his Kennedy foe!

Now Frank Sinatra and Robert Kennedy were not close –
Frank ranted and raved and scared away most!
And with Robert Kennedy's War on Crime
Many of Frank's friends were doing jail time!

But Sinatra was friends with Joe DiMaggio
Together, they pulled a few pranks, you know!
But when Marilyn died, Joe DiMaggio cried
And blamed the Kennedys for her demise!

Thus Marilyn's death was truly a waste –
A Giancana plan that was made in haste!
Marilyn's murder was a political crime
That was covered up in the nick of time!

One more tale must yet be sung
Of Frank the German, an evil Hun
Who killed for Giancana without remorse
And entered Marilyn's house with force!

A Greek girlfriend named Eugenia Pappas
Knew too much and created a fracas –
Eugenia told Penny of an August night
When Frank and his friends ended Marilyn's life!

Frank told Eugenia of Marilyn's final cries
When they taped her mouth as she bravely died –
The sedatives gradually took effect
As Marilyn took her final breath!

THE QUATRAINS OF CAMELOT

Eugenia was warned, "Don't hang with Frank!
Or some day you will get the yank!
His German eyes seem blue and true
But some day he'll get rid of you!"

The love affair was initially quite strong
But didn't really last that long
Like most romance, it eventually fades
And the lovers go their separate ways!

Frank told Eugenia, "You know too much!"
Now that we have broken up –
The secret of Marilyn's demise
Must never meet the public eyes!

She went with Frank on a Mafia yacht
In a final effort to patch things up –
But the orders came from Giancana's crew,
"Eugenia, I must get rid of you!"

Frank was given an awful choice –
To kill Eugenia himself or from one of the boys!
He held Eugenia to his breast –
And fired a bullet into her chest!

Frank said, "I will forget you never!"
Then threw her body in the Chicago River –
Near Ashland Avenue she was found
In early spring, when the thaw came round!

Penny's mother was then imposed
To view Eugenia's body decomposed –
Eugenia's mother was so distraught
She could not view her daughter's loss!

"I'll never forget the horrible sight
Of Eugenia's body in the night –
My daughter's best friend committed no crime –
She knew too much, so it was the end of the line!"

The Chicago police did their very best
And called Frank Schweihs to take a test –
But the Chief Investigator, Richard Cain
Was a member of the Chicago Gang!

Eugenia's murderer was never arrested –
The Chicago police never really contested
The testimony of a Mafia hitman –
Who would go on to kill again and again!

Simple murders are never solved
When politicians lack resolve!
So Eugenia Pappas remains a name
Synonymous with the Marilyn game!

One thing that you have to wonder –
What if the Mafia's role had been uncovered?
Had the investigation not been circumvented –
Could John Kennedy's death have been prevented?

Which takes us back in time
To a murder on St. Valentine's
Giancana played a role –
But never would he pay the toll!

Jeanne Carmen was Marilyn's closest friend
And talked with Marilyn near the end
She says one duty for our nation –
Is to help restore Marilyn's reputation!

The men who committed this treachery
Would one year later in Dallas be –
And the failure to solve Marilyn's crime
Would put John Kennedy next in line!

Marilyn became a pawn, you see
In this Mafia-Kennedy rivalry
An innocent lamb, Marilyn's murder foretold
Of greater tragedies yet to unfold!

THE QUATRAINS OF FDR

FDR was a wealthy young cad –
A very socially active lad
He loved the ladies and they loved him,
Now is that really much of a sin?

Franklin was struck with polio while middle aged
But that couldn't keep him from the political stage!
He couldn't walk – his legs were bent,
But he went on to become our President!

As the years went by, some Congressman claimed
That FDR didn't seem the same –
His memory, it seemed, was no longer first rate
And it became difficult for him to concentrate!

They organized a team of erudite doctors
From the Mayo Clinic and even Harvard –
And what did the physicians find, pray tell?
Franklin had a positive VDRL!

Now, one thing is certain, you must believe –
Presidents don't suffer from social disease!
Typhoid, or cholera, or perhaps some strange bug –
But a social disease is swept under the rug!

People might look at us with unease
If you or I get a social disease!
But if our dear President gets the clap
All his advisors must shut their trap!

And so the report of the erudite physicians
Disappeared in the usual political tradition –
"The President's fine," they said with a sigh –
And shot arsenic and mercury salts in his thigh!

FDR died of a cerebral hemorrhage –
That's really a form of political rhetoric!
He died of a bleed in the brain, that's true
But that's what a .38 caliber bullet will do!

*It was a most unusual stroke
With swelling on the left side of his face and throat –
A stroke causes bleeding in the brain's Willis circle –
The face shouldn't swell, nor should it turn purple!*

*Dr. Howard Bruehn said he moved Franklin to bed
And that's when he pronounced our President dead!
But Daisy Suckley said three men moved FDR
Before Dr. Bruehn arrived from the yard!*

*The least they could do was get their story straight
So lies to the people they could perpetuate!
Now why would they put FDR back to bed?
Change his suit to pajamas, and cover his head?*

*Did Franklin really die in the afternoon?
Or was he dead that morn when they entered the room?
I suspect Franklin died late in the eve –
Was it foul play that forced him to leave?*

*The Warm Springs group needed time
To clean up Franklin from the crime!
They phoned Eleanor Roosevelt in D.C.
And told her to her appointments keep!*

*Franklin's body was returned by train –
Back to the White House he slowly came
There the body lied in state
While others were left to contemplate!*

*Joe Stalin was upset – he liked dear old FDR –
The Yalta conference made Stalin a star!
"Check the arsenic levels!" was Stalin's demand
But no one would listen to the Russian command!*

*Harry Hopkins and the Brain Trust core
Needed someone to beat Dewey in '44 –
They went with Franklin, sick though he was –
Because he still commanded the people's trust!*

Winston Churchill, Franklin Roosevelt and Joseph Stalin at Yalta

*FDR's health and memory were poor
And he shouldn't have run for his final tour!
The experts all seemed ill at ease –
For no one seemed to know, what was his disease?*

*But in the spring of '45
FDR was still alive!
Life was now painful and no more fun –
Did someone provide FDR with a gun?*

*The question still lingers that Stalin raised –
What was the illness in FDR's final days?
Were polio or social diseases at fault?
Or did he receive too many arsenic salts?*

*The wartime generals made a big fuss
At FDR and the Hopkins Brain Trust!
They were too friendly with the communists
And gave up too much at the Yalta conference!*

The Polish people were really livid
That Poland was to Stalin given –
Did FDR cave in to Stalin's forces?
Didn't Russia kill the Poles in the Katyn forest?

Harry Truman didn't trust the Reds –
He viewed the Communists as a threat –
The Cold War would start anew
But none dare call this an American coup!

And why did Daisy Suckley leer
That security guards were nowhere near?
If FDR died of a cerebral stroke
Security guards could not give hope!

FDR's right hand did shake and falter
As he signed the treaties made in Yalta!
But if he had decided to take his own life
The swelling should have been on the right!

Franklin's son was in the Pacific
But Eleanor was quite specific –
James Roosevelt would stay away –
And miss his Father's final day!

"Franklin died like a soldier," Eleanor said
And wouldn't let anyone look at his head!
"There will be no viewing of the President
And no autopsy for this White House resident!"

But how many soldiers die from a stroke –
As on the battlefield they try to cope?
Was Eleanor trying to tell us more –
That some foul play might have been in store?

"A closed casket is what I insist
And talk of foul play should cease and desist!
Please remember, we are at war –
Talk of conspiracy should be no more!"

*But does the President's wife have the right to declare
That an autopsy shall not be done anywhere?
Shouldn't the people be advised
Of how their President really died?*

*If you or I die from a sudden cause
The coroner must investigate, that's the law!
But if you die as a President in history
Your cause of death may remain a mystery!*

*And what could the Hopkins Brain Trust do
If a proper investigation were to ensue?
It would reveal Roosevelt's true malady –
And hurt his Presidential legacy!*

*This story has been told by three doctors to me
I have no reason to doubt their veracity!
Two were Department Chiefs in general surgery
And the other was President of the American Podiatry!*

*Dr Howard Bruenn shared some scuttlebutt
With Dr. Harlan Sowell, an old Naval Bud--
He wrote that FDR's fatal Warm Springs stroke
Was really a .38 caliber assassination poke!*

*"This is absolutely outrageous!" –
Those are the words of the sages –
"Let's not re-open the books –
Or consider a second look!"*

*Perchance, what might be discovered?
Are there actions yet uncovered?
Would it hurt for the people to see
The real truth behind our history?*

*The elderly people we tend to ignore
'Oft hold the key to days of yore!
In order to understand the last –
We must talk to legends of the past!*

Dr. Howard Bruenn

*"You're crazy not to know
That your replacements are in tow!
Men who are younger and stronger –
Are destined to be around longer!"*

*"I feel sorry for the human race –
Fighting over land and space!
With each future generation
Facing another annihilation!"*

*"Work is healthy, don't you know –
It keeps the mind from wandering low!
You do your duty and comply –
But never watch the world go by!"*

*"We are mechanical bodies that fail –
That is our human travail!
We strut around through life –
Forgetting our eventual plight!"*

*"We are machines that eventually die –
Burning oxygen and fuel to carbon dioxide –
Like some old fashioned motor car –
We end up buried in a yard!"*

*Did FDR's death signify
That you could hide how a President died?
And was J. Edgar taking notes –
In case of future proletariat revolts?*

*Was FDR too friendly with the Russians –
Which caused domestic repercussions?
Were the Generals up in arms
Over Stalin's persuasive charms?*

*Did the Cold War begin
Before World War II. did end?
Were Harry Hopkins and the Brain Trust
Too close to the communist thrust?*

THE QUATRAINS OF CAMELOT

Years from now, they may exhume FDR's grave
In order to quiet the conspiracy knaves!
But if they find FDR's skull with a hole –
They'll just say it was from the gravedigger's hoe!

We try to fill the empty spaces
While maintaining social graces!
Hoping that by looking back –
We might find some hidden track!

Do you believe in Santa Claus –
In fairy tales and toys with gloss?
Or is life just one giant ravine –
That swallows up your hopes and dreams?

We construct our world
With a religious twirl –
Hoping as we go
That Someone's in control!

Do you believe in the virgin birth –
When Christ came down unto the earth?
Was it a Divine Proclamation
That led to the enunciation?

Or should we simply accept by faith
The rulings that our Leaders make?
Suspecting with fear and trepidation –
There might be an alternate explanation!

Suicide or murder? Who's to say?
The truth will wait another day!
Of course, there was no official investigation –
So we're left with rumor and speculation!

After his death, FDR's medical records were lost –
They'd been placed in the Bethesda Naval Hospital vault!
Three weeks later they would disappear –
But historians say, "There's no conspiracy here!"

THE UFO QUATRAINS

Dr. J. Allen Hynek

UFO's don't officially exist –
At least that's the U.S. government drift!!
If you see one flying by
It's probably just a meteor high!

Dr. J. Allen Hynek taught astronomy
Outside Chicago, at Northwestern University
I attended his class as a senior in '67 –
He talked about more than just the heavens!

Dr. Hynek was a civilian scientist for the Air Force –
In charge of analyzing Project Bluebook UFO reports
He showed a pass in his wallet for all to see –
That if a UFO landed, he'd get past Security!

Now, why would the Air Force issue a pass
In the dreadful chance that a UFO should crash?
And then turn around and issue a proclamation
That UFO's are a figment of the imagination?

*Dr. Hynek talked of UFO chases
That involved Air Force jets and pilot aces!
The pilots were told not to file a report
Or their careers as pilots would soon be cut short!*

*UFO's were seen at radar stations
Making all sorts of weird gyrations!
They flew faster and higher than any known plane
And attempts to catch them were always in vain!*

*They were called Foo Fighters during World War II.
They would follow the German and American planes, too!
When the pilots reported what they'd been seeing
They were told, in fact, that they must be dreaming!*

*Then it happened in the early fifties
The Air Force gave orders they thought were nifty –
"Tell our pilots to shoot them down!
We can't have saucers flying around!"*

*But when our pilots started their gunning
The results they found were rather stunning!
The pilots' planes would quickly sour
As their planes lost all their electrical power!*

*Now, let's use a little logic –
If this was some sort of secret project
Would we give orders for our planes to fire
And lose a multi-million dollar fighter?*

*If these saucers are truly under guidance
They must have some sort of alien pilots –
Some kind of intelligent Being –
That knows how to pilot a flying machine!*

*In the summer of 1947
A UFO fell out of heaven!
At Roswell, New Mexico, they discovered
Alien bodies that were recovered!*

The bodies were placed in coffins small
And to Wright Patterson they were hauled!
The government had an explanation soon –
This was nothing but a weather balloon!

Dr. Hynek talked of alien beings –
Some were gray and some were green!
Some were short with polydactyly
And others tall with arachnodactyly!

The public must never be told
So the military can maintain its hold –
"If we keep secret the technology in the wreckage
Our side would have a military advantage!"

So the military keeps trying to shoot them down
With space-based lasers they continue to hound!
But with advanced technology and electrogravitic power
We could end the oil crisis in less than an hour!

The military has a special team
That goes to every crash site scene –
They carry off bodies, dead or alive
Before the news media can arrive!

It's the greatest cover-up that's ever gone on –
More secret than the atomic bomb!
Military men in the still of the night –
Keeping everything out of sight!

Dr. Steven Greer started Project Disclosure
He encouraged military men to reveal secret folders!
Alien beings have visited since man was born –
But Presidents and Congressmen are not informed!

Dr. Greer found that the CIA and the President
Were not informed of the secret precedent –
That the military could knowledge withhold
Without the President being told!

THE QUATRAINS OF CAMELOT

Are there alien beings that have visited us
By getting on some intergalactic bus?
Living among us in our atmosphere –
And studying the world that we hold dear!

Extraterrestrial biologic entities – EBE's –
That's what the government calls these Beings!
And while they don't officially exist
They're all classified according to risk!

Betty and Barney Hill
Talked of Grays that gave them a chill –
They scraped their skin and extracted DNA –
Then sent them on their merry way!

Then the crew of Apollo 11
Saw something in the heaven!
But when they returned back to the ground –
They were told not to discuss what they had found!

Astronaut L. Gordon Cooper of Gemini-5
Said alien beings have been captured alive!
The incident at Roswell was no fluke –
But the government won't reveal the truth!

The question now is, what do you do?
With information that's too hot to view?
What would religious leaders say
If aliens were allowed to have their day?

And how would citizens react
To find we're not alone, in fact?
Would people panic and then decide
To all commit mass suicide?

Would religious leaders accept the reality
Of an alien religious duality?
Or would it be necessary to convert
All the beings to just one church?

Will a World Council decide the religion
For everyone within the dominion?
Or will each group be allowed a choice
According to the people's voice?

Who do you call God?
Buddha? The Divine? Allah?
It's what you believe that counts –
That helps you adversity to mount!

Is God a multi-headed Chimera –
With religions comprising different genera?
Does an all-inclusive God please everyone –
From the earth to the distant suns?

Or does one God get the call
And decide to rule above all?
One controlling, unifying Being –
Who acts without ever being seen!

As the genetic pool reforms
And integration is the norm –
Will there be a single face –
And one religion for the race?

Or will each disparate faction
Engage in counter-productive action –
Fighting for their Holy Ground –
With battles raging 'round and 'round!

One movie that gave everyone a chill
Was "<u>The Day The Earth Stood Still</u>" –
Alien beings were there employed
To keep mankind from being destroyed!

But what would the people say of a President
Who claimed that alien beings were sent
To monitor our planet's birth
And wait for peace to rule the Earth?

THE QUATRAINS OF CAMELOT

The government's position
Is to ridicule the opposition –
The witnesses lack the ability
To defend their credibility!

Is it a government art
To keep people in the dark?
To protect our religion and God
From people who poke and prod?

What if alien beings
Visited our earthly scene?
Would missionaries be sent
To make the aliens repent?

The earth revolves around the sun–
This the Catholic Church did shun!
What other revelations
Have been labeled speculation?

You'd best keep your mouth shut –
If you're on the up and up!
Astronauts and pilots
Are told to keep quiet!

Navy Secretary James Forrestal
Planned to tell it all –
But his apparent suicide
Would act the truth to hide!

Is there an alien lunar base
That the astronauts saw face to face?
They came to call them Santa Claus –
But NASA silenced all their calls!

Will aliens let us rule the earth
With radioactive bombs that burst –
Waiting for some great destruction
That would limit our reproduction!

"We have to avoid panic on all accounts!"
This is what the government mounts –
Better to leave things unseen
Than admit the truth about alien beings!

Until then, the government maintains the delusion
That UFO's are merely optical illusions!
While plane chases and radar images and UFO stations
Are merely figments of the imagination!

Is it really a confabulation –
A product of our imagination –
That alien beings would travel near
And challenge concepts we hold dear?

Some Beings don't look like us –
There's no need to make a fuss!
Some live in water, others breathe air –
Must we be so debonair?

RESTRICTED SOM 1-01
TO 1201—3—11—1
MAJESTIC—12 GROUP SPECIAL OPERATIONS MANUAL

EXTRATERRESTRIAL
ENTITIES AND TECHNOLOGY
RECOVERY AND DISPOSAL

TOP SECRET/MAJIC
EYES ONLY

WARNING! This is a TOP SECRET-MAJIC EYES ONLY document containing compartmentalized information essential to the national security of the United States. EYES ONLY ACCESS to the material herein is strictly limited to personnel possessing MAJIC-12 CLEARANCE LEVEL. Examination or use by unauthortized personnel is strictly forbidden and is punishable by federal law.

MAJESTIC-12 GROUP   *April 1954*
MJ---12 4838B

THE KINGFISH QUATRAINS

*Senator Huey Long was known as the Kingfish –
Power he would never relinquish!
But after September 8, 1935
Huey would no longer be alive!*

*Senator Long was a powerful man
Who harbored Presidential plans –
He was running for the Presidency in '36
And was giving Franklin Roosevelt fits!*

*Now Seymour Weiss, Long's right-hand man
Along with hundreds of Huey's fans
Received a tax evasion notice
From FDR's Internal Revenue Service!*

*Huey Long and Dr. Ochsner didn't agree
On what the best type of society should be –
Dr. Ochsner was opposed to socialistic ways
And Huey thought big oil companies should pay!*

*Huey's Share-Our-Wealth platform
Called for major corporate reform –
Rich people would their money lose
To help the poor who had no shoes!*

*Each family would have its own personal homestead
And excess wealth to the poor people would spread!
Long proposed a new tax on the oil barons –
But would he leave Wall Street barren?*

*Would Huey Long have been good for the nation?
Was there a plan for his elimination?
Do democracies always reflect the people's voices?
Or do they sometimes get help to make the right choices?*

*Did Huey's death begin the mystery
Of how politicians alter history?
There's no conspiracy in the park
If lone gunmen take the mark!*

Dr. Karl Weiss was a political activist
Who disagreed with Huey's politics!
Three straws were drawn, as the story goes
And Karl was the one who they chose!

Dr. Weiss spent time in a European nation
And saw the power of Hitler's persuasion –
He observed what a charismatic leader could do
With a trusting electorate who approved!

Now FDR and Huey had a major schism
About Harry Hopkins, Huey spoke with derision –
He spent hours talking to Americans on the radio
Along with Father Charles Coughlin on RKO!

Dr. Weiss waited at the Governor's office in Baton Rouge
But was his presence there nothing more than a ruse?
The bullets in Huey were calibers .38 and .45 –
Dr. Weiss's .32 Browning was not a suspect prime!

The official story was that Dr. Weiss threw a punch
And the bodyguards jumped in the melee all at once!
Huey Long took two bullets as he ran to the door
And Dr. Weiss took 62 shots, as they riddled his corpse!

So the official story of Huey's demise
Is that Dr. Weiss planned a surprise –
He threw a punch, and in the resulting fight
Huey's bodyguards accidentally shot Huey – twice!

Now J. Edgar Hoover happened to be on the phone
And he put out the story that Dr. Weiss acted alone!
But no one as yet had identified Dr. Weiss –
So where did Hoover get his advice?

Drs. Vidrine, Lorio, and Cook heard of the emergency –
They rapidly assembled and took Huey to surgery!
They gave him blood and repaired his colon
But a small artery near his kidney was still a-going!

Hours later, they had to make a decision –
Should they go back through the old incision?
Huey was still talking and implored –
Would the doctors re-explore?

THE KINGFISH QUATRAINS

*The physicians decided not to go back
And Huey died eighteen hours after that –
Huey lived thirty hours in all
After he was shot in the Governor's hall!*

*Huey's desperate pleas went unheeded
As he lay in his hospital bed still bleeding –
Was he just ahead of his time?
Or was his death a political crime?*

*Seymour Weiss, Huey Long's right hand man
Had numerous contacts with the Mafia clan –
Frank Costello later told Meyer Lansky on the sly –
The doctors had their orders to let him die!*

*Eight bodyguards told eight different stories
Of how Huey Long met his glory!
Evidence was lost and records were smeared
And Dr. Weiss's gun just plain disappeared!*

*"This was obviously a lone gunman!" Hoover declared
Before the gun smoke had cleared the air!
"It's important to get a name announced –
To satisfy the public on all counts!"*

*Despite protests from around the nation
The FBI decided there would be no investigation!
FDR dropped the tax cases against all Huey's men –
Was this a reward or was he making amends?*

*Why do we hate
And fail to relate?
Do we face our own demise
If we fail to compromise?*

*Why do we suffer before we die?
That's a right of passage I decry!
Best to run and play –
Before they take you away!*

*We are all inter-connected –
Our lives can be mis-directed!
One man can control the fate
Of an entire nation-state!*

THE QUATRAINS OF CAMELOT

Is there an all-seeing eye
That would secretly spy?
To destroy international tyrants –
And create a one-world alliance!

It must be nice to be organized –
To live a life without surprise!
Everything is nice and neat –
Until the Reaper comes to greet!

Must each generation find anew
Some international glue –
That would unite the disparate nations –
And prevent their annihilation?

They always send a proxy –
Like they don't have the moxie
To face the coming storm –
They avoid the public scorn!

Will I see the faces of death
That portend my final breath?
Will I pass quickly in the night
Or face my final days with fright?

Don't make the citizens mad –
That rule is ironclad!
The government must be protected –
The lone gunman will be dissected!

"To be taken before your time –
That's not what I had in mind!
We never know what fate has in store –
As for me, I could have done more!"

And to this day, you can hear the pleas
As the sound echoes through the Baton Rouge trees –
"Won't someone help me?" Huey implores
And the politicians close their doors!

THE "UNIFIED" SOLUTION

THE DEALEY PLAZA SHOT SEQUENCE EXONERATES LEE HARVEY OSWALD AS A SHOOTER

Josiah Thompson recently stated that the Dealey Plaza shot sequence may never be satisfactorily resolved – this is a puzzle that has eluded researchers for over forty years. I decided to take a fresh look at the problem, and to find out if a solution could be found that merged the known acoustics data with the Zapruder film observations, as well as those of eyewitnesses to the assassination of President John Fitzgerald Kennedy.

While the acoustics data can hear, it cannot see. And, while the Zapruder film can see, it cannot hear. But is it possible to match the time gaps on the acoustic data with documented observations in the Zapruder film? Remember, the acoustics data allows only five shots, with only one frontal shot from the Grassy Knoll and four rear shots, as described by D. B. Thomas.

Over the years, many solutions have been offered to explain the location and number of shots fired in Dealey Plaza during the assassination of President John Fitzgerald Kennedy on November 22, 1963. There is only one solution, however, that successfully combines the acoustics data, the Zapruder film observations, witness observations, and a three dimensional ballistics analysis. I have called this the "unified solution" because it explains the greatest amount of accumulated data.

Let's begin with the easier salvo, the second salvo, which acoustics shows to be two shots – a frontal shot from the Grassy Knoll followed six tenths of a second later by a rear shot. Witnesses relate the final shot to be a double sound, likened to a burst from an automatic weapon. There is the smell of gunpowder as follow-up cars pass by the Grassy Knoll, which is to the front and right of JFK. John Kennedy's head in Zapruder frame 312 is suddenly thrown back and to the left, and bone fragments are embedded in motorcycle Officer Hargis's vest, riding to the left and rear of Kennedy.

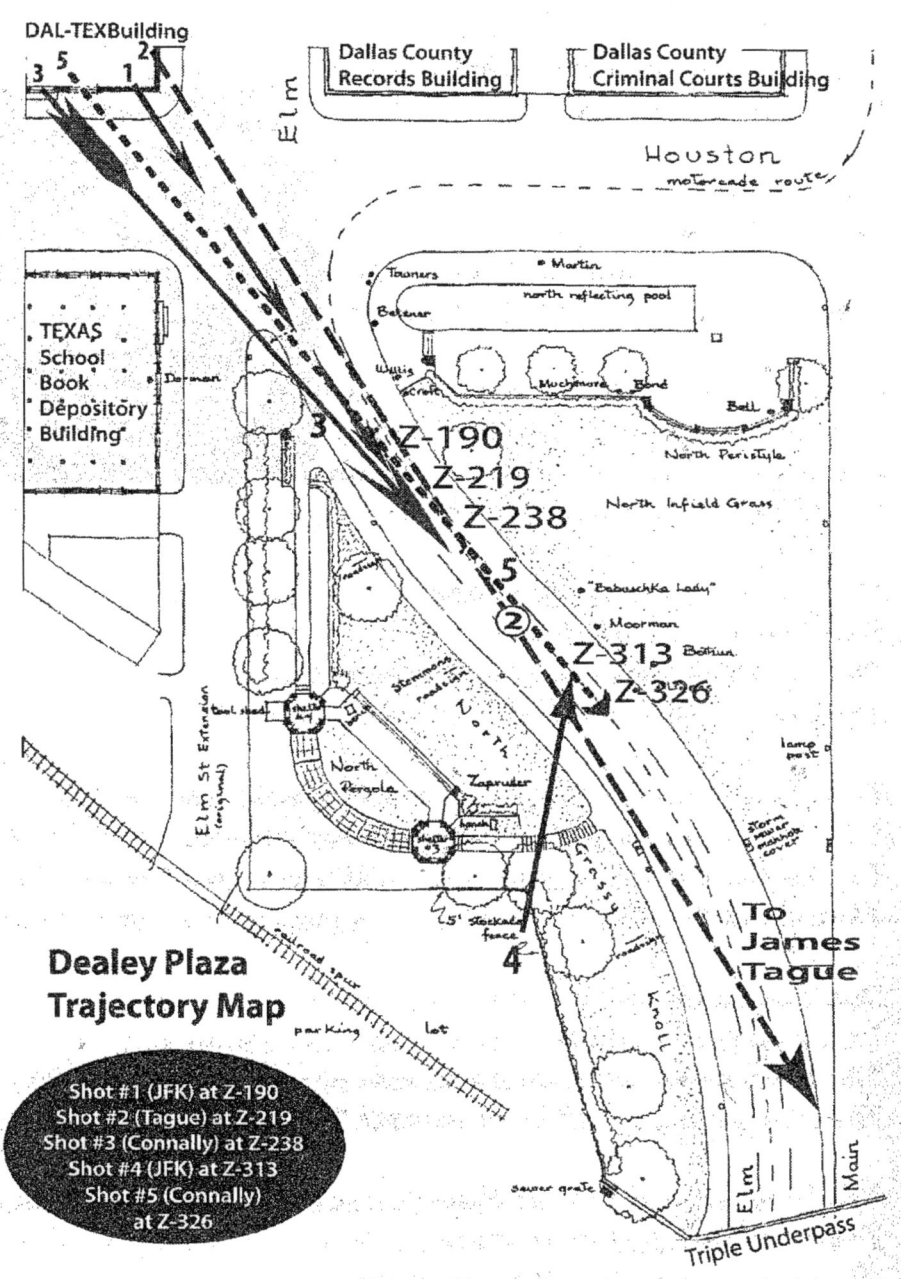

Acoustics shows that six tenths of a second later, at Z-326, a rear shot is fired. Governor Connally's right wrist is shattered, and Connally drops his Stetson hat, as seen in the Zapruder film. Fragments of this bullet crack the inside of the windshield, which was not cracked when viewed earlier in the Altgen's photo at Z-255.

So far, we have established two shooters – a Grassy Knoll shooter who fired the fatal shot from the front right, and a rear shooter who missed Kennedy and hit Governor Connally in the right wrist. A three dimensional reconstruction suggests that the rear shooter missed Kennedy – only because the Grassy Knoll shot suddenly moved Kennedy's head to the left six tenths of a second earlier.

Now let's go to the first salvo of shots. The general consensus of most students of the Zapruder film is that the Kennedy neck shot occurs around Z-190 and that the Connally shoulder shot occurs around Z-238. (The Warren Commission attempted to combine these two shots into a single shot halfway between – at Z-223.) Governor Connally relates that President Kennedy was shot first and that, as Connally turned around, he was subsequently shot. The time gap between these two shots is 48 frames.

Acoustics shows the first salvo to consist of three rear shots. The first and third shots are 2.7 seconds, or 49 frames apart. If Kennedy is hit by the first shot (Z-190), then Connally must have been hit with the third shot (Z-238).

This suggests that the second shot, which acoustics places at Z-219, must be the missed shot, which first strikes Elm Street, and then strikes the curb in front of James Tague on Main Street near the Triple Underpass, sending up a chip of cement that strikes Tague on the cheek.

In fact, Sheriff Decker, in the lead car, states that after he heard the first shot, he turned around and saw a small cloud of debris, as the missed (second) shot struck Elm Street.

THE QUATRAINS OF CAMELOT

Where are the rear shooters located? If one traces a line from James Tague near the Triple Underpass back to JFK's position at Z-219, and then extrapolates this line back, the point of origin is not the Depository, but the Dal-Tex building. This position allows significant concealment for the shooters and easier escape than from the Book Depository.

In three dimensions, a shot fired at Z-219 from the Dal-Tex building that is too high, will miss JFK and the limousine (which tilts downward on Elm Street), strike Elm Street, and be in line to hit the curb in front of James Tague. The serendipitous shot to James Tague mandates a shooter in the Dal-Tex. **There are no shot solutions to James Tague from the Depository.**

Evidence that the first shot (the neck shot) occurred around Z-190 includes Hugh Betzner who states he took his photo (at Z-186) before the first shot, and Phil Willis, who states he took his photo (at Z-202) after the first shot was fired. Witness Mary Woodward stated that, upon hearing the first shot, she saw Kennedy bring his hands up to his neck.

Where did the first shot at Z-190 originate? The Warren Commission determined that shots from the Depository were blocked by the Depository Oak Tree from Z-166 to Z-210. Since a shot at Z-190 is blocked by the Depository Oak Tree, I will place the location of this rear shooter at the Dal-Tex building as well. The bullet enters JFK's upper shoulder and, traveling downward, exits his neck, where a tracheostomy is later performed by the Parkland surgeons. (See diagrams below.)

Where did the Connally shot at Z-238 originate? The bullet enters Connally's right shoulder (near the axilla posteriorly) and exits at the right nipple, traveling on a 28 degree downward angle, as Connally is turned to his right, looking back. In his book Six Seconds in Dallas, which conducts a trajectory analysis, Josiah Thompson places this shot from the east end of Dealey Plaza, which includes the Dal-Tex Building and excludes the Depository.

ANALYSIS OF THE JFK BACK WOUND

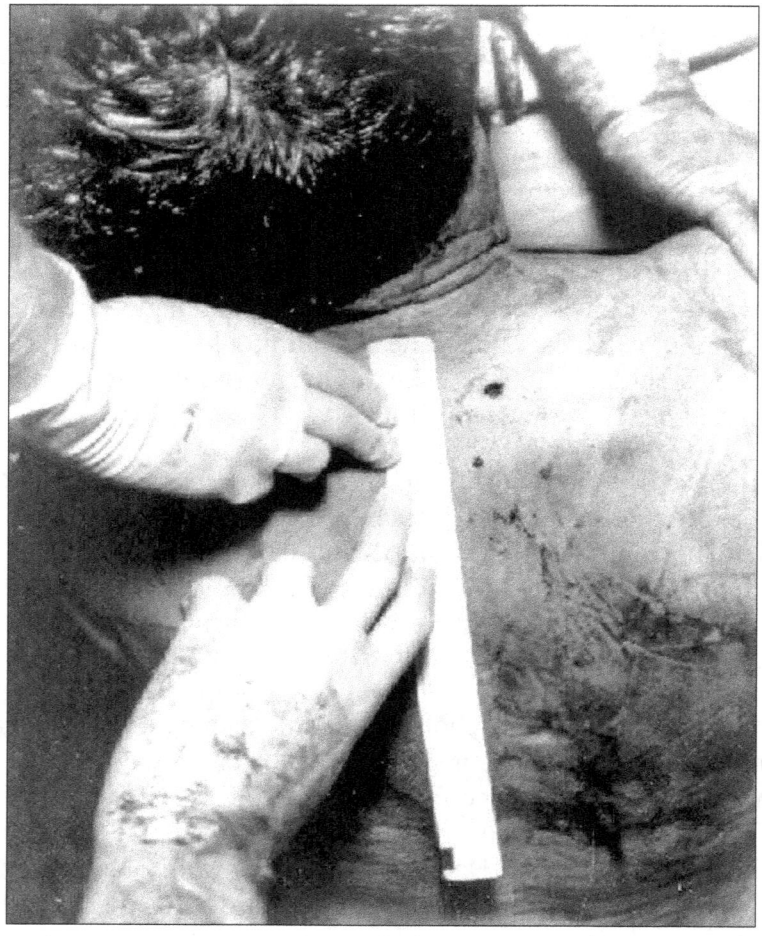

The JFK autopsy photo showing the back wound entry.

Note that the large, baseball sized, exit wound in the back of JFK's head, as described to me by the Dallas Parkland surgeon, Dr. Charles Crenshaw, has been "blacked out".

Secret Service Agent Clint Hill also related that "the right rear portion of the head was gone and was in the back seat!"

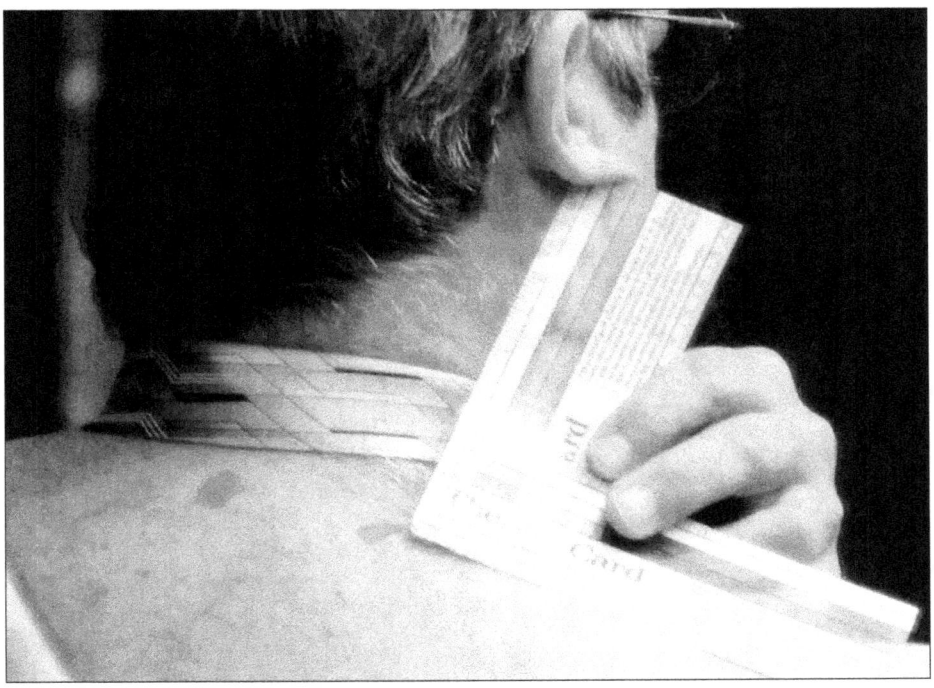

I have placed a red dot on my upper shoulder at the corner of a ruler that measures 14 cm from the stylomastoid foramen and 14 cm from the acromion process, as measured by the Bethesda pathologists. Two inches to the left of this red dot is another red dot placed at c7 — the midline "notch" you can feel in the back of your neck below your neck tie or collar.

This argues that the JFK back wound enters at the c7 level, travels downward to nick the transverse process at t1, seen on x-ray, then exits at the sternal notch at t2. The bullet never strikes significant bone, leaving a small exit wound at the throat.

ANALYSIS OF THE JFK BACK WOUND

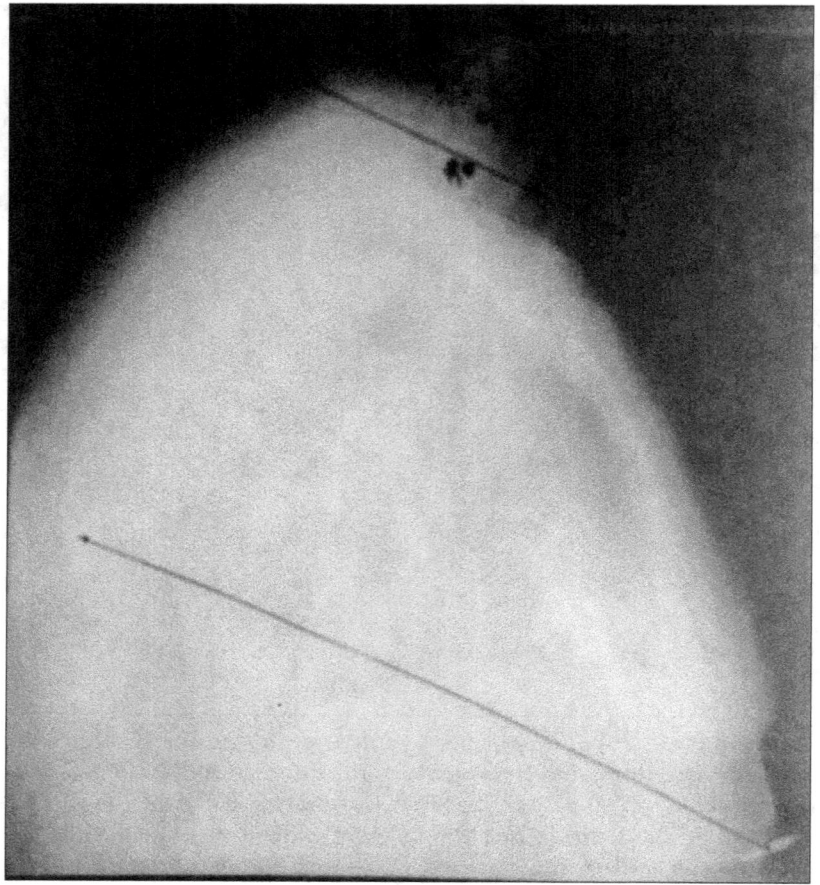

I taped coins on my body at the corresponding entrance and exit wounds of the JFK neck wound (upper line) and the Connally wound (lower line). I then took a lateral chest x-ray and drew a line between the exit and entrance wounds.

JFK's wound enters at the right upper back and exits at the sternal notch in the neck. Connally's wound enters at the right armpit and exits just below the right nipple.

Note that the two trajectories are parallel, suggesting that they were fired from the same location at similar times from the rear. This argues that the JFK neck wound and the Connally anterior chest wound were both exit wounds from an elevated rear location.

THE QUATRAINS OF CAMELOT

The "Grassy Knoll" is to the right and front of JFK.

Note: Motorcycle Officer Hargis behind and to the left of JFK has fragments of bone embedded in his vest after the assassination!

Secret Service Agent Clint Hill, who is seen standing on the left running board of the trailing car, stated that "The back of the head was gone," after the assassination.

The Picket Fence: Before and After

Motorcade approaching Grassy Knoll.

Motorcade simulation with Dal-Tex Building and Book Depository in background

326 ANALYSIS OF THE JFK BACK WOUND

Simulated view of JFK approaching the Grassy Knoll

Grassy Knoll shot to JFK from behind picket fence

THE QUATRAINS OF CAMELOT

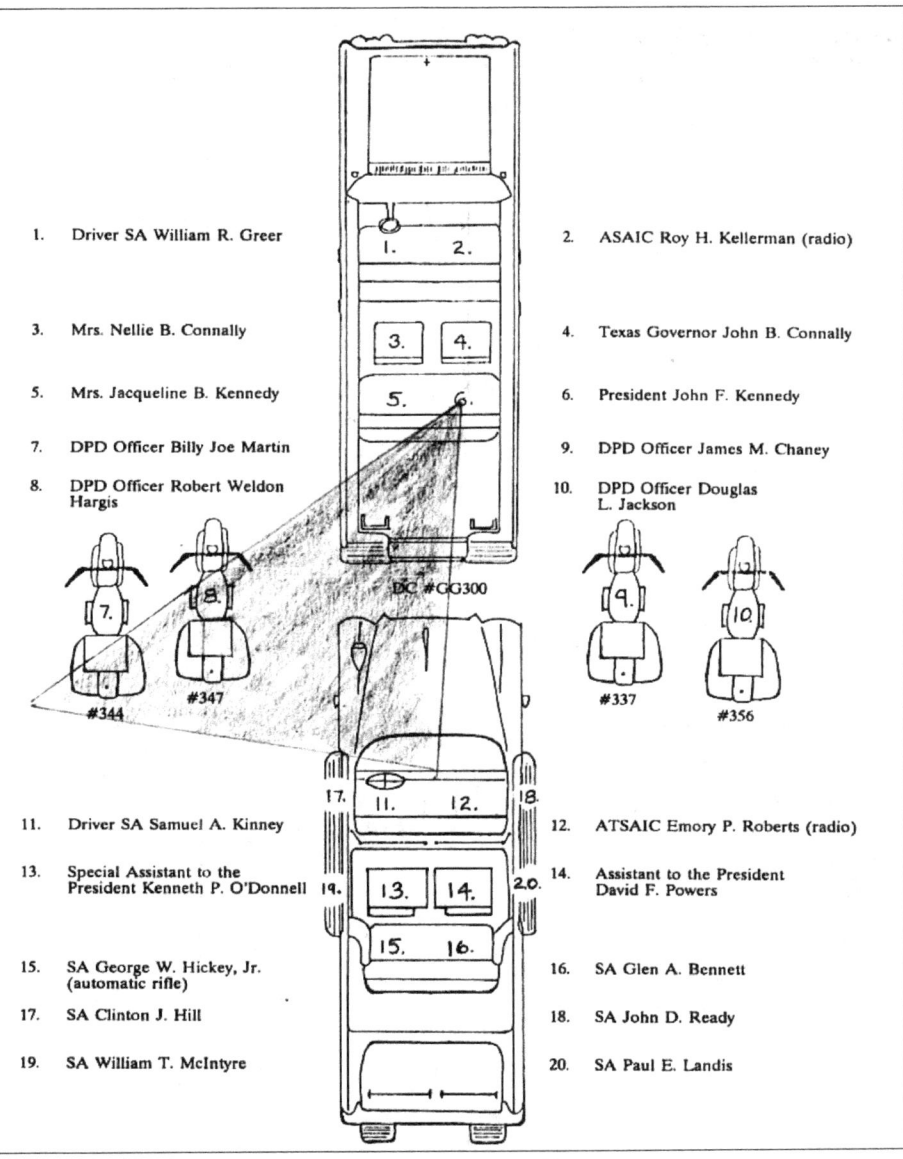

1. Driver SA William R. Greer
2. ASAIC Roy H. Kellerman (radio)
3. Mrs. Nellie B. Connally
4. Texas Governor John B. Connally
5. Mrs. Jacqueline B. Kennedy
6. President John F. Kennedy
7. DPD Officer Billy Joe Martin
9. DPD Officer James M. Chaney
8. DPD Officer Robert Weldon Hargis
10. DPD Officer Douglas L. Jackson
11. Driver SA Samuel A. Kinney
12. ATSAIC Emory P. Roberts (radio)
13. Special Assistant to the President Kenneth P. O'Donnell
14. Assistant to the President David F. Powers
15. SA George W. Hickey, Jr. (automatic rifle)
16. SA Glen A. Bennett
17. SA Clinton J. Hill
18. SA John D. Ready
19. SA William T. McIntyre
20. SA Paul E. Landis

I have drawn the splatter pattern of the JFK head shot from the Grassy Knoll, located to the front and right of JFK.

Fragments of bone were embedded to the left and rear of JFK, in Officer Hargis's vest on motorcycle #8!

ANALYSIS OF THE JFK BACK WOUND

Best chance for a shot to hit James Tague is an early shot from the Dal-Tex Building

Only chance for a Book Depository shot to hit James Tague is well after the assassination

THE QUATRAINS OF CAMELOT

The missed shot to James Tague View from the Dal-Tex building

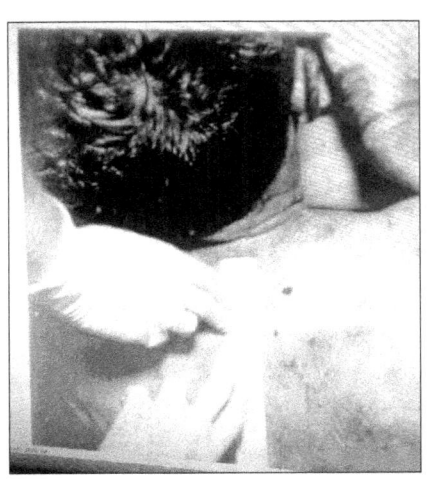

Official photo of the back of JFK's head — notice the "darkened area" at the right rear that appears to have been shaded

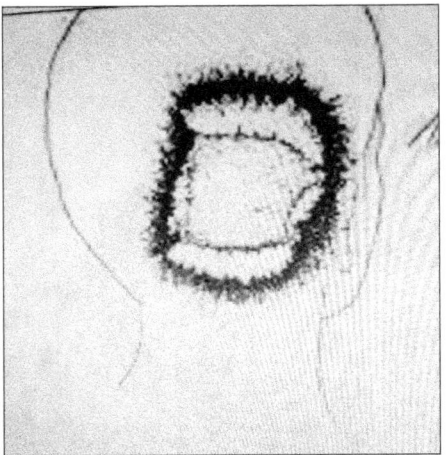

A pictorial representation of President Kennedy's head wound, as described by Dr. Robert N. McClelland of Parkland Hospital

"I'm just a patsy."

Bill Truels and Judyth Vary Baker

Bill Truels and Madelaine Brown

Dealey Plaza witness Jean Hill and Jim Marrs, 1992

Dr. Cyril Wecht, who challenged the Warren Commission findings, and Dr. Bill Truels (Robert Groden is seated to the left)

DISCUSSION UNLIMITED INC. presents

THE WARREN REPORT: THE WHOLE TRUTH?

MR. MARK LANE, Attorney and former New York State Assemblyman, does not accept the findings of the Warren Commission Report and will present a critical analysis of the Report.

A PANEL OF PROMINENT ATTORNEYS WILL CROSS-EXAMINE MR. LANE:

MR. JOSEPH A. BALL, attorney for Warren Commission during the investigation.

MR. HERMAN F. SELVIN, former president L.A. County Bar Association.

MR. A. L. WIRIN, noted civil liberties and constitutional attorney.

8:00 P.M., Friday, December 4, 1964
Beverly Hills High School Auditorium
241 So. Moreno Drive, Beverly Hills

Admission: $1.50   Students: $1.00
For ticket information call NO 3-0424

SUMMARY

To summarize the first salvo of three shots, the first shot enters JFK's upper shoulder and, traveling downward, exits his neck, striking the back of the seat in front of him.

The second shot is too high (as the limousine is now moving downhill), passes just over the limousine, striking Elm Street and then the curb in front of James Tague, with a small chip of cement striking his cheek.

The third shot would have hit JFK, but Kennedy is now moving to his left towards Jackie, and the bullet hits Connally's right shoulder instead.

Because the three rear shots on the acoustics in the first salvo are so close together (with gaps of 1.7 seconds and 1.0 second respectively), **the simplest shot solution places two rear shooters in the Dal-Tex building firing the first salvo of three shots.**

If one now analyzes the time frame between the two salvos, as measured on the acoustics, there are fourteen Zapruder frames missing between the two salvos. Just before the fatal head shot, there are a series of very rapid movements, such as Driver Greer's head turning around in just one frame.

Yet the limousine appears to maintain a constant speed of 12 miles per hour. This suggests that the limousine slowed down just before the fatal head shot, and that frames were edited out to maintain a constant speed. Several witnesses, including William Newman just 15 feet away, maintained that the limousine slowed down just before the fatal head shot.

Keep in mind that the Zapruder film "accidentally" broke in two places, and had to be spliced back together at exactly the two points where Kennedy was shot! These were called accidental splices, with two frames even being "accidentally" reversed! So it is not unexpected that frames might be missing.

SUMMARY

How many bullets would this leave inside the limousine? The first bullet exits JFK's neck and most likely strikes the metallic back of the seat in front. The second bullet was a missed shot, striking Elm Street, and then the curb in front of James Tague. The third bullet shattered Connally's tenth rib, exited his right chest and stayed within the car. The fourth bullet was an exploding round and would leave only small shards. The fifth and final bullet struck Connally's right wrist and stayed within the car.

Thus, three bullets (CE567 and CE569 were labeled) stayed inside the limousine—one which struck JFK and two which struck Governor Connally. A total of five bullet fragments were found inside the car. This study suggests that the five fragments came from a total of three bullets.

The Grassy Knoll shot created such a controversy that LBJ was forced to form the Warren Commission in order to legitimize the "Lone Gunman" explanation. In 1963, the public mostly trusted the news media and the government to tell the truth. The public was unaware of a "Deep State" that holds an alternate agenda. Former CIA director, William Casey, once stated, "We'll know our disinformation program is complete when everything the public believes is false!"

What conclusions can one draw from this "unified solution" of the Dealey Plaza shot sequence? **First, the Depository was a decoy, complete with a planted gun and a phony "shooter's lair".** One witness, F. Lee Mudd, was on the north side of Elm Street and fell to the ground when shots were fired – he claimed they originated from the Dal-Tex. If shots originated from the Depository, why did people in front of the Depository run toward the Grassy Knoll instead?

Second, Lee Harvey Oswald was an unwitting patsy or decoy, since no shots originated from the Depository. This also explains why there were no powder burns found on Oswald's face after supposedly firing three shots from a rifle.

Many individuals claim to have been involved in the JFK assassination, but only one of them has provided this "unified" explanation – only one individual, in my opinion, has got it right. His name is James Files, a Mafia-CIA gunman who claims to be the

Grassy Knoll shooter. Files places two shooters in the Dal-Tex building (including Chuck Niccoletti and Johnny Roselli), not the Depository, which is contrary to all the popular explanations.

Files states that Officer Tippit was not shot by Oswald. He states that, after the assassination, a manhunt ensued for Oswald, and that Officer Tippit, who had mistakenly stopped at least two people earlier, mistakenly stopped the wrong man – a Mafia related individual – and asked for identification. The man refused, and killed Officer Tippit, rather than be identified and enter the public spotlight.

This shot sequence analysis suggests that Lee Harvey Oswald (who was in the Depository) was not a shooter. The actual perpetrators may have involved members of the Chicago mob who had previously worked with the CIA in attempting to kill Fidel Castro.

It should also be noted that a previous assassination attempt against JFK was thwarted by the FBI three weeks earlier on November 2nd at Soldier Field in Chicago. Special Agent Abraham Bolden later attempted to inform the Warren Commission, but he was falsely accused by the Mob, arrested and imprisoned, and the truth was suppressed by the FBI for over 30 years.

Finding a solution to the Dealey Plaza shot sequence is like trying to match all the faces on a Rubik's cube – except that all the faces will probably never match, due to the many counterarguments and conflicting witness observations.

This unified solution is the best match when combining the acoustics with the Zapruder film, three dimensional analysis, and many of the witness observations. In the following paragraphs, I will discuss some of the counter-arguments.

COUNTER-ARGUMENTS

Some claim that the neck wound is too small to be an exit wound. However, if a bullet does not strike bone, the entry and exit wounds can be the same size. In addition, a frontal shot fired from the Grassy Knoll to the neck around Z-190 has less than a one second window of opportunity to be fired without striking Secret Service agents, motorcycle policemen, or people on the south side of Elm Street.

Some claim that the back wound did not probe deeply, so it must have been a "dud" bullet, that later purportedly fell out on the stretcher at Parkland. As a trauma surgeon, I can say that bullet wounds often do not probe due to muscle movements. In addition, I have never seen a bullet "fall out" of a wound – even when palpable under the skin, they are often pesky to remove, and require excision with a scalpel. Also, in a phone conversation with Dr. Gary Aguilar, Dr. Boswell stated that, at autopsy, a probe was passed from the back wound and out the neck wound. Furthermore, all the structures that would be expected to be injured by a through-and-through bullet, including the cupola (or tip) of the lung, were found to be injured at autopsy.

Some claim that only a small hole was in the back of the head. But reviews of Parkland doctors, nurses and other witnesses by Dr. Gary Aguilar, as well as a personal conversation I had with Dr. Charles Crenshaw, described a "baseball sized" exit wound in the right posterior skull. Dr. Crenshaw also described an entry wound in front of the right ear. This is consistent with a shot from the Grassy Knoll to the right and front of JFK with a large exit wound posteriorly.

Why do the bullets match Oswald's rifle? Bullets can be fired into water, then reloaded onto another larger casing with a "sabot" ring, as described by Jim Marrs in his book, <u>Crossfire</u>. When fired through a slightly larger gun, they will retain the original rifling ridges. This technology was available in the sixties. It should also be noted that Oswald's rifle had a misaligned site and did not smell of gunpowder.

In conclusion, I believe that the Dealey Plaza shot sequence has been solved. This "unified solution" requires two shooters from the Dal-Tex building and one shooter from the Grassy Knoll, who would only fire as a last resort.

The minor injury to bystander James Tague at the Triple Underpass was serendipitous, in that it requires **placement of a shooter in the Dal-Tex building** – there are no solutions for a shot from the Depository to miss Kennedy, strike Elm Street, and then strike the curb in front of James Tague.

Governor Connally, holding onto his Stetson hat until the final rear shot was fired, as seen on the Zapruder film, was also serendipitous, in that it further refutes the "single bullet theory", which mandated that JFK and all of Connally's wounds were caused by a single bullet. As Dr Cyril Wecht points out, you cannot hold onto a Stetson hat after a bullet shatters the largest bone in your wrist!

The final bit of serendipity was the placement of the Depository Oak tree by Mother Nature, which blocks a Depository shot from Z-166-Z-210 – which means that the Kennedy neck shot at Z-190 had to come from somewhere else!

Finally, the Grassy Knoll shot is the obvious proof of a conspiracy, as concluded correctly by the House Select Committee on Assassinations in 1979.

A Mafia-CIA gunman, James Files, now in Federal prison and claiming to be the Grassy Knoll shooter, is the only person who has echoed this seemingly unlikely explanation, which avoids the Depository as a shooting location. Files later stated that he was accused of firing too soon, and that the final rear shot would have killed JFK. He was told to only fire from the Grassy Knoll as a last resort, but Files claimed that if he had waited any longer, Jackie Kennedy would have been directly behind JFK and in the line of fire.

This "unified solution" is a scientific analysis that combines the acoustic data with the Zapruder film and a three dimensional ballistics analysis – something that has never been done before. This shooting solution represents the "best fit" of the available data. It happens to exonerate Lee Harvey Oswald as a gunman.

OUR HISTORY IN A NUTSHELL

> *We'll know our disinformation program is complete when everything the American public believes is false.*
> William Casey, CIA Director, 1981

1. In the case of Senator Huey Long, Dr. Weiss's gun simply disappeared in the Sheriff's possession for fifty years – it was the wrong caliber for the bullets in Huey Long and had to be retrieved from Dr. Weiss's car after the assassination! The bullets did, however, match the bodyguards' guns.

2. Hundreds of residents on Saipan knew that aviation heroine Amelia Earhart, who was on a spy mission from FDR in 1937 to photograph illegal Japanese Pacific installations, with special Fairchild wing cameras, had been captured after crash landing and was recovering from burns at the Garapan prison, but the media simply described this as a mass hallucination!

3. FDR's cold blooded gunshot murder in April, 1945 at the Little White House in Warm Springs was covered up when J. Edgar Hoover threatened all the witnesses. FDR and his Brain Trust were too friendly with Joe Stalin, and Allen Dulles in Bern, Switzerland was anxious to get the Cold War started! FDR was never taken to the nearby hospital for his supposed stroke!

4. In July, 1945 Secretary of Defense, James Forrestal and future President John F. Kennedy view German UFOs in Europe. JFK and James Forrestal become proponents for UFO disclosure and oppose wars of intervention and nuclear weapon development. JFK writes a diary of his European trip. German UFOs fly to the moon and Mars, but the public is told that German UFO's couldn't fly. Forrestal is later suicided by his own intelligence agency.

5. Marilyn Monroe was "suicided" in 1962 by the Chicago Mafia, as a request from the CIA after Robert Kennedy had visited, in an effort to end Robert Kennedy's political career. Marilyn died from a fatal suppository of Nembutal and chloral hydrate, courtesy of the Deep State and a Mafia team sent from Chicago.

6. The John Kennedy assassination in 1963 involved a fatal headshot from the Grassy Knoll, when the rear shots failed to kill JFK. This required the police, the FBI, the news media and LBJ to cover this up. Witness William Newman, standing at the Grassy Knoll, was closest to JFK and told me that he was never asked to testify by Allen Dulles and the Warren Commission! The Soviet Union had agreed ten days earlier to JFK's proposal for a joint moon project, but the deep state wouldn't allow it!

7. My Northwestern University Astronomy professor, Dr J. Allen Hynek in 1967, who was the civilian head of the government's Project Blue Book, read declassified UFO files in astronomy class. Despite widespread skepticism among the populace, he was a firm believer in the existence of UFOs and four types of extraterrestrials! Our final exam even included characteristics of aliens, such as arachnodactyly and polydactyly, as seen in the movie, *E.T. the Extra-Terrestrial*, where Dr. Hynek consulted.

8. Martin Luther King was purportedly killed by lone gunman James Earl Ray. But Dr. William Pepper found a conspiracy that included an Alpha 184 six-man sniper team in Memphis, as well as a surveillance team on the roof of the fire station near the Lorraine Hotel, and a café owner in the bushes behind his café with a rifle.

9. Senator Robert Kennedy was killed in 1968 at the Ambassador Hotel in Los Angeles. Dr. Cyril Wecht pointed out that powder burns on RFK's temple and shots from the rear were fired only two inches away. Yet Sirhan Sirhan was behind a steam table in front of RFK. The new security guard, hired by CIA middle-man, Robert Maheu, stood behind RFK and admitted to pulling out his gun. Acoustics and bullet holes revealed 12 shots fired. Photos by a college student in the kitchen were in possession of the Los Angeles Police, who then lost them and never made copies or saved the negatives!

10. Two things bothered me about the official version of the OKC bombing of the Murrah Building in 1995. First, the seismic tracing recorded two sharp bomb explosions (not from a falling building) ten seconds apart. The local TV stations showed the OKC bomb squad carrying out unexploded bombs from inside the building, which was explained away as a secret cache belonging to the ATF – which the ATF later denied.

I treated first responders at a first aid tent near the Water Resources Building, which later had to be demolished, and they were concerned about the possibility of unexploded ordinance. Retired Air Force General Benton K. Partin stated in his OKC bombing report to the US Congress that bombs inside the building were the major factor in the destruction. Joe Harp, based on his experience with military explosives, identified the additional bombs removed from the building as being military in nature. Neither of these experts were permitted to testify at the McVeigh or Nichols trials.

The Murrah Building was ordered demolished one month later without performing a scientific forensic analysis of the residual bomb residue.

Second, how could a ground level fertilizer bomb leave no toxic ammonia smell, and damage 136 buildings with a concussion that rattled the glass in my office building ten miles away?

Twenty-eight years later, Dr. Michael Salla held an exopolitics interview with Deep State informant Sean David Morton about Area 51. During this interview, Sean briefly deviated from this discussion and calmly stated that, after being embarrassed at Waco and Ruby Ridge, the government decided to create a false flag event and infiltrate the Sovereign Patriot movement, trying to get them to "blow up something." He went on to say that

THE QUATRAINS OF CAMELOT 343

Timothy McVeigh was an agent provocateur, that this was not a fertilizer bomb but a thermobaric or concussion bomb, and that McVeigh was never executed.

One of the execution witnesses, Susan Carlson, a reporter for WLS-AM Radio in Chicago, stated on the air that McVeigh "appeared to be still breathing, or what appeared to be shallow breathing, even after being pronounced dead." In an unusual move, McVeigh's lawyers blocked the state mandated autopsy, while the government, who "owns" the body, declined to request organ donations, which typically pay the state $200,000. Most unusually, McVeigh refused all appeals, in order to speed up his own "execution"!

According to a 2010 ruling by Salt Lake City Judge Clark Waddoups, sealed court records later revealed the involvement of the CIA with prosecutor Merrick Garland, who had insisted that over 100 OKC bombing records, involving over 1,000 pages and 22 surveillance videos, remained secret (and remain sealed to this day).

In letters to his mother and sister, McVeigh confided that he worked for the Army Special Forces as a sharpshooter on covert missions – his death certificate stated "US Army." It would seem that Timothy McVeigh was a CIA asset who was "sheep dipped" as a right wing militia member. Who ever thought that sniper training tactics, such as remaining motionless for hours, would come in handy for faking your own "execution"? Local ATF members were texted to stay home that morning.

But this all seems preposterous. Why would our government blow up its own federal building and then sentence Terry Nichols, who declined to participate with McVeigh, to life in prison for building a fertilizer bomb that never existed? Would our government kill hundreds of innocent men, women, and children, and then falsely blame its political opponents in order to put them in jail and justify expanded government intervention? Do governments really perform false flag events on their own citizens for some greater cause?

11. It took over a year for night "elevator repair crews" hired by the new owner to plant Thermite explosives, with residue found in the debris of the twin towers, to create a perfect false flag demolition of the 911 towers and motivate our country to go to war. It took over a year for night "elevator repair crews" hired by the new owner to plant Thermite explosives, with residue found in the debris of the twin towers, to create a perfect false flag demolition of the 9/11 towers and motivate our country to go to war in the Middle East. The Pentagon outer wall damage, once the smoke cleared, was seen to be too small a hole for a plane, but not for a missile, and the demolition of Building #7 was not done by firemen as reported, who are not trained to plant explosives.

As of the writing of this book, the public believes that Senator Huey Long was killed by Dr. Weiss, Amelia Earhart and her navigator Fred Noonan simply got lost and disappeared, FDR died of a "cerebral hemorrhage", flying saucers and extraterrestrials simply don't exist, Marilyn Monroe committed suicide, James Forrestal committed suicide, John Kennedy was killed by lone gunman Lee Harvey Oswald, Martin Luther King was killed by lone gunman James Earl Ray, Robert Kennedy was killed by lone gunman Sirhan Sirhan, and the twin towers were brought down on orders from Osama bin Laden!

In short, there is a deliberate effort underway to dumb-down the population. I doubt that our government will ever permit the truth to be told. Thus, it is up to independent journalists to break free from their corporate bonds and plant the seeds for true disclosure. I leave it to the readers to do their own research and arrive at their own conclusions The Pentagon outer wall damage, once the smoke cleared, was seen to be too small a hole for a plane, but not for a missile, and the demolition of Building #7 was not done by firemen as reported, who are not trained to plant explosives.

Who Will Tell The Children?

Dealey Plaza Field Trip

DISCLOSURE TIMETABLE

1. Americans are informed that antigravity vehicles exist and can travel underwater. The public is in disbelief until an antigravity vehicle is demonstrated. College and high school physics books are amended to explain antigravity and antigravity propulsion.
2. Electrogravitic propulsion is explained to the public and used for space travel within our galaxy.
3. Zero point free energy, using Nikola Tesla technology, is revealed to the public, which will end our reliance on fossil fuels.
4. Medbeds, manufactured on the moon, will be released to the public, which cure cancer and other ailments using DNA frequency. The technology has been known for decades. Anti-aging technology will also be introduced.
5. The public is informed that time is not linear and that government sponsored projects allow us to visit the past and the future.
6. Some individuals, with hybrid DNA, are able to change their physical appearance. Read William Tompkins' book, *Selected by Extraterrestrials* for more detail.
7. The public is informed that our space program has traveled to planets outside our solar system using portal technology and wormhole technology. These journeys take hours or weeks, not centuries and involve merchant ships trading goods and services.
8. The public learns that "soul swapping"- the transfer of consciousness from one body to another is routinely performed by our government. This technology was taught by extraterrestrials at Area 51 and includes soul transfer to clones by our intelligence agencies.
9. The above revelations will prepare the public for the biggest revelation of all – that friendly extraterrestrial Beings exist and that some of them look like us and walk among us in a government sponsored Envoy program. We will join the Galactic Federation and work with other Beings to live and work in the galaxies.

10. Our government – the Deep State – will finally admit it's involvement in the murders of Senator Huey Long, FDR, James Forrestal, Marilyn Monroe, President John Kennedy, Martin Luther King, Robert Kennedy and John Kennedy, Jr. The Deep State will also admit its involvement in child and drug trafficking and viral manipulation to create pandemics.

11. Our government will admit to the existence of unfriendly Beings and our negotiations with them in 1954 to obtain UFO technology in exchange for allowing abductions and genetic experimentation. The Germans had already developed some of this technology with the assistance of unfriendly extraterrestrials and had traveled to the moon and Mars by 1945. Operation Paperclip was Allen Dulles' project to import Germans after the war to further develop this extraterrestrial technology.

12. Unfriendly extraterrestrials have now been expelled from our solar system. It is up to us to end wars and learn to live peacefully before any of these revelations can be released to the public.

13. Now that people have been officially informed that extraterrestrials exist and walk among us, our society owes an apology to Valiant Thor. Largely ridiculed by the press and the Deep State, he arrived as an extraterrestrial emissary from 1957 to 1960, lived at the Pentagon, and urged President Eisenhower to stop nuclear proliferation, end the Cold War, and make peace with the Russians. Eisenhower was later overruled by Allen Dulles and the CIA's MJ12, but Val Thor's policies were later adopted by President Kennedy, who pushed for the nuclear proliferation treaty and a joint US-Russian space program, which ended with the CIA-sponsored JFK assassination only weeks later. Since then, we have been embroiled in perpetual wars, continued dependence on fossil fuels, and plans by the Deep State to block public disclosure of zero point energy, and anti-gravity spaceships.

Who Will Tell The People?

The People wondered, "Where hast thou gone, Oh Mighty King? And who were the perpetrators of this loathsome deed?"

But no one dared tell the People. For, if the People should rise up against their new King, who could stop them?

Thus did the future Kings fear the Corruptors and their Power, for none dared call it Conspiracy.

So it was decided, rather than share the truth, to let the People live their Delusion.

Thus did the Myth endure.

The Tale Of Camelot

Dealey Plaza Field Trip

ABOUT THE AUTHOR

Dr. Bill Truels is a practicing general surgeon and wound surgeon in Oklahoma City. He grew up in Chicago and graduated from Northwestern University in 1967. He obtained a Master's Degree in biochemistry from Indiana University in 1969 and graduated from the University of Illinois Medical School in 1973. He obtained his surgery training at the University of Oklahoma and St. Anthony Hospital and began private practice in 1979 in Oklahoma City.

Dr. Bill Truels

"I was a freshman at Northwestern University when President John Kennedy was assassinated," Dr. Truels relates. During his lifetime as a physician, Dr. Truels has acquired an extensive verbal history from his patients and fellow physicians that he shares in his other six books: Breach of Faith, Common Ground, Life After Medical School, Alternate American History 101, The Lancer Chronicles, and Poems from the Heartland.

Dr. Truels is not himself a researcher, but more a chronicler of events told to him. Be prepared for a fresh look at the deaths of Huey Long, FDR, Marilyn Monroe, JFK and RFK. This information derives from conversations with patients and older physicians, as well as JFK witnesses and researchers, and will require further research for verification.

This book provides a good starting point for students wishing to study the JFK assassination, as it details all the various factions who were hostile to JFK and wanted him removed from office.

A word of warning – be prepared to laugh – and cry – at this powerful tribute to John Fitzgerald Kennedy and to the researchers who have worked so hard to bring the truth to light!

www.ingramcontent.com/pod-product-compliance
Lightning Source LLC
Chambersburg PA
CBHW050325010526
44119CB00003B/106